THE
CARDINALS OF
CAPITOL HILL

The Cardinals of Capitol Hill

THE MEN AND WOMEN WHO CONTROL GOVERNMENT SPENDING

Richard Munson

GROVE PRESS
NEW YORK

Published by Grove Press
A division of Grove Press, Inc.
841 Broadway
New York, NY 10003-4793

Published in Canada by General Publishing Company, Ltd.

Library of Congress Cataloging-in-Publication Data

Munson, Richard.
    The cardinals of Capitol Hill : the men and women who control government spending / Richard Munson.—1st ed.
    Includes bibliographical references and index.
    ISBN 0-8021-1460-1
    1. United States. Congress. House. Committee on Appropriations. Subcommittee on VA, HUD, and Independent Agencies. 2. United States. Congress. Senate. Committee on Appropriations. Subcommittee on VA-HUD-Independent Agencies. 3. United States—Appropriations and expenditures.   I. Title.
JK1430.A72M86   1993
328.73'07658—dc20   92-43854

Manufactured in the United States of America

Designed by William McCarthy

First Edition 1993

10   9   8   7   6   5   4   3   2   1

To Daniel and Dana

CONTENTS

House of Representatives Appropriations Committee, 102nd Congress

DEMOCRATS

Jamie L. Whitten, Mississippi, chair
William H. Natcher, Kentucky, vice chair
Neal Smith, Iowa
Sidney R. Yates, Illinois
David R. Obey, Wisconsin
Edward R. Roybal, California
Louis Stokes, Ohio
Tom Bevill, Alabama
Bill Alexander, Arkansas
John P. Murtha, Pennsylvania
Bob Traxler, Michigan
Joseph D. Early, Massachusetts
Charles Wilson, Texas
Norman D. Dicks, Washington
Matthew F. McHugh, New York
William Lehman, Florida
Martin Olav Sabo, Minnesota
Julian C. Dixon, California
Vic Fazio, California
W. G. ("Bill") Hefner, North Carolina
Les AuCoin, Oregon
Bernard J. Dwyer, New Jersey
Steny H. Hoyer, Maryland
Bob Carr, Michigan
Robert J. Mrazek, New York
Richard J. Durbin, Illinois
Ronald D. Coleman, Texas
Alan B. Mollohan, West Virginia
Lindsay Thomas, Georgia
Chester G. Atkins, Massachusetts
Jim Chapman, Texas
Marcy Kaptur, Ohio
Lawrence J. Smith, Florida
David E. Skaggs, Colorado
David E. Price, North Carolina
Nancy Pelosi, California
Peter J. Visclosky, Indiana

REPUBLICANS

Joseph M. McDade, Pennsylvania
John T. Myers, Indiana
Clarence E. Miller, Ohio
Lawrence Coughlin, Pennsylvania
C. W. Bill Young, Florida
Ralph Regula, Ohio
Carl D. Pursell, Michigan
Mickey Edwards, Oklahoma
Bob Livingston, Louisiana
Bill Green, New York
Jerry Lewis, California
John Edward Porter, Illinois
Harold Rogers, Kentucky
Joe Skeen, New Mexico
Frank R. Wolf, Virginia
Bill Lowery, California
Vin Weber, Minnesota
Tom DeLay, Texas
Jim Kolbe, Arizona
Dean A. Gallo, New Jersey
Barbara F. Vucanovich, Nevada
Jim Lightfoot, Iowa

VA, HUD, AND INDEPENDENT AGENCIES

DEMOCRATS

Bob Traxler, Michigan, chair
Louis Stokes, Ohio
Alan B. Mollohan, West Virginia
Jim Chapman, Texas
Chester G. Atkins, Massachusetts
Marcy Kaptur, Ohio

REPUBLICANS

Bill Green, New York
Lawrence Coughlin, Pennsylvania
Bill Lowery, California

Senate Appropriations Committee, 102nd Congress

DEMOCRATS

Robert C. Byrd, West Virginia, chair
Daniel Inouye, Hawaii
Ernest F. Hollings, South Carolina
J. Bennett Johnston, Louisiana
Quentin N. Burdick, North Dakota
Patrick J. Leahy, Vermont
James R. Sasser, Tennessee
Dennis DeConcini, Arizona
Dale Bumpers, Arkansas
Frank R. Lautenberg, New Jersey
Tom Harkin, Iowa
Barbara A. Mikulski, Maryland
Harry Reid, Nevada
Brock Adams, Washington
Wyche Fowler, Jr., Georgia
Robert J. Kerrey, Nebraska

REPUBLICANS

Mark O. Hatfield, Oregon
Ted Stevens, Alaska
Jake Garn, Utah
Thad Cochran, Mississippi
Robert W. Kasten, Jr., Wisconsin
Alfonse M. D'Amato, New York
Warren Rudman, New Hampshire
Arlen Specter, Pennsylvania
Pete V. Domenici, New Mexico
Don Nickles, Oklahoma
Phil Gramm, Texas
Christopher S. Bond, Missouri
Slade Gorton, Washington

VA, HUD, AND INDEPENDENT AGENCIES

DEMOCRATS

Barbara A. Mikulski, Maryland, chair
Patrick J. Leahy, Vermont
J. Bennett Johnston, Louisiana
Frank R. Lautenberg, New Jersey
Wyche Fowler, Jr., Georgia
Robert J. Kerrey, Nebraska

REPUBLICANS

Jake Garn, Utah
Alfonse M. D'Amato, New York
Don Nickles, Oklahoma
Phil Gramm, Texas
Christopher S. Bond, Missouri

INTRODUCTION

IN THIS ERA of massive federal deficits the annual budget has become the paramount business of American society. The choices politicians make about spending determine government policies, and these choices are made increasingly by the few representatives and senators who sit on the House and Senate Appropriations Committees, particularly by those who chair each panel's thirteen subcommittees—the cardinals of Capitol Hill.

This book seeks to explain how appropriators work by tracing the actions of one subcommittee through an annual budget cycle as it divided some $81 billion among twenty-four federal departments and agencies concerned with veterans, housing, space, science, and the environment. I chose to follow the Veterans Administration, Housing and Urban Development, and Independent Agencies Subcommittee (the VA-HUD panel) because it controls the most discretionary money used to fund domestic government programs. In addition, its fiscal 1992 deliberations were particularly dramatic. Efforts both to kill and to protect NASA's space station illustrate well the political machinations involved in congressional appropriations.

Despite extensive media coverage of federal policies and politics, few people—either inside or outside Washington—understand how the cardinals control and exercise their power of the purse. Reporters condescendingly concentrate only on pork barrel politics, how appropriators direct substantial federal spending toward highways, sewers, and other federal projects in their own districts. Lawmakers on authorizing, or policy-making, committees merely complain about how appropriators usurp their power. Recent Republican presidents, wanting to increase their own power with a line-item veto, have painted the cardinals simply as big spenders responsible for the federal deficit. All these views, however, are imperfect and incomplete.

While some of their deeds are less than admirable, the cardinals of Capitol Hill perform a noble enterprise: As elected representatives of the people they fund the federal government and choose among competing interests. This book tries to illuminate their actions, with the hope that improved public understanding of the appropriations process will help moderate the public's cynicism toward government, enhance the accountability of lawmakers, and reduce the monumental debt we leave our children.

Richard Munson
Washington, D.C.

The Cardinals of Capitol Hill

1

THE POWER OF THE PURSE

MEETING SECRETLY IN an ornate room on the second floor of the United States Capitol, thirteen senior Democratic members of the House of Representatives spent just three-quarters of an hour to allocate almost three-quarters of a trillion dollars. This group, known as the College of Cardinals because of its power and the secrecy of the rituals by which it divvies up the federal pie, is the most potent and mysterious council in Washington. These chairmen of the thirteen Appropriations subcommittees touch every American, for they determine how much money will be spent on highways, meat inspection, B-2 bombers, drug rehabilitation centers, low-income housing, and sewers. In essence, they and their thirteen Senate counterparts control the federal government.

For Bob Traxler and the other cardinals, the May 14, 1991, meeting, although an annual ritual, occurred at a particularly ominous time. The assembled lawmakers had to write a federal budget for fiscal 1992 that responded to swelling unemployment lines, a war in Iraq, and the collapse of the Soviet Union, but their options were limited by a massive federal debt of nearly $4 trillion.

Jamie Whitten, chairman of the House full Committee on Appropriations (and of its Subcommittee on Rural Development, Agriculture, and Related Agencies) called the session to order, and the cardinals took their seats around the oval conference table within the

3

inner sanctum of room H-218. These experienced politicians displayed a jovial collegiality and confidence, having worked together for years, having seen presidents come and go. Their average age was sixty-eight, and three—Jamie Whitten of Mississippi, William Natcher of Kentucky, and Sidney Yates of Illinois—were in their eighties.

A small cadre of senior staff slipped into chairs squeezed along walls lined with portraits of former committee chairmen. These thirteen subcommittee staff directors, known by the purposefully unassuming title of "clerks," and Whitten's front-office aides had been maneuvering and negotiating about the spending allocations since the president formally delivered his budget proposal to Congress on the first Monday in February.

Traxler and his colleagues took a few moments to adjust to Whitten's slurred Mississippi drawl, but the group soon nodded its agreement about the seriousness of Washington's deficit. None of the appropriators accepted responsibility for this mountainous liability. Quite the contrary. Whitten expressed personal pride in cutting the budget requests of every president since Franklin Roosevelt.

Turning to federal spending for fiscal year 1992, which was to begin some five months hence on October 1, 1991, the chairman lamented the constraints imposed by the recent budget summit agreement with which congressional and White House leaders tried to tackle the deficit. It was painful enough that growth in discretionary spending had been limited to 5 percent, barely enough to keep pace with inflation. More troubling to most cardinals was the new restriction against paying for increases in domestic spending with decreases in defense spending. Whitten announced that the "fire wall" erected between domestic and defense funds meant at least $8.7 billion in fully justified needs could not be met. Traxler, wanting more money for space, science, and environmental programs, moaned out loud.

Whitten finally distributed a single sheet of paper listing proposed lump-sum spending allocations for the thirteen subcommittees. The chairman, too clever simply to dictate their adoption, suggested that individual cardinals were free to offer changes. "Yet in order for that allocation to change," Traxler admitted later, "I'd have to steal it

4

away from other subcommittees. And they're not going to give me a penny. Not one penny."

Still, there was much bitching and speechmaking. William Natcher, the intense but gentlemanly Kentuckian, asked that $1 billion be added to his pot for education, reflecting the sentiment of House Democrats. Neil Smith from Iowa renewed his annual plea for more money to fight crime and drugs. And Traxler of Michigan put his fellow cardinals on notice that he couldn't afford the orbiting space station with his $81 billion allocation. But in the end no cardinal volunteered any of his money for education, crime, or space, and no one could suggest a more salable plan than Chairman Whitten's.

This short, subdued meeting marked the first formal step in an annual February to October cycle that sets budgets and priorities for every federal department and agency. Yet it masked lengthy, tumultuous, behind-the-scenes bargaining.

If political power is displayed by physical location, the House Appropriations Committee enjoys substantial authority. The panel's three-office suite on the second floor of the Capitol is mere steps from the House floor. The only office with similar access is the Speaker's. In fact, Whitten's suite used to be the Speaker's until shortly after the Civil War, when Schuyler Colfax decided that the just-completed eastern wing of the Capitol, with its view of modern town houses, was nicer than the view (and smell) down the Mall, on which cows grazed and through which a canal, often rank during Washington's sticky summers, meandered. In recent years, with the Mall hosting one of the nation's grand vistas of monuments and museums, several Speakers have eyed Whitten's rooms longingly. Tip O'Neill, for instance, was talking with the chairman one morning about a particular program when he inquired loudly, "Jamie, why is your office nicer than mine?" Appropriations staff became even more alarmed when Jim Wright's wife dropped by shortly after her husband had been elected Speaker, with a notepad and interior designers in tow. But Whitten retained his office.

If power is traced by who travels to whose office, appropriators and their staff are at the top of the heap. "Admirals and generals come to visit me and not vice versa," boasted a Defense Subcommittee staff member. Another expressed amazement at the Washington elite who come begging. "Here I am a simple staffer, and I'm constantly called by cabinet secretaries and agency directors," he said. "It's a heady experience, and I quickly learned that power increases as power is exerted."

Appropriators control the only legislation that must be approved every year. "It's not the end of the world if we postpone the Clean Water Act or a tax measure," said a cardinal. "But the entire government will close down if the train of appropriations doesn't run on time." The very necessity of their actions creates a climate that favors accommodation over confrontation, comity over conflict. While cardinals of the majority party dominate the allocation process, their subcommittees are perhaps the only institutions on Capitol Hill that maintain a tradition of bipartisanship.

But power in Washington is finally measured by the terms of the adage "Follow the money." In this city obsessed with political strength, the cardinals and their clerks are the ultimate power brokers. They wield their clout by being able to eliminate projects in the districts or states of defiant lawmakers or to cancel the favorite programs of presidents. Sometimes, such discipline is dispersed mercilessly, as Republican Senator Don Nickles learned after challenging Democratic Senator Robert Byrd on a budget resolution; the Senate Appropriations chairman simply made sure that Amtrak train service wasn't restored in Nickels's home state of Oklahoma. As one cardinal put it, "Opposition is punished—endlessly."

Other times these controllers of the federal purse exert quiet authority by disbursing favors to friends. It's no surprise that lawmakers tend to support a cardinal's legislation that directs pork barrel projects to their districts. "Appropriators earn favor by what they do," observed a representative. "They offer a quid for your quo."

Cardinals may control a smaller share of the federal budget than they did thirty years ago, but they still oversee all discretionary spending, and within Congress they remain the deal makers to see since they alone possess the ability to "take care" of congressional districts. When budgets are tight, their ability to determine the fate of

6

government projects translates into enormous political influence. "We're the only game in town," boasted an appropriator. "Everything else in the federal budget—interest on the federal debt, Social Security, and other entitlement programs—is on autopilot."

Appropriators, of course, are products of their environment, influencing and being influenced by the executive branch and other legislators. Cardinals battle constantly with the administration over specific funding levels, as well as over more generic issues involving spending caps, accounting procedures, line-item vetoes, and balanced budget amendments. Despite these struggles, Housing Secretary Jack Kemp declared flatly, "The Appropriations Committee is the most powerful committee in the history of the democratic experience." Within Congress members of the authorizing committees complain vehemently that appropriators are seizing political turf and taking credit for all the image-boosting, voter-influencing pork barrel projects. But a key legislator on an authorizing committee admitted candidly, "The Appropriations Committee stepped into a power vacuum that developed over many years, and it will take a very long time for us to regain power."

THE EARLY DAYS

Our nation's founders, skeptical of concentrating power in the presidency, clearly wanted Congress to control federal spending. Article I of the United States Constitution declares: "No money shall be drawn from the Treasury, but in consequence of appropriations made by law. . . ." Expanding on this provision in one of his *Federalist Papers,* James Madison wrote: "This power over the purse may, in fact, be regarded as the most complete and effective weapon with which any constitution can arm the immediate representatives of the people, for obtaining a redress of every grievance, and for carrying into effect every just and salutary measure."

In the early years of the Republic, however, the House Ways and Means Committee and the Senate Finance Committee exercised minimal supervision of the federal budget. The president's fiscal powers peaked during the Civil War, when the administration freely spent soaring sums without congressional approval. Representatives, recognizing that the Ways and Means panel had become burdened to the point of immobility with its jurisdiction over taxes, tariffs, and spending, decided in 1865 to divide those responsibilities and create a Committee on Appropriations; the Senate followed suit two years later. Significantly, the chairman of the Ways and Means Committee—considered by one historian to be "as powerful as any member of Congress had ever been"—decided to take control of Appropriations, "the power center of the next century." (A Mathew Brady photograph of Thaddeus Stevens, the first Appropriations chairman, hangs in the committee's conference room.)

Appropriators soon established thirteen subcommittees, including the forerunner of today's VA-HUD panel, then named Sundry Civil. But other lawmakers became annoyed by the group's growing power, and the executive agencies increasingly chafed under new congressional restrictions. In 1885, on the committee's twentieth anniversary, rank-and-file members of the House rebelled and stripped appropriators of control over more than half the spending bills, including the critical budgets for the military, agriculture, roads, and harbors. The Senate took similar action in 1899. The resulting hodgepodge remained fairly constant until World War I, when federal spending again soared. In 1921 appropriations stood at $6.5 billion, over six times the prewar average. With eight different committees going their own ways, congressional budgeting suddenly seemed chaotic.

Seeking management reforms, lawmakers passed the Budget and Accounting Act of 1921, requiring the president to submit to Congress an annual budget for the United States, and they established a Bureau of the Budget (now known as the Office of Management and Budget, or OMB) controlled by the White House and a General Accounting Office (GAO) responsible to the legislature. Perhaps more far-reaching, the reform measure also reconsolidated congressional spending decisions within the Appropriations Committee. But hoping to restrain the committee's clout, lawmakers restated a restriction against cardinals' inserting new legislation within their bills; this detachment of appropriations from authorizations, also practiced by the British Parliament, sought to separate spending decisions from policy making. There the structure has essentially rested.

Throughout the 1950s and early 1960s Clarence Cannon ruled the House Appropriations Committee autocratically, in ways that would be unthinkable today. The conservative Democrat, for instance, denied the chairmanship of the commerce subcommittee to Sidney Yates simply because he thought Yates was too liberal. Indeed, Cannon abolished the subcommittee and transferred its jurisdiction to another panel ruled by a more economy-minded appropriator. (Yates, after leaving the House for an unsuccessful Senate race, returned in 1965, gained a new seat on Appropriations, and now chairs the Interior Subcommittee.)

Cannon and most of his colleagues viewed themselves as strict guardians of the Treasury, determined to cut spending rather than start new programs. According to the chairman, "You may think my business is to make appropriations, but it is not. It is to prevent their being made."

When Cannon died in 1964, the gavel passed to George Mahon, a far more conciliatory and accommodating leader. Such attributes allowed Mahon to survive the demands from an increasingly liberal Democratic caucus for more social programs. Appropriations soared during Mahon's tenure, but the committee's share of total federal expenditures fell. Entitlements and other mandatory spending, over which appropriators were given no authority, grew from 23 percent of the budget during the Kennedy administration to a whopping 63 percent in fiscal 1992. This transformation, according to a political scientist, was "a deliberate effort by Congress to unshackle itself from its fiscal guardians." Entitlement payments to individuals—such as Medicare and pensions for veterans—were inaugurated with little concern about long-term costs, as politicians focused more on the rights of those to be assisted than on the price of such assistance.

THE DEFICIT AND THE BUDGET AGREEMENT

In the year before Jamie Whitten banged the gavel down on the May opening of the fiscal 1992 appropriations cycle, federal spending had been the overriding concern of Congress. The size of the budget is staggering, difficult to comprehend even for those working in the rarefied world of Capitol Hill. While families worry about $100 grocery bills and business executives fret about a $1,000 piece of equipment, Congress allots billions of dollars. Former Senator Everett Dirksen conveyed the unreality of federal budgeting with a quip now etched in our language: "A billion here, a billion there, and pretty soon you're talking about real money."

By this definition, the federal deficit has clearly become real money, although its size is a moving target. When President Bush submitted his budget in February 1991, he projected the fiscal 1992 deficit at a record $281 billion; several months later estimates rose to $399 billion. (When the year was over and accounts were settled, the figure reached "only" $290 billion, largely because the government temporarily postponed spending money to close failed financial institutions.) To gain some perspective on $290 billion, consider that figure in terms of seconds ticking on the clock. One million seconds pass in only 11.5 days. One billion seconds, a thousand times longer, last 31.7 years. Two hundred and ninety billion seconds span a whopping 9,193 years—roughly the time since the Neolithic era, when prehistoric peoples first learned to plant crops and produce pottery.

The federal government's total debt exceeds $4,300,000,000,000, and Washington pays almost $600 million each and every day just to cover the interest on that mortgage. To eliminate the debt, every American would need to contribute an extra $17,250 in taxes; a family of four would face a $69,000 bill from the IRS.

Massive deficits are a fairly recent phenomenon. Thomas Jefferson set the tone for the nation's early approach to federal budgeting by writing, "I place economy among the first and most important of republican virtues, and public debt as the greatest of the dangers to be feared." Abraham Lincoln added, "As an individual who undertakes to live by borrowing soon finds his original means devoured by interest, and next no one left to borrow from—so must it be with a government." The Great Depression and World War II altered that commitment, in part because of the magnitude of the deficits but also because of a "new economics" ascribed to John Maynard Keynes, with its ideas about deficit spending as a proper tool for governments to offset downswings in the economy. In the midst of economic upheaval President Franklin Roosevelt gave up trying to balance the federal budget. Wanting to put Americans back to work, he reversed a cost-cutting order and pumped $1 billion into the Public Works Administration. Washington borrowed the funds to fulfill Roosevelt's dream, and it has been borrowing them ever since.

The government's annual deficit remained modest until the 1970s, when higher energy prices and an accompanying recession sent the fiscal 1975 shortfall to $53 billion. Several pundits issued dire warnings, but few worried as long as the economy generated enough new wealth to underwrite the deficits. Many economists, in fact, suggested that deficits were healthy if the government was building highways, schools, and research institutes that increased the nation's productive capacity. They compared such government spending with a corporation's investment in a factory, arguing that just as the business repays its bonds with increased revenue from its new facility, so the government should be able to finance the national debt with the new wealth that flows from the nation's productive investments.

Lawmakers passed the Budget Act of 1974 to bring some discipline to federal budgeting and to check President Richard Nixon's regular impounding of funds. Yet the new law did little to control the imbalances, which became severe in the 1980s, after President Ronald Reagan convinced Congress to cut taxes and boost defense spending. With revenue decreasing and expenses increasing, the annual shortfall swelled above $212 billion in fiscal 1985. Robert Walker, a frustrated Republican representative from Pennsylvania, declared, "The fact is the budget process has failed miserably. It is coming apart at the seams."

Congress subsequently tried a new approach in 1985 with the

11

Gramm-Rudman-Hollings law, which required lawmakers to hit falling deficit targets every year or face across-the-board spending cuts, which are known as sequesters. Although appropriators complained bitterly about sequesters, the Gramm-Rudman-Hollings Act inadvertently empowered the cardinals. Since the law enables a single lawmaker to block any spending above a subcommittee's allocation with a simple point of order (a parliamentary procedure on the House or Senate floor), each cardinal uses every nickel allotted to him and then rejects virtually all amendments. "The result," explained a clerk, "is that spending bills usually end up as they are first written by the subcommittee chairmen."

Prophecies of outrageous inflation and financial collapse failed to materialize; in fact, the economy enjoyed its longest, if modest, peacetime expansion throughout most of the 1980s. But the deficit, as described by former White House economist Charles Schultze, had become like a termite gnawing away at America's economic infrastructure, depressing our living standards and reducing federal policy makers' latitude to deal with emerging economic problems or emergencies. By the decade's end Washington was forced to devote almost $200 billion a year just to meet interest payments on the debt.

With a slow economy providing less revenue than expected and a savings and loan bailout costing far more than anyone imagined, the federal deficit became *the* political issue by mid-1990. A series of editorials in *The Washington Post* predicted imminent Armageddon: "The Coming Budget Disaster," "Deficitology," and "Yes to Taxes." More and more economists prophesied alarming consequences. Even "Keynesians," who favored government spending to increase national wealth, suggested the current debt was probably twice as large as it should be.

President George Bush jump-started a budget summit in late June 1990 by agreeing to accept some "tax revenue increases," and the nation's political leaders spent long hours at Andrews Air Force Base, just outside Washington, trying to craft a set of politically acceptable tax increases and spending restraints. Jamie Whitten participated in the negotiations only briefly, leaving after lecturing the participants about how such high-level confabs were unnecessary and threatened the constitutional separation of powers. The Appropriations chairman argued that Congress should resolve budget problems on its own, without interference from the White House.

Robert Byrd, in contrast, wanted to bargain and make his mark as chairman of the Senate Appropriations Committee, a post he had assumed only a year before after stepping down as majority leader. His goals were clear: to eliminate the sequester constraints that Gramm-Rudman-Hollings placed on his panel and to find additional money that appropriators could allocate to domestic programs. The West Virginia senator prepared poster-size charts showing how President Reagan throughout the 1980s had squeezed $326 billion from domestic spending, while defense expenditures soared $569 billion above a baseline. Domestic spending, complained Byrd, "was the poor little runt puppy in the litter. He's underfed, and gradually he's becoming more and more undernourished."

Having made little progress with substantive arguments, Byrd lashed out at the arrogant attitude of White House negotiators. The Senate Appropriations chairman, a stickler for protocol, initially directed his anger at White House Chief of Staff John Sununu, who regularly propped his feet on the conference table. "I'd be embarrassed if any of my staff treated members of Congress this way," declared Byrd after a frustrating day of directionless discussions. Emphasizing the distinction between staff—even senior White House staff—and elected officials, the chairman added, "I don't think President Bush would be happy either." Sununu put his feet on the floor.

Not much later, after Budget Director Richard Darman had cavalierly dismissed another Democratic suggestion, Byrd barked, "You may not think you need me, but there'll be no agreement without me." Realizing the truth to the chairman's stern assertion, Darman asked to begin one-on-one negotiations with the Senate's top appropriator. Darman and Byrd eventually reached a series of agreements on budget procedures and increased appropriations, but rank-and-file representatives, in a dramatic 1:00 A.M. roll call, refused to embrace other aspects of the summiteers' package, particularly a politically risky gasoline tax increase. Bush subsequently vetoed Congress's stopgap spending measure, and government operations halted one weekend in early October 1990. Pundits proclaimed the demise of national leadership.

Further discussions on Capitol Hill finally produced a combination of compromises, including Medicare cutbacks and tax increases for the wealthy, aimed at trimming $492 billion over five years from the projected deficit. The broad outlines of the Byrd-Darman agreement, however, remained intact. Congress approved the measure just two weeks before election day, and most politicians, anxious to return home and campaign, had little idea of specific provisions within the complex deal.

Lawmakers slowly realized throughout 1991 that Darman had won two strategic victories: He had restricted the ability of appropriators to siphon money from defense to domestic programs, and he had gained for the OMB the power to "score" a particular expense as defense or domestic spending. The White House budget director asserted that these new powers would eventually save billions of dollars. Appropriators, however, had enjoyed substantial triumphs of their own, particularly the substitution of spending caps for deficit targets and sequesters. According to Representative Bill Green, ranking Republican on the VA-HUD panel, "The budget agreement made appropriators more masters of our own fate than we had been."

The Budget Enforcement Act of 1990 also increased spending authority about 13 percent for fiscal 1991, nearly triple the rate of inflation. To put this another way, appropriators could disburse an extra $40 billion for domestic discretionary programs. Bob Traxler alone lifted funding authority for space programs $1.7 billion, raised veterans' affairs spending $1.6 billion, and swelled environmental accounts $607 million. The OMB, as might be expected of a Republican administration, didn't tout this spending increase aspect of the agreement. In fact, Darman told reporters that domestic spending would be frozen, disguising the actual increase with exaggerated estimates of what appropriators would have spent without an accord.

Compared with the OMB and appropriators, the House and Senate Budget Committees lost big. With the agreement setting caps for domestic, defense, and international spending and with the OMB scoring the accounts, the budget panels had little to do. Admitted a senior Budget Committee staffer: "The summit made this a frustrating place to work." The frustration became particularly evident when the Senate committee tried to draft its fiscal 1992 budget resolution. Committee veteran Bennett Johnston suggested that Tim Wirth not bother with his proposal to increase education spending because the panel's actions were meaningless. "Then why is there a Budget Committee?" asked the Colorado senator. After Johnston explained that the group's recommendations were merely advisory, a flabbergasted Wirth inquired, "It makes absolutely no difference what we do?"

"Absolutely no difference," replied the Louisiana senator, who was also a member of the Appropriations Committee. To make his point even more clear, Johnston declared, "Appropriators don't even know what we do."

THE BUSH BUDGET

Cardinals do care what the administration proposes, and they traditionally use White House numbers as the basis to begin the annual appropriations process. By the time President Bush sent his fiscal 1992 proposals to Capitol Hill on February 4, 1991, the federal agencies and OMB had spent six months devising draft budgets.

Planning for the fiscal year that was to begin in October 1991 commenced in the spring of 1990, when assistant secretaries throughout the government asked their program directors for legislative ideas and spending requests. By September most agencies had established budget working groups to examine their accounts. Cabinet secretaries and agency administrators sent departmental strategies to the Office of Management and Budget in October. The OMB's four program associate directors (PADs), the top lieutenants responsible for ensuring that agency requests reflect the president's priorities, routed their recommendations to Richard Darman on November 18. The budget director delivered his "passbacks" to the agencies just before Thanksgiving, forcing many assistant secretaries to spend their holiday deciding which OMB cuts to appeal.

Agency leaders approached appeals differently. Housing and

Urban Development Secretary Jack Kemp, a headstrong conservative who continued to have personal designs on the White House, aggressively challenged OMB's tinkering with his plan. Less assertive administrators appealed only a few changes with the PADs, seldom with Darman, and very rarely with the president himself. Appropriators don't normally participate in the administration's drafting process. In fact, Representative Bob Carr, ranking Democrat on the Transportation Subcommittee, admitted to not even knowing how the OMB is structured or operates.

Once President Bush gave his final approval during the second week of January 1991, the now-massive document was sent to the Government Printing Office, where tight security protected against leaks. On the morning of February 4, 1991, couriers dropped off copies at the offices of each lawmaker and at the press galleries. Legislative assistants across Capitol Hill feverishly filled the next several hours reading selected sections of the huge tome in order for their bosses to supply reporters with brief reactions. Journalists attended Darman's morning press conference for an overview before heading to the early-afternoon briefings at each agency, where they could ask detailed questions. Appropriations staff spent much of the day—and the rest of the week—on the phone with budget officers at the agencies, probing assumptions, clarifying nuances, and splitting hairs over the structure of accounts.

The White House budget clearly favored agencies controlled by Bob Traxler's subcommittee. Bush targeted the National Science Foundation for a whopping 17.5 percent rise to $2.7 billion, three-quarters of which would go toward scientific research. Despite NASA's embarrassing cost overruns, the president proposed raising space spending 13 percent, bringing the agency's budget to $15.7 billion, of which $2.03 billion would be devoted to the space station. The administration sought a 9 percent increase in the Environmental Protection Agency's operating budget, largely to implement the recently reauthorized Clean Air Act. And veterans were to obtain a $1 billion, or 4.8 percent, boost, mostly to cover higher health care costs.

With the administration's budget request in hand, the cardinals and clerks began their regular eight-month sprint to have all thirteen bills approved by the House of Representatives, amended by the Senate, reconciled in conference committees, and signed by the president before the new fiscal year began on October 1. Said a senior staff member half-seriously, "We move quickly so we hear fewer squeaks and run over more people."

2

The Allocation

Richard N. Malow obtained his copy of the 2,029-page Bush budget at 8:00 a.m. on Monday, February 4, 1991. Within two hours the clerk for Bob Traxler's subcommittee, therefore a key player in the unfolding drama, purposely wandered through the Appropriations Committee's central office, encouraging the staff to match the president's large funding increases for science, space, and the environment. Privately, however, Dick Malow warned Traxler not to expect such a large allocation from Chairman Jamie Whitten.

The allocation of the federal budget among the thirteen Appropriations subcommittees is the most closed, the least understood, but the most consequential annual process within the Congress of the United States. Surprisingly, the bulk of the multibillion-dollar judgments are not made by elected officials on the House floor, by members of the Appropriations Committee, or even by the thirteen cardinals. "The central office staff ensures Whitten is aboard," revealed a senior appropriator, "but the allocation is a staff-driven process."

While most Americans cheered the air war over Iraq, Malow and the other subcommittee staff directors each spent the early days of February preparing a short written summary for Whitten's staff of what the president had—or should have—sought for the federal departments, agencies, and commissions whose funding he controlled. Commented one clerk: "We ask for the world, knowing we won't get it."

19

Appropriators would spend some $721 billion for fiscal year 1992, but this number is misleading. Approximately $208 billion of that total was for mandatory programs—such as Medicaid, crop insurance, and pensions for veterans—over which the committee has little control; these programs are funded more or less automatically, and their beneficiaries are identified by separate legislation. The remaining $513 billion of discretionary spending authority represented about a third of the $1.4 trillion federal budget. (Most of the rest was for Social Security, other entitlements, and interest on the government's debt—all outside the cardinals' domain.)

Because the 1990 budget agreement set spending limits for defense (about $291 billion) and international aid (about $22 billion), what remained for the cardinals to allocate was some $200 billion of domestic discretionary spending. Although $200 billion is only a fraction of total federal spending, it remains a substantial sum, equaling only slightly less than the combined annual sales for General Motors and Exxon, America's largest industrial corporations.

The "college of cardinals" usually split this domestic discretionary money into thirds: one for Traxler's VA-HUD Subcommittee, one for Natcher's Labor, Health and Human Services and Education Subcommittee, and one divided among the eight other panels controlling domestic programs. With money tight, however, even minor adjustments to this informal calculus affect federal programs dramatically—one reason why cardinals hold enormous power.

Serious negotiations over each panel's share of the federal pie began during the February congressional recess, when lawmakers were out of town. A team of four central office staff members—Dennis Kedzior, John Mikel, Gregory R. Dahlberg, and George P. Arnold—met with each subcommittee clerk to determine his subcommittee's desires. "We heard thirteen temper tantrums that week about what's desperately needed," reflected Kedzior. "And since we can't fully satisfy each clerk's pleas, we're viewed as the front-office heavies."

The initial discussions often dragged on for several hours, with subcommittee staff outlining their money and political problems, as well as the scorekeeping conflicts that might arise with the OMB over

20

The Federal Budget in the Last Four Decades
(in billions of dollars)

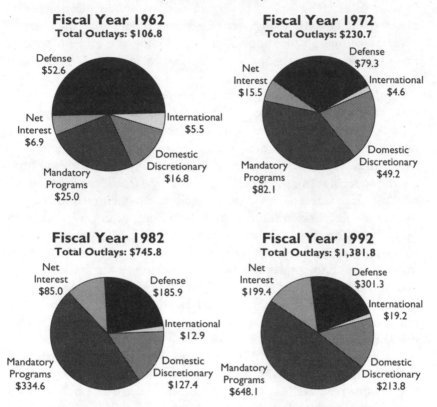

Fiscal Year 1962
Total Outlays: $106.8

Defense
$52.6

Net Interest
$6.9

International
$5.5

Mandatory Programs
$25.0

Domestic Discretionary
$16.8

Fiscal Year 1972
Total Outlays: $230.7

Defense
$79.3

Net Interest
$15.5

International
$4.6

Mandatory Programs
$82.1

Domestic Discretionary
$49.2

Fiscal Year 1982
Total Outlays: $745.8

Net Interest
$85.0

Defense
$185.9

International
$12.9

Mandatory Programs
$334.6

Domestic Discretionary
$127.4

Fiscal Year 1992
Total Outlays: $1,381.8

Net Interest
$199.4

Defense
$301.3

International
$19.2

Mandatory Programs
$648.1

Domestic Discretionary
$213.8

The portion of the budget spent on mandated spending has increased dramatically over the last four decades, as has the interest on the federal deficit. (Figures not adjusted for inflation.)

a particular account's being classified as defense or domestic spending. For each agency or program, two numbers were key: last year's appropriation and the president's current proposal. Clerks employed the benchmark that would paint the most dire picture possible in order to justify a large allocation. But Kedzior, who had been orchestrating this process for several years, remarked, "They can't pull much over on us. We get a gut instinct about who the greedy bastards are."

Whitten's staff again and again returned to a single question for the clerks: "What do you really need to get your bill through the House?" They placed enormous importance on finding the mix of compromises required to pass spending legislation and fund government operations.

The front-office team eventually proposed a dollar amount for each subcommittee and asked the clerk if he could live with it. Initially, of course, each staff director declared emphatically that the number would cause political suicide (and even the end of democracy as we know it). Malow asserted that with "only" $81.2 billion funding the space station, as favored by NASA and President Bush, meant he must close veterans' hospitals, abandon low-income housing projects, and cancel scientific research. Unwilling to cut allocations to other subcommittees further, Kedzior rejected Malow's trade-offs, believing that significant fat could be trimmed from VA-HUD's housing and environmental budgets. The front-office staff also thought NASA was bloated, but they held no strong biases toward any particular space agency account, other than to ensure that Chairman Whitten obtained funds for the advanced solid rocket motor being built in his Mississippi district.

After haggling with the thirteen clerks, Kedzior, Mikel, Dahlberg, and Arnold returned to their Capitol office suite and added up the bottom-line requests. As expected, the total exceeded by billions what the budget would allow, so Kedzior and his colleagues began the balancing act. After comparing a multitude of alternative allocations, they laid out their recommended numbers to Frederick G. Mohrman, the burly staff director of the full committee.

Fred Mohrman is an old hand, having served as clerk of the interior panel for many years before becoming Whitten's chief assistant in 1986. He is, in fact, only the ninth staff director in the hundred years of the House Appropriations Committee. Viewed by colleagues as plodding and uninspiring, but competent and formidable, Mohrman describes his job flatly: "I'm not the brightest, and I'm not the cutest, but I'm there every day because the work of funding the federal government must be done." Several lawmakers volunteered that they would not want to face the tough-talking Mohrman in a political fight.

Dennis Kedzior, by contrast, is articulate, charming, and well liked by clerks and cardinals, even if he doesn't give them adequate allocations. His eleven-year tenure with the Appropriations Committee follows time at the Department of Transportation and the House Budget Committee. Despite the lowly title of staff assistant, Kedzior is Mohrman's right-hand man and does the outreach (which Mohrman despises) to the OMB, the Budget Committee, and House leaders to ensure that appropriations bills run through the system on time and with the minimum of conflict.

Kedzior explained his group's consensus allocations to Mohrman, pointing out the probable problems and predicting who would scream about what. The staff director made only minor changes, and the next day he informed Chairman Whitten of the plan.

At this point in the budget drama the subcommittee chairmen aren't players in the bargaining. "We're really not involved to any appreciable extent until the cardinals' meeting," admitted Bob Traxler. According to a senior staff member, "I can't talk to the chairmen yet because they don't understand the complexities of the budget or the scorekeeping machinations we must perform to stay within the spending caps."

Key appropriators, however, were already being lobbied on several fronts. The most formal pressure from congressional colleagues comes in the form of the Budget Resolution, which is recommended by the Budget Committee and approved by the full House. Yet since the 1990 budget summit agreement had already set a framework for federal spending, taxes, and the deficit, the fiscal 1992 resolution, adopted in mid-April, served mostly as a rhetorical statement by the Democratic majority. It conveyed political positions but avoided budget choices. To cover suggested education increases, for instance, the resolution included $1.8 billion in unspecified spending reductions, a cop-out that thrust the burden (as well as the power) of budgeting onto the appropriators.

Democratic leaders also pressured the cardinals to distinguish their party from Republicans. To demonstrate that Bush was not a real "education president," for instance, Speaker Thomas Foley and Majority Leader Richard Gephardt yearned to show that the Democratic Congress provided more money for schools. Yet Whitten, a veteran appropriator more concerned with adjusting specific programs than with setting broad political strategy, felt little need to take signals from his party's bosses.

The administration, of course, tried to direct the cardinals' actions through the priorities expressed in its budget proposal. But the White House attempted more aggressive lobbying techniques, too. Richard Darman, for instance, traveled to Capitol Hill several times in March and April to press Whitten for more money to NASA and its space station. Although such meetings between the OMB director and the Appropriations chairman are not unusual, Darman's focus on a particular agency was. Whitten listened politely but ignored the White House staffer. As an OMB official put it, "The chairman blew Darman off." The two men never got along, in part because Whitten, the elderly country lawyer, couldn't relate to the young, fast-talking Ivy Leaguer. "Darman's a fine young man," the chairman declared, "but he's a power-grabbing prankster." Distrust between the two men had festered during the previous year's budget summit, when Whitten felt participation by White House aides threatened Congress's control of the federal purse. Real animosity exploded on April 25, 1991, when Darman ordered a small, but disruptive, spending cut of thirteen ten-thousandths of 1 percent (or $13 for every $1 million in almost every government account) because a supplemental spending bill had slightly exceeded the budget ceiling; Whitten viewed the action as petty and as evidence of the OMB's having too much authority.

President Bush, unlike his predecessors, entered the allocation fray personally by sending a letter to Whitten seeking "special consideration" for NASA. But the chairman, who was soon to celebrate his fiftieth anniversary in Congress, wasn't impressed by notes from 1600 Pennsylvania Avenue, and he firmly believed that the president had no role in his committee's allocation decision.

Outside Congress and the White House, an unusual alliance of lobbyists also tried to increase Bob Traxler's allocation. Informally called the 602(b) Coalition after the section within the Budget Act that defines the allocation rules, the four-year-old group exemplifies the odd bedfellows that find one another in Washington. Meeting every Monday morning, an executive committee of aerospace contractors, scientists, housing activists, veterans, and environmentalists plotted ways to encourage the cardinals to allocate more money to the VA-HUD panel and their favorite federal agencies: NASA, National Science Foundation, Department of Housing and Urban Development, Department of Veterans Affairs, and Environmental Protection Agency. Senior appropriators, however, dismissed the outsiders' efforts, claiming that the 602(b) allocation is perhaps the only major political decision on which lobbyists lack leverage.

During the fourth week of April, about a month before the cardinals were to meet, Kedzior and his team returned to each clerk with a specific number. They met each staff director separately, fearing that several might gang together to stage a raid on a weaker subcommittee. The clerks were not told of the allocations for other panels, but they knew that their own number was insufficient to avoid conflicts among the competing agencies and departments within their jurisdiction. "We were not very popular that week," Kedzior admitted. "We heard a lot of explosions and screaming." The central office staff maintained no reserve, so if a clerk wanted to appeal the draft allocation to Mohrman, he'd have to take the money from other subcommittees. Few tried.

The interior panel's staff members, even though they fared relatively well, took the lower-than-wanted allocation personally, comparing themselves with puppies that had been kicked and moaning about how any shortfall would hurt Native Americans they supported. Kedzior expected such complaining. "The subcommittees that worry me most are the ones that don't say anything," he explained. "If they don't holler, we know we screwed up by giving them too much money." Malow, despite his reputation as an aggressive negotiator, resisted approaching the shrewd and gruff staff director. He proceeded instead to explore options for distributing his $81.2 billion among twenty-four agencies, coming to an initial conclusion that he must trim most programs or kill a major initiative.

While the clerks began dividing up their own budgets, Mohrman and Kedzior went to the other side of the Capitol and shared their spreadsheets with James H. English, staff director for the Senate Appropriations Committee. Although House and Senate appropriators later battled heatedly over specific spending accounts, senior staffs on both sides, favoring efficiency over controversy, wanted the lump sum allocations by the two chambers to be as similar as possible.

Two days before the House cardinals met in May, Mohrman gathered the clerks and revealed the final fiscal 1992 allocations for all thirteen subcommittees. Known for his bland recitations, the staff director gave what he described as his "ABC speech," emphasizing how the elementary process of dividing the federal spending pie was complicated by the diverse interests represented in the room. Although none of the assembled staff was satisfied with his allocation, each knew that the deal was set, that the front office had done its best to balance the disquiet.

The allocations didn't propose any radical restructuring of the government. Rather, they offered a modest—but in political terms significant—reordering of Bush's domestic priorities, reflecting the staff's best judgment of what would sell in the Democrat-controlled Congress. Among the most notable changes were a $3.3 billion increase for education and health spending and a $1.3 billion cut for Traxler's subcommittee, which funded NASA. The Interior Subcommittee obtained $1.1 billion more than the president requested for natural resources development, national parks, and Native American programs. Transportation lost almost $1 billion.

STAFF

Appropriations staff members enjoy substantial power, but defining the extent of their authority is difficult. Claiming to express what other lawmakers think but are afraid to admit, Representative Norm Dick declared flatly that the staff controls the Appropriations Committee. Such a conclusion, counters the staff, goes too far. "The staff is powerful only if it can deliver, only if its chairman is on board,"

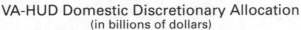

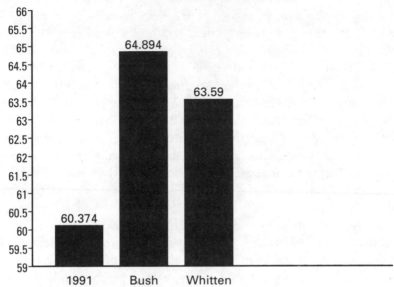

VA-HUD Domestic Discretionary Allocation
(in billions of dollars)

said one. "Our role is to inform policymakers of their choices and to force them to make the tough decisions," commented another. A third defined "clerk," a holdover title from the nineteenth century, as "the ultimate misnomer for an influential employee, but it still denotes a subordinate."

Compared with other Capitol Hill offices, staff power on Appropriations is certainly concentrated. Some 150 legislative committee staffers in the House contribute to the Environmental Protection Agency's authorization, but only one Appropriations staff member decides how much to spend on which environmental programs. Clerks also possess more independence and flexibility than their colleagues on authorizing committees, largely because they manage complex technical and accounting items that most lawmakers are reluctant to tackle; authorizers, however, want to debate abortion, environmental standards, and other policy issues personally.

Kedzior, Malow, and their colleagues claim to be the last bastion of professionalism within Congress. They pride themselves on being nonpartisan specialists, on being pragmatists concerned primarily with making the government work, and on recognizing the price of policy. House Appropriations employees assert they could work for anyone, Democrat or Republican, and they refer to themselves as "professional staff" rather than "majority staff." When Whitten became chairman of the full committee, he made no personnel changes. When Bob Traxler replaced Edward Boland as cardinal of the VA-HUD panel, Malow and the subcommittee staff concentrated on breaking in the new chairman rather than worrying about their own jobs. Even Republican appropriators suggested that most of the current staff would remain if the Grand Old Party won control of the House.

Clerks are a confident and competent lot. Demanding and aggressive, they yell regularly at lobbyists and administration officials who make unrealistic requests or take too much time. Despite such abuse, these outside observers commented frequently on the funding team's brilliance, hard work, and genuine concern for public service.

To ensure that staff members understand how the federal fiscal system works, recruits are plucked from the budget offices of federal agencies to spend a year as detailees on one of the subcommittees. The experience within an agency enables them to appreciate the operations of a large department and the concerns of the OMB. Commented a clerk: "Having seen firsthand the screwups within bureaucracies, we tend to be fiscally conservative." Full-time jobs are offered to only a few detailees who excel. To protect against partisanship, they are immediately rejected if endorsed by a Democratic or Republican member of Congress, if they ever worked for a politician, or if they participated in election campaigns. Candidates must endure three grueling interviews, first with the subcommittee clerk, then with staff director Fred Mohrman, and then before all thirteen clerks, sitting around the conference table in the committee's central office. Technically Mohrman hires all Appropriations personnel; as a result, Dick Malow, the VA-HUD clerk, was ultimately accountable in 1991 to the staff director and Whitten, although on a day-to-day basis he reported to Bob Traxler, the VA-HUD cardinal.

For a budget officer or analyst, serving on the Appropriations Committee is viewed as the pinnacle of one's career. Malow welcomes new staff members to the VA-HUD panel by declaring flatly, "This is the best job you'll ever have." A similar speech was given to Malow when he joined the subcommittee more than two decades ago. "We're indoctrinated with the fact that the House Appropriations staff is a select corps of professionals," said a staff member. "Again and again the message is clear: We are the brains and power that make the system work. These are intoxicating words."

Although the staff professionals could earn far more as lobbyists, they are well compensated, with annual salaries for clerks and central office staff set a bit above $100,000. Perhaps an equivalent benefit in the status-conscious world of Capitol Hill is the attention lavished on these deal makers by cabinet secretaries, generals, and other members of Washington's elite.

Compared with other congressional staffers, who tend to spend only a few years on Capitol Hill before returning to school, joining a lobbying firm, or taking some other job, Appropriations personnel are seasoned veterans. The average tenure of clerks in 1991 was slightly more than twenty years; several have been managing federal budgets since Lyndon Johnson was in the White House.

The Appropriations staff is divided into five layers: full committee, subcommittee professionals, associates, minority staffers, and investigators. The professionals in the central office—led by Fred Mohrman and Dennis Kedzior—take responsibility for the 602(b) allocation and overriding issues that affect all thirteen subcommittees, such as sequesters. In the grand conference room just off the House floor and overlooking the Mall, they also work with the parliamentarian and the Rules Committee to set the terms for the floor debate of bills and with the Office of Management and Budget and the Congressional Budget Office to calculate whether spending caps have been breached.

The small staff of each subcommittee, in suites scattered throughout the Capitol and the Rayburn House Office Building, operates as its own fiefdom. The VA-HUD panel, controlling $81 billion for twenty-four separate departments and agencies, includes only three professionals—Dick Malow, Paul Thomson, and Michelle Burkett—

and one rotating administrative assistant. The central office staff members don't presume to pressure the subcommittees on specific accounts, although they occasionally remind a clerk of Chairman Whitten's personal interest in a particular provision. "We leave subcommittees to make their own decisions," explained Kedzior.

The third layer consists of associates working in the offices of lawmakers on the Appropriations Committee. As a benefit of committee membership, each appropriator receives enough extra payroll from the House to hire two legislative assistants ostensibly to track his interests on the subcommittees. While the responsibilities of associates have increased slightly during the past decade, particularly over items of parochial interest to their bosses, these legislative assistants rarely participate in negotiations over key provisions of a spending bill.

Reflecting their peripheral role in the House appropriations process, six minority staffers operate out of cramped offices in the Longworth House Office Building. According to a clerk, "We have to go out of our way to remember that the minority staff are there." (The more influential Republican staff members are the associates for the ranking minority members on the subcommittees.)

The final staff component is a little-used surveys and investigations team, composed mostly of former FBI agents and accountants, who are called upon periodically to examine questionable actions by particular agencies.

Overseeing the distribution of the federal budget by a small number of personnel is possible only because staff relies heavily on other professionals. Of particular importance are the budget officers at the federal agencies, with whom appropriators share a long-standing compact to exchange accurate and confidential information. Also periodically called upon are specialists at the Congressional Budget Office, General Accounting Office, and Congressional Research Service within the Library of Congress.

The central office and subcommittee professionals—the senior staff—are a closed and insular clan. They trust few outsiders. With the unusual combination in Washington of tremendous authority and tenure, they don't fear the political threats of individual representatives. And as a busy elite they essentially ignore most lobbyists.

For the most part, these attitudes are beneficial to the committee and Congress, ensuring that the appropriations process operates efficiently and with limited pressure from partisan political factions. But the staff also smacks of an "old boy network." The central office professional team and all thirteen clerks are white men. The first female secretary was hired in 1973, the first female professional came on board in the early 1980s, and the first black professional was hired in 1990. (This staff composition reflects the domination of white male lawmakers on the committee. Of the total fifty-nine House appropriators in 1991, only three—Marcy Kaptur, Nancy Pelosi, and Barbara Vucanovich—were women, and only three—Edward Roybal, Louis Stokes, and Julian Dixon—were minorities.)

The resulting culture used to be exhibited at the staff's periodic social events, wild melees at which participants acted like fraternity brothers. According to a professional staff member, "The whole scene was quite crude and male." It was, in essence, a bonding experience, but one that was not open to those outside the clan. More recently spouses and the few professional women working for the subcommittees have invited themselves to staff parties, which predictably have become less raucous. But the combative language and bawdy jokes continue, evidence that Appropriations remains a male domain. Bragged a senior staff member: "We're still a pretty crass crowd."

ALLOCATING AUTHORITY

The institutional character of the Appropriations Committee changed after Watergate as a more liberal Congress approved numerous "reforms" designed, in part, to break the panel's hammerlock on government spending. Impatient with seniority rules that had entrenched southern conservatives, the Democratic caucus began to select cardinals by popular vote. According to a contemporary Appropriations staffer, quoted by political scientist Allen Schick, "All of a sudden, the subcommittee chairman is playing to an audience and that audience has to vote on him every two years to put him back in his chair. That has a great deal to do with how the committee is reacting to the fiscal situation. There doesn't seem to be a tendency in the committee to cut so much anymore because they are doing what the Democratic Caucus wants them to do."

Junior appropriators, moreover, became more outspoken, less willing to follow the dictates of their chairmen. "Before the sea change of the early 1970s," lamented a cardinal, "new members were expected to sit quietly and learn from their elders. Only if freshmen were lucky did the chairman pass them a question to ask at a hearing. Today, in contrast, not only do junior members ask questions, but some of them actually introduce amendments on the House floor challenging their own chairmen."

Although Appropriations remains the most bipartisan of congressional committees, interparty bickering has increased. When Silvio Conte served as the House panel's ranking Republican throughout the 1980s, it didn't seem to matter that the minority party didn't participate in the allocation process since Conte informally worked with Whitten to get what he wanted. Relations changed in February 1991, after Conte died suddenly and the more conservative Joseph McDade took over and demanded increased control. When Whitten, as usual, informed the ranking Republican of the allocations only after the cardinals had met, McDade filed a formal protest, calling the process "troubling and at present unsatisfactory." Joined by the committee's twenty-one other minority members, McDade declared that the allocations "heavily influence, and in some instances dictate, the future funding decisions of each of the subcommittees" and complained that "there is no consultation, no solicitation of opinions and no sharing of information prior to the time the allocations are brought forth in full committee for ratification." Whitten promised to investigate ways to open the process, but no one on the panel expects new procedures.

Dynamics also have changed between the House and Senate Appropriations Committees. According to political scientist Richard Fenno's 1966 study, House appropriators typically outmaneuvered their Senate counterparts, who had to spread their attentions over several committee assignments. Most of this disparity in power disappeared during the past two decades as Senate cardinals became more assertive and hired more staff. While the House maintains a slight strategic edge by initiating appropriations bills, the relationship between the two bodies now depends mostly on the personal clout of individual House and Senate cardinals.

Appropriators on both sides of the Capitol, however, have seized more responsibility for legislating as other lawmakers fail to resolve tough policy issues. In 1989, for instance, it was the money panels that defined "obscene" art that federal funds couldn't support, moderated a dispute between environmentalists and Pacific Northwest loggers over cutting trees inhabited by threatened spotted owls, and reformed reporting requirements for lobbyists and consultants.

Appropriators are not supposed to legislate in their bills, following the historical split between spending and policy-making, and their regular forays into the domain of authorizers are a constant source of tension within Congress. The dynamic, however, is not simply one of authorizers objecting to the actions of appropriators. In fact, chairmen of authorizing committees frequently want the cardinals to embrace legislative language that their own panels won't consider or endorse. Said one senior authorizer: "While we don't want appropriators running roughshod over us, a good relationship with a cardinal lets us accomplish a lot of things we wouldn't be able to do otherwise."

The difference between authorizers and appropriators can be compared with who does the shopping. The authorizing committees prepare the grocery lists, but appropriators decide if it will be two or three cans of peas and if it will be the 89-cent or 99-cent variety. But in the case of appropriators, the choice is actually between two or three satellites and between the $100 million or the $200 million variety.

The day-to-day relations between authorizers and appropriators often depend upon the power—perceived or real—of the authorizing chairman. Representative John Dingell, for instance, is viewed on Capitol Hill as a strong leader who protects aggressively the turf of his Energy and Commerce Committee. House appropriators regularly call Dingell and his staff to check proposed language within spending bills. "Such courtesies are not extended to weaker chairmen," said a senior legislative staffer, "but the cardinals don't want to see John Dingell challenging them on the House floor."

Dingell and other House authorizers, however, have little influence over Senate appropriators, and because of the coincidence of seniority, a few senators direct the authorizing *and* the equivalent appropriations panels. Senator Bennett Johnston, for instance, oversees the Energy and Natural Resources Committee as well as the Energy and Water Development Appropriations Subcommittee; if the Louisiana Democrat can't push bills through his more politically contentious authorizing panel, he can ignore House authorizers and tack legislative measures onto his appropriations bill.

The legislative committees, of course, establish environmental standards, define legal banking activities, set trade policies, and impose taxes—all of which are outside the scope of appropriators. Yet agency officials and lobbyists increasingly turn to appropriators, recognizing that dollars control policy. Numerous administration leaders stated flatly that cardinals and clerks are better informed, have more facts, and make wiser, less partisan judgments. "Appropriators don't get distracted by some of the sideline issues that consume authorizers," said a NASA executive. "Virtually unique in Washington, they measure milestones and results."

ALLOCATING JURISDICTION

When Clarence Cannon reigned in the 1950s, the Appropriations chairman regularly adjusted the jurisdiction of each subcommittee to suit his political aims or whims. Jamie Whitten, in contrast, hasn't altered the basic structure of the thirteen panels since he took control in 1978. Stable as it currently is, the present arrangement doesn't make a great deal of sense. Even appropriators express confusion over why one subcommittee determines funding for Defense Department operations, another finances the development of nuclear weapons, a third oversees the construction of military bases, and a fourth supports veterans.

History provides a few explanations. Cannon, for instance, wrestled control of nuclear power and weapons away from the Pentagon in the 1950s by arguing that such projects were public works that should be managed by a separate Atomic Energy Commission and monitored by his Energy and Water Development Subcommittee.

Jurisdictional allocations now evolve slowly. When the president's budget arrives early each year, a computer at the Appropriations Committee reveals scores of new budget accounts. While about 90 percent of the changes simply reflect new names for existing programs, the panel must decide which subcommittee controls each fresh initiative. Most often the central office staff gives the new program to the appropriations panel that typically oversees the relevant federal agency. Sometimes, however, an individual cardinal expresses a personal interest in a particular program.

On a few occasions disputes erupt. The last serious debate concerned a $500 million account to close military bases, part of the Defense Department's downsizing. Since the Military Construction Subcommittee had financed the development of bases, it wanted to control how they were dismantled. But the defense panel wasn't willing to pass up half a billion dollars without a fight. So Whitten gathered leaders of the two panels to argue it out, and after several hours the military construction unit walked away with the account.

Members of Congress periodically submit proposals to alter subcommittee jurisdictions. Representative George Brown, chairman of the authorizing Science, Space, and Technology Committee, wants a single funding panel to review all science projects. Representative Sonny Montgomery, who thinks veterans should avoid competition from HUD and independent agencies, often suggests a separate Appropriations unit to support the nation's retired military. And some conservatives argue that the controversial National Endowment for the Arts should be transferred from the protection of liberal Sidney Yates and his Interior Subcommittee.

Appropriators, who have a vested interest in the status quo, scoff at such suggestions. Commented a clerk: "The current system works, and people are reasonably happy, so why change?"

ALLOCATING ASSIGNMENTS

Appropriations is the committee of choice for most lawmakers. A former member of Congress described the job's attraction succinctly: "The most delicious of all privileges—spending other people's money." Competition is fierce for the fifty-nine House and twenty-nine Senate seats. When Marcy Kaptur was first elected to Congress from Toledo, Ohio, in 1982, her closest political adviser took her aside and declared that the best leverage is where the money deals are cut. The congresswoman had to wait eight and one-half years until her courtship of senior Democrats finally paid off. Even then she had to knock out five challengers in balloting of the Democratic Steering and Policy Committee, which makes the party's panel assignments.

Speaker Thomas Foley enabled other politicians to obtain the prized post later in 1990, when he added two Democratic slots to Appropriations, continuing a slow expansion of the committee's size. The panel had lost one Republican and two Democratic members after the November 1990 election, but because more Democrats were elected to the House, the committee could have kept a fair party balance simply by filling all three vacancies with Democrats. But Minority Leader Robert Michel desperately wanted to name a Republican to Appropriations. Jamie Whitten objected to the expansion, complaining in part about the physical constraints of getting a larger group together in its modest-sized committee room. The Speaker, however, decided to satisfy the Republican leader rather than the Appropriations chairman.

Within the Appropriations Committee, the real power struggle focuses on subcommittee assignments since some panels have far more authority than others. Former Marine John Murtha, for instance, controls $270 billion of defense spending, while Julian Dixon oversees only $0.70 billion for the District of Columbia. New panelists tend to be relegated to the thankless District of Columbia and Legislative Branch Subcommittees, which control relatively little money and provide no benefits to an appropriator's home district.

When an appropriator died, retired, or was defeated at the polls (a rare event), the cardinals used to divvy up subcommittee assignments in private, smoke-filled meetings. But in 1974 Representative David Obey, now the top appropriator of the Foreign Operations Subcommittee, pushed through reforms that specified more open procedures. Now if there's a Democratic vacancy on a subcommittee, all Democratic appropriators gather in the central office, one wall of which is covered by a big tote board that lists the current members of each subcommittee. Those wanting a new assignment and the few who are on three subcommittees (and who can protect only two of those slots) must give up one of their seats. Green cards are placed on the tote board to designate vacancies. The staff director calls the roll by seniority on the full committee, and each appropriator without two assignments gets a chance to move his name to one of the green cards. The most senior appropriators, of course, already have plum assignments and don't move.

The straightforward process, however, has its complexities. For instance, if an appropriator is willing to abandon both of his or her current subcommittee assignments, a process known as rolling the dice, he or she will be called ahead of more senior members. The decision is not necessarily a gamble—if you have the right connections. One appropriator rolled the dice only after learning from helpful central office staffers that Whitten planned soon to expand his favorite current subcommittee, ensuring that he could get the post back.

The assignment meeting is one that no appropriator misses since decisions made there determine a member's political future. The atmosphere is usually tense, except among the central office staffers, who compare themselves with Vanna White on "Wheel of Fortune" as they turn over green cards when assignments change.

Appropriations is an exclusive committee for House Democrats, meaning that its members generally cannot serve on other legislative panels. Four appropriators, however, are designated to sit on the Budget Committee, as a cardinal put it, "to make sure the Budget Committee doesn't do anything stupid." House Republicans also typically serve only on Appropriations, but their relatively fluid rules allow more exceptions. The smaller number of senators, in contrast, must sit on several committees; Barbara Mikulski, chairman of the Senate Veterans Affairs, Housing and Human Development, and Independent Agencies Appropriations Subcommittee, also works on two authorizing panels, Labor and Human Resources, and Small Business.

House appropriators typically have two subcommittee assignments, while their Senate colleagues tend to be spread more thinly across four or five panels. Usually for political gain, a few hardworking House members serve on three subcommittees, but they're automatically considered the most junior members of their third panels.

Reflecting the independence of Appropriations subcommittees, sometimes referred to as grand duchies, cardinals are usually elected according to their seniority on a subcommittee rather than on the full committee. This practice produces some odd results. Representative Louis Stokes, for instance, had been on Appropriations a few more years than Bob Traxler, but because Traxler had served continuously on the VA-HUD panel a bit longer than Stokes, he chaired that subcommittee during the fiscal 1992 funding cycle while Stokes served as its significantly less powerful ranking Democratic member.

Republican appropriators, having slightly different procedures, revised their subcommittee assignments in early 1991 upon the death of Silvio Conte. Representative Jerry Lewis decided to leave the VA-HUD panel in order to obtain the Republican vacancy on the defense panel that has substantial authority over military contracts for his Southern California district. Taking his place on VA-HUD was a more junior Californian, Bill Lowery, who transferred from the smaller Treasury-Postal Service and General Government Subcommittee. Lowery started his new assignment halfway through the panel's hearings and only a few short weeks before Traxler revealed his unexpected and controversial "mark" for the twenty-four agencies.

3

MARKUP

ONLY ONE DAY after the cardinals met, Bob Traxler called the House VA-HUD subcommittee together to consider his recommendations for distributing $81.2 billion among the federal agencies concerned with veterans, housing, space, science, environment, and consumer affairs. A score of lobbyists and journalists began lining up about noon outside the panel's unmarked offices on the first floor of the U.S. Capitol, hoping to witness the proceedings. Marty Kress, NASA's director of congressional affairs, situated himself strategically away from the group so he'd have a chance to shake hands with the arriving chairman and once again quickly request support for space programs.

Traxler was eating lunch around the corner in a private dining room with Representative Bill Green, the panel's ranking Republican. The subcommittee's tight allocation for fiscal 1992—$1.3 billion below what the president suggested—had convinced the cardinal that a major project within his budget had to be slashed, but that choice had been difficult for this man with a temperament that favors collegiality and consensus. Green bolstered the cardinal's resolve to make bold spending decisions. After dessert and a brief discussion of which panel members would support them, Traxler turned toward the VA-HUD office, encountered Kress, and offered a noncommittal "We'll do our best." The NASA lobbyist looked worried.

About ten minutes after 1:00 P.M. on May 15, the subcommittee

39

staff ushered the lobbyists and journalists into the conference room, just one floor below the full committee's suite. Panel members surrounded the rectangular table, as clerk Dick Malow assumed his position on Traxler's left. The associates sat in chairs along the walls. Everyone but the chairman and the professional staff were frantically reading the just-distributed markup notes that listed the chairman's recommended funding for twenty-four separate departments, agencies, and commissions. Halfway through the document an associate muttered, "Oh, my God!"

Traxler took off his coat, revealing bright red suspenders that matched his tie. The stocky, bespectacled chairman sat down, rapped his knuckles on the table, and called the session to order. Malow passed a piece of paper to Louis Stokes, the panel's ranking Democrat, who read the prepared motion for the subcommittee to go into executive session. Traxler asked the clerk to call the roll. Although no lawmaker lifted his eyes from the critical document before him, each endorsed the motion. After less than three minutes in the room the lobbyists and journalists were ushered out.

"Now we can get down to business," Traxler declared as he began to describe how money was tight thanks to a smaller-than-expected allocation. "It's going to be a year of tough choices."

The chairman spent ten minutes painting a bleak fiscal forecast before distributing two additional sheets of paper, titled "Station In" and "Station Out." The first described the array of cuts in veterans', housing, science, and environmental programs that Traxler believed would be necessary if $2 billion were designated for NASA's space station. The second summarized the markup notes, which eliminated the space agency's pet project.

"I take no pleasure in striking funds for the station," the chairman said. "We simply don't have enough money to support everything."

Station supporters gasped. Bill Lowery, a Republican from San Diego, looked back on the event and commented, "I was aware that the station was controversial and could be trimmed, but I had no idea until I walked into the markup that the entire project would be killed."

Jim Chapman, a strong NASA supporter, never expected Traxler would dare eliminate a multibillion-dollar project. The decision caused the Texas Democrat "parochial panic" since a large share of the space station's funding had been going to the Lone Star State. It took several minutes before Chapman could muster his thoughts and rise to the project's defense. NASA, he eventually countered, had conformed to all the redesign specifications that the subcommittee had requested in late 1990, and the station now offered enormous potential for astronauts in near-zero gravity to develop commercial products and conduct scientific experiments.

As had been planned over lunch, Bill Green complained even more adamantly than Traxler about how the space station's rising costs were eating into all the subcommittee's other programs. NASA's flagship project, he declared, was unnecessary and unaffordable.

Appropriators lodged claims and counterclaims for almost two hours, until Traxler finally suggested a straw poll on his "Station

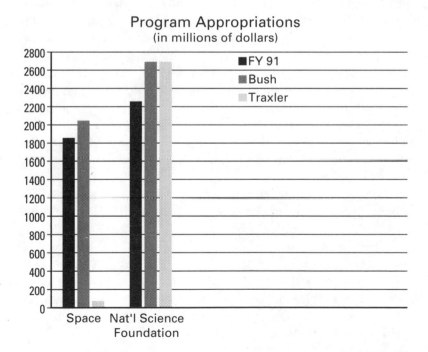

Program Appropriations
(in millions of dollars)

Out" scenario. Malow again called the roll. As Traxler expected, Democrats Louis Stokes, Chester Atkins, and Marcy Kaptur and Republicans Bill Green and Lawrence Coughlin voted against the space station. Joining Chapman and Lowery was Joseph McDade, who as the ranking Republican on the full Appropriations Committee is a member of every subcommittee. With Democrat Alan Mollohan abstaining, the vote was 6–3. If the House and Senate concurred, the $40 billion space station was shot down.

Having carried the day, Traxler became a diplomat, acknowledging that Chapman and Lowery might want to introduce an amendment on the House floor to restore funding, and he promised not to block consideration of such a provision when the Rules Committee set the terms for floor debate, but two conditions had to be met. To provide a level playing field with his own plan, Traxler first demanded that an amendment provide the full funding requested by the administration. "We can't nickel and dime the station and ever have it be operational," he said. "We should either seriously build the project or kill it." Second, Traxler demanded that the amendment not be based on accounting gimmickry, an increasingly common practice among budget-strapped appropriators. Chapman and Lowery agreed to these terms, and the panel briefly discussed—but didn't decide—whether an amendment should be brought before the full Appropriations Committee or just to the House floor.

"Traxler was a perfect gentleman," reflected Lowery. "He understood our concerns and desire for an amendment." The cardinal could be gracious because he was confident of winning a floor fight since his conditions seemed to require that Chapman and Lowery fund the space station by cutting popular housing, science, and environmental programs. Traxler was so assured of his position that he even offered the services of subcommittee clerk Dick Malow to draft the hostile amendment. Chapman and Lowery, knowing well the clerk's concerns with the NASA project, declined that offer.

After the station vote the rest of the bill was "well greased," in Malow's words. He and the chairman spent several minutes describing the highlights. Clear winners included the Environmental Protection Agency, which received $355 million more than the administration sought, and medical care for veterans, which rose $175 million. Suffering in addition to NASA was Housing Secretary Jack Kemp's new HOPE program (Homeownership and Opportunity for People Everywhere), which obtained $655 million less than President Bush requested.

McDade argued that more money should be given to HOPE, a controversial initiative designed to sell public housing to poor tenants. The senior Republican lectured at length about the bankruptcy of traditional public housing programs and the need for new approaches, but Republican Bill Green, who had served as the regional housing director in New York City before being elected to Congress, rebutted McDade's charges aggressively. Without calling for a vote, Traxler intervened and asked Paul Thomson, the subcommittee staff member in charge of HUD's accounts, to "find a bit of money from another account and supplement the HOPE proposal." Away from McDade's scrutiny, Thomson later shifted only $5 million from one part of the HOPE initiative to another.

After answering several procedural questions, Traxler again rapped his knuckles on the table and adjourned the meeting. "Three hours had passed," reflected an associate staffer, "and the tension had exhausted me."

Several lobbyists and journalists had remained in the hallway, hoping for news of the panel's actions. Traxler, who usually avoids the media, knew he had to promote his plan if he was to block a floor amendment, so the chairman put on his jacket, assumed a cordial smile, and walked out the door, distributing copies of his "Station In" and "Station Out" papers to the small crowd. The space station decision, he declared, "reflects the fact that our federal government's budgeting has hit a dead end. We simply can no longer afford huge new projects, with huge price tags, while trying to maintain services that the American people expect to be provided."

Chapman appeared a few minutes later, looking shell-shocked. Acknowledging that he'd probably introduce a floor amendment, the Texas Democrat said, "If we want the space station, we're going to have a battle on our hands."

***

43

Reactions to the panel's markup were mixed and passionate. Most independent commentators commended Traxler for being a courageous and responsible lawmaker who made a tough but necessary choice to reduce federal spending, something politicians frequently talk about but rarely do. Canceling the station would eventually save taxpayers billions of dollars, and the media, at least, tended to support the move. *Business Week* editorialized: "Earth to Congress: Scrap the Space Station." *Time* magazine commented that "NASA's proposed house in the sky will cost too much and do too little."

White House spokesman Marlin Fitzwater, in contrast, complained that House Democrats had turned the space station into a partisan issue and were trying to destroy one of the personal priorities of the president and vice president. Traxler, noting his panel's bipartisan vote, called the White House charges "a total fabrication" and "a disgraceful suggestion."

Housing advocates, environmentalists, and space scientists quickly supported Traxler's move. "Something has to give," said the president of the National Low Income Housing Coalition. "For our constituents, if it's a question of building housing for a half dozen astronauts in space or building housing for humans down here, it's an obvious choice."

HUD Secretary Jack Kemp didn't care about the station, but he seethed about several of Traxler's housing provisions. In fact, he promised to recommend a presidential veto of the entire bill—his first of several such threats—if his department didn't receive at least $865 million for HOPE. (The subcommittee provided only $210 million.)

Knowing the natural hesitancy of other lawmakers to challenge a cardinal, space station supporters on Capitol Hill were skeptical of their chances to restore funding. Robert Walker, ranking Republican on the Science, Space, and Technology Committee, stated simply, "The decision can't be reversed without major pressure from the administration." George Brown, the Science, Space, and Technology Committee's new chairman, was more blunt: "The space station looks like it's defunct."

Traxler's unexpected decision staggered aerospace contractors, which employed an estimated twenty-five thousand station workers scattered across the country. A leading industry lobbyist moaned, "Since I don't see how we can turn this vote around in the House, perhaps our best strategy is to hope for something from the Senate and then settle on a reasonable compromise."

Barbara Mikulski, Traxler's counterpart as chair of the Senate VA-HUD subcommittee, was a recent convert to the space station, but she didn't want to shoulder full responsibility for saving the project. The Maryland senator expressed such feelings just after the House panel's markup, at a reception for American lawmakers and dignitaries hosted by Queen Elizabeth II, in town to dedicate a British exhibition at the Library of Congress. Traxler's action dominated the garden party conversation. When Representative George Brown spotted Mikulski, he lumbered across the lawn and towered before her. "What are you going to do about the space station?" pleaded the cigar-chomping chairman of the House Science, Space, and Technology Committee.

Angered at being boxed into a corner at a public event, Mikulski shot back. "Me?" she cried, pointing her finger aggressively up at Brown. "The question is: What are *you* going to do?"

Elsewhere on the British Embassy grounds Traxler ran into Vice President Dan Quayle, who directed the National Space Council, which coordinated NASA and military space efforts for the administration. The two men exchanged only brief comments, with Quayle saying that the vote was "a real setback." As the vice president moved on to greet other politicians, he remarked to Traxler, "Let's talk about the station soon." They never did.

HEARINGS

Dick Malow, Paul Thomson, and Michelle Burkett clearly had not written the complex markup notes during the evening between the cardinals' meeting and the subcommittee's markup. In fact, they and Traxler had worked intensely on the document for almost three weeks after having obtained from the central office staff a fairly firm

45

indication of their panel's allocation. To be even more accurate, they began their budget-setting process in mid-February with a series of hearings at which administration witnesses tried to justify their spending requests.

Appropriators pride themselves on being hard workers who roll up their sleeves and examine the minutiae of government operations. During the fiscal 1992 cycle the thirteen House subcommittees heard from more than fifty-two hundred witnesses at 271 hearings. The record of their effort totaled more than ninety-eight thousand printed pages. "All members of our committee put in extremely long hours and give much time and thought to the difficult decisions we must make," boasted Jamie Whitten.

Hearings are Congress's best opportunity to explore whether the administration spent its money as lawmakers required, and appropriators frequently use the occasions to assert their authority. Traxler, for instance, lectured NASA officials against using "budget gimmicks that effectively run around the Congress and the appropriation process," and he blasted agency officials for signing service contracts before appropriators had provided sufficient money to fulfill those contracts. The chairman also ordered the Department of Veterans Affairs to consult with the subcommittee before reprogramming money. "We are not going to insist that there be no opportunity to review the committee's decisions," said Traxler, "but we do expect to be consulted, and we need to know when you put a stop on a program and why you are putting the stop on it."

Each subcommittee handles its hearings differently. Unlike others, the Transportation Subcommittee shows its queries to agency officials ahead of time, and the defense panel is the only one that allows staff members to ask questions. Most hearings are technically open to the public, but conference rooms for the VA-HUD and Treasury-Postal Service subcommittees are so small that few people other than witnesses, panel members, and associate staff can attend.

Press coverage varies dramatically. Defense Secretary Dick Cheney testified in the midst of Operation Desert Storm and attracted more than two dozen television cameras and about seventy-five reporters. (Noting the media's presence, all members of Senator Daniel Inouye's subcommittee showed up, a rare event for busy senators.) Just one hour later, however, Energy Secretary James Watkins appeared before a separate Senate panel and attracted only two newsletter reporters and the subcommittee's chairman. Cardinals and clerks often complain that less than a handful of reporters take the time to understand the complexities of the federal budget or the implications of specific appropriations.

Demonstrating that Washington loves Hollywood, the VA-HUD panel tried to add a little flair to this otherwise businesslike procedure by having Ron Howard, the actor and film director who had just released *Backdraft,* testify in favor of funding for the National Fire Academy. With scores of reporters and young staffers clamoring to see the celebrity, Traxler scheduled Howard's appearance at one of the House's larger hearing rooms. (The high-profile event didn't translate into money, however, as the chairman noted in his report that he was "unable to provide additional funding." Yet later in the year Senator Barbara Mikulski inserted an additional $2.26 million for the U.S. Fire Administration facility, which happens to be in her state, Maryland.)

Over the past decade hearings have become shorter and less intense. "Since the Reagan and Bush administrations disliked government innovation, we've had fewer new initiatives to consider," explained a clerk. Another staff director suggested that politicians devote less time to hearings because of growing constituent demands and increased campaign fund-raising requirements.

Agency officials still take the events seriously, believing that a poor performance will jeopardize their funding priorities. Almost all are briefed extensively by their budget officers, some gather their assistant secretaries or associate directors to review the "company line," and a few even stage mock hearings to practice their responses. The exception was HUD's Jack Kemp, who as a confident former appropriator decided simply to deliver his basic stump speech on the benefits of homeownership. The housing secretary even refused to meet beforehand with his budget officer and, as a result, proved unable to answer most questions about his department's budget, being forced again and again to have his staff later supply written answers for the record.

Hearings sometimes produce dramatic confrontations between

47

senior administrators and appropriators, with the members of Congress usually having the upper hand—but not always. When OMB Director Richard Darman tried to justify his office's budget request before the House Treasury–Postal Service and General Government Subcommittee, members of the panel used the occasion to pitch their favorite proposals to the budget czar. Representative Nancy Pelosi, a liberal Democrat from San Francisco who was new to Appropriations, passionately described the plight of her constituents whose homes and offices had suffered extensive damage from the October 1989 Loma Prieta earthquake. Striking a partisan note, she complained that the Bush administration's Federal Emergency Management Agency (FEMA) had failed to provide funds quickly to the affected region.

The well-briefed and quick-witted Darman waited patiently for Pelosi to finish before explaining that the administration's past budget requests for FEMA were far above what Traxler's subcommittee had provided; blame, he suggested, might be better directed at Congress than the White House. Then, with a sly smile, Darman asked the congresswoman why she had voted the previous day for the Democratic Budget Resolution that virtually zeroed out funding for FEMA and her constituents. Pelosi's face went ashen. After several seconds she quickly glanced at her associate staffer, who with raised eyebrows silently admitted that he, too, had not known what was in the resolution. An OMB official later said, "Darman really nailed her, didn't he?"

Appropriators, however, usually win these encounters since they control the purse strings. Representative Neal Smith, for instance, complained at length about the lack of cooperation from the State Department's Congressional Affairs Office. Even Representative Harold Rogers, who usually defended the Bush administration as the Commerce, Justice, State, and the Judiciary Subcommittee's ranking Republican, declared, "I'm as frustrated as the chairman is with the State Department's congressional relations office. On the one hand, they can be unresponsive, rude, and arrogant. On the other hand, they can be unresponsive, rude, and arrogant." When the subcommittee endorsed Smith's proposal to slash the office's budget by 87 percent, two State Department staffers blanched and staggered out of the conference room.

Several weeks before his hearing, each agency's budget officer delivers to the subcommittee staff a thick set of budget justifications. Painstakingly prepared, the books provide a far more detailed defense of each line item than the president's initial budget submission. The Environmental Protection Agency's justification alone spanned 648 pages.

The VA-HUD staff grilled the budget officers extensively about items in the justification books, looking for information rather than confrontation, wanting to understand, for instance, the housing agency's assumptions for occupancy rates at federal housing projects. Malow, Thomson, and Burkett posed scores of questions to the career civil servants: "Suppose the subcommittee did x, what would the outcome be?" or "I have a particular number in mind for an account; what can we fit into it?" On some occasions they had budget officers run dozens of different variations through their Lotus programs. "We want the facts, not the spin," said Malow. "Budget officers are the only ones who are honest with us."

Although they are employees of the executive rather than the legislative branch of government, budget officers often are treated as adjunct staffers of the VA-HUD subcommittee. In addition to providing detailed, nonpartisan information about the agency's assumptions and intentions, these officials serve as early-warning sirens for appropriators, cautioning that certain actions would prompt a thousand letters from angry constituents and lobbyists. "I certainly have my duty to the agency," explained an administration official, "but I also feel a responsibility to the senators and representatives so they don't get blindsided by political problems." Trusted budget officers even critique the parochial funding requests from lawmakers and offer insights into the viability and wisdom of specific earmarks. No doubt they benefit from this close relationship, too. By cooperating, the civil servants protect their scarce money from dubious projects and their actual bosses from controversy.

***

For hearing witnesses, the design of the VA-HUD conference room instills both informality and trepidation. Department heads sit across a rectangular table from the lawmakers, five feet apart, an arrangement that encourages dialogue rather than speeches. On the wall behind and above the chairman, however, a fresco portrays a bare-breasted woman in a red dress surrounded by fires, crows, black-cloaked women, and other signs of desolation.

Traxler began each hearing with short words of welcome and a quick statement of the agency's overall request for money and personnel. After the secretary or agency director introduced his senior staff and summarized his prepared statement, the chairman and the ranking member each asked questions for fifteen minutes. Traxler then solicited short statements or queries from the other panel members, alternating by seniority between Democrats and Republicans.

Junior appropriators often use hearings to focus on agency projects in their districts, taking the opportunity to encourage the administration to fix particular problems. Jim Chapman, for instance, urged William Reilly to rethink the EPA's strict regulations on toxic emissions from wood-preserving businesses, several of which are in Chapman's district. The administrator responded that an existing Superfund site in northeastern Texas is a wood preserver's operation, and "we are now paying the price for that." This put-down didn't stop Chapman's parochial efforts. When FEMA leaders appeared before the panel, the Texas Democrat sought more money for a Houston-Galveston project. At the NASA hearing Chapman stated frankly, "I'm from Texas, and the Johnson Space Center is in my state. I'm very interested in its role in the space station."

The bulk of each House hearing, which usually lasts two full days for the larger agencies and departments, features the cardinal conducting a systematic review of the justification books. Traxler read from a double-spaced text provided by one of the three professional staff members, who sat on his left side and whispered suggestions into his ear. Copies of the questions were distributed to other panel members only just before the chairman asked them, a practice instituted after Republicans had leaked queries to administration officials. Traxler checked off the questions as he asked them, and only periodically did he stray from the prepared text.

The chairman, in essence, sought answers to two broad questions. First, what did the agency do with the money appropriators gave it last year? And second, what does the agency want to do with the money appropriators will give it this year? Framing the follow-up queries, however, is an art form because, as Malow explained, "Department secretaries and agency directors try to provide only one-half to one-quarter of an answer."

Michelle Burkett prepared more than sixty pages of questions for EPA Administrator William Reilly, who executed perhaps the most artful dodge in response to questions about pollution prevention. Asked why the EPA proposed slashing in half the budget for its Office of Pollution Prevention, Reilly sidestepped the query with "It is very difficult to try to put dollar amounts against something that is in essence an ethic within the agency."

Hearings often provide clues to what the cardinal is planning for his markup. At his session with NASA officials, for instance, Traxler quickly moved from congratulating Administrator Richard Truly on the recent launch of the space shuttle *Atlantis* to posing a series of tough questions about the agency's cost overruns on the space station, Hubble telescope, Mars observer, advanced solid rocket motor, and gamma ray observatory. NASA, more than any other agency to appear before the panel, heard the cardinal's lamentations about tight budgets and the tough decisions that lay ahead.

For some new members, Appropriations hearings prove to be frustratingly narrow, particularly compared with those by the more aggressive legislative panels. Authorizers often hold meetings across the country and solicit the views of diverse interest groups and private-sector leaders. Appropriators remain in Washington and talk mainly to bureaucrats; their witnesses tend to concentrate on money matters rather than policy. Lamented Representative Marcy Kaptur: "Appropriators are the recipients of information rather than independent investigators searching for information."

Staff members often use hearings to force a commitment from an agency, as Dick Malow did with the National Science Foundation on its construction of two eight-meter telescopes, one in Chile and the other in Hawaii. The previous year appropriators had provided $4 million to purchase initial glass for both projects, but with an under-

51

standing that the British Commonwealth nations would pay half the total $176 million cost. By the fiscal 1992 hearings no international partner had made a commitment, and Malow wanted to ensure that at least one full telescope would be built if the United States put up its share. The clerk wrote a series of questions for Traxler that compelled National Science Foundation officials to accept that understanding publicly. "There's the value of hearings," declared Malow as he later read from the transcript. "Now no one from NSF can claim not to know the deal."

Malow was graduated from the University of Michigan with a degree in political science, but the white-haired, bespectacled, and lanky clerk has become one of the nation's leading experts on engineering and science projects. "Malow might not have the academic credentials," said a lobbyist, "but he asks commonsense questions, and he's a quick study who isn't snowed by the technical jargon of researchers." To underline the clerk's influence, a NASA executive remarked, "Malow has put his mark on almost every project we have. His fingerprints are everywhere."

A 1989 profile in *The Wall Street Journal,* entitled "How a House Staffer Wields Great Power over Policy Decisions," suggested that Malow has long been the space agency's true administrator. Malow, however, is the classic clerk, understanding his place relative to elected officials. Just before the *Journal* article appeared, he worried not whether the piece would be flattering toward him (as it was) but whether Whitten and Traxler would think it overemphasized the role of staff and insufficiently praised appropriators. Fortunately for Malow, the cardinals took no offense.

Malow usually avoids the spotlight and runs a closed shop. The VA-HUD panel is the only Appropriations subcommittee that doesn't even designate its office with a sign. The professional staffers often lock their doors, and the office has few telephone access lines. When the new phone system was installed, Malow, not wanting to be bothered by outsiders, made sure that incoming calls wouldn't roll over to other numbers. In fact, the clerk accepted only one direct line; another phone number is given only to spouses, and a third is open for calls from the central office.

Although the clerk funds others to develop state-of-the-art technologies, he personally shuns computers and other modern machines.
With a traditionalist's view toward the role of professional staff,
Malow refuses to use a word processor and instead dictates letters
and memos for the central office secretaries to type. It was a conces-
sion by the staff director even to install a computer for tracking the
hundreds of funding requests from members of Congress, and he
swore never again to deal with such newfangled equipment when the
system malfunctioned during the middle of the fiscal 1992 budget
cycle.

After spending eight weeks talking with government officials, the
VA-HUD panel opened its doors in late April to the public. Already
tired of hearings, the professional staff universally hated this exposure to "outside witnesses." "These are the four worst days of the
year"; "We're subjected to predictable and painfully boring speeches
from lobbyists"; "Fewer than five percent have anything intriguing to
say" were the common complaints. Traxler himself found reasons to
be elsewhere for most of these sessions, leaving it for junior panel
members to endure the testimonies.

By tradition, these public hearings are open to anyone on a first-
to-call, first-scheduled basis. They proved to be a cattle show, with
some 150 witnesses each given five minutes to make his or her pitch.
A typical participant was the Washington representative of a trade
association who wanted to impress his clients that he had appeared
before the powerful Appropriations Committee on their behalf. The
director of the Water and Wastewater Equipment Manufacturers
Association even had her assistant bring an Instamatic camera so
pictures of the testifying lobbyist could be included in the group's
newsletter.

Public witnesses clearly depict the disparate pressures on Traxler's
panel. The U.S. Catholic Conference, representing some eight thousand elementary and secondary institutes, wanted more funding to
remove asbestos from schools. The National Utility Contractors'
Association desired additional money for the construction of sewers.
The Cherokee Nation of Oklahoma proposed increased spending for
Indian housing. The lieutenant governor of Massachusetts sought

$100 million to clean up Boston Harbor. The American Gastroenterological Association wanted the Department of Veterans Affairs to expand its research on digestive diseases. Ralph Nader's Public Interest Research Group proposed more money for the Consumer Product Safety Commission.

Though the staff abhorred the four days with public witnesses, some appropriators used the occasion to score political points back home. For instance, discussing the Environmental Protection Agency's sewer budget were presidents of local water companies from the districts of Representatives Marcy Kaptur, Louis Stokes, and Chester Atkins. Having encouraged the Washington-based reporters for their local papers to cover the hearing, these lawmakers declared undying support for their water companies. Kaptur praised her constituent profusely: "I would just like to say, for the record— and I will use my privilege as a member of the committee to say—that I don't think we could have a finer director of our water division than we do in the city of Toledo."

THE LOBBYISTS

In addition to their five minutes of formal testimony, hundreds of lobbyists spend endless hours trying to influence appropriators and the professional staff, who typically try to avoid the petitioners. "I could meet with lobbyists all day every day of the week," protested Paul Thomson. "Rather than offer anything new, they simply reiterate their points. I don't have time to make them feel good." Despite such complaints, appropriators quietly admit they couldn't work without lobbyists. In fact, a few outside advocates, chosen over the years for their reliability, discretion, and honesty, enjoy considerable influence on the funding process. "I often turn to a couple of lobbyists to identify problems and suggest remedies," admitted a clerk. "Several provide valuable questions for our hearings and technical language for our reports."

Lobbyists often ask Malow to speak before their groups, hoping to learn of the subcommittee's plans—information the influential clerk gives out sparingly—and to endear themselves in a social setting with him. The staff director, however, remains focused on business. Lamented a lobbyist: "I've never been able to jolly him, to get him to have a few drinks and lighten up."

Agency officials also go to great lengths to impress Appropriations staff, believing well-organized visits to federal facilities will translate into more money. Park Service personnel regularly invite Interior Subcommittee professionals to see the latest developments at Yellowstone, and they tend to throw in a rafting trip down the Snake River. The Defense Department is probably the most aggressive, carting loads of congressional staff aboard jet fighters, tanks, and aircraft carriers; in the macho language of appropriators and aircrew, a Defense Subcommittee staffer on such a trip "blew his lunch in the backseat of an F-18."

The NASA lobbying machine is legend among appropriators. Since John Glenn and his colleagues were extolled for possessing "the right stuff," astronauts have paraded around the country, fostering public support for the space program; NASA even sponsors space cadet clubs in public housing projects. Aerospace contractors supplement the agency's efforts by working with political action committees, high-priced lobbyists, and thousands of workers (read voters).

Yet NASA's golden image on Capitol Hill has been tarnished. "I used to get mail regularly praising the space agency," said a representative. "But since the *Challenger* exploded and the Hubble telescope malfunctioned, that mail has stopped." NASA Administrator Richard Truly also didn't enjoy the tight relations his predecessors had with appropriators. Former chief James Fletcher used to talk regularly with Malow, sharing information about current projects and brainstorming about new initiatives. Truly, in contrast, believed NASA had become too beholden to the Appropriations Committee, and he maintained an arm's length relationship.

Despite the setbacks and tensions, a cardinal warned, "NASA and its advocates possess phenomenal political clout. Never bet against 'em." Top on the astronauts' agenda for fiscal 1992 was the space station, and according to a NASA official, "The station is so critical to the agency that our top executives would fall squarely on their swords if Congress killed the project."

***

With posts in virtually every congressional district across the country, veterans also can muster a substantial lobbying campaign, and over the past decade they have focused increased attention on appropriators. In 1991 they enjoyed the added benefit of Operation Desert Storm. Politicians, said a delighted lobbyist, "were competing to see who was more manly about giving more money to our military heroes."

Appropriators, however, view veterans as a difficult constituency to please. Despite President Bush's request for a billion-dollar increase in their medical care budget, a significant shift from the regular cuts proposed by the Reagan administration, veterans cried for more.

Since fiscal 1988 leading veterans' groups have jointly prepared an annual Independent Budget, a book-length set of recommendations on how the Department of Veterans Affairs should spend its money. According to a lobbyist, "Appropriators initially thought the Independent Budget was nice but forgettable, but today we find that they insert full paragraphs into their own report." Yet appropriators, while praising the overview of demographic and economic trends affecting veterans, called the budget request extremely unrealistic. In fact, the report itself admits that it "does not rely only on the arbitrary restraints and artificial limitations of the federal budget process."

What veterans lack in budget realism, they make up for with patriotic displays and unreserved lobbying. Several times throughout the year they sponsor large Washington conferences and, replete with military caps, swarm across Capitol Hill. "We find that veterans in wheelchairs are particularly effective lobbyists," said a group leader. "We're shameless about getting what we want."

Housing advocates, in contrast, rarely cooperate with one another. Some favor large public housing developments, others support shelters for the homeless, and all feel righteous about their cause. With passage of the Cranston-Gonzalez National Affordable Housing Act of 1990, the inherent tension temporarily gave way to collaboration. Representatives of some sixty housing groups gathered together in February 1991 to promote funding for the new initiative, particularly the HOME Investment Partnerships that were to provide flexible grants for states and cities to expand the supply and affordability of housing. But the broad coalition slowly splintered until only a small subgroup, nicknamed HOME Alone, remained to concentrate on increased appropriations for the block-grant program. That cluster arranged for its local activists to meet with VA-HUD appropriators in their congressional districts, for its members to send postcards to Traxler, and for its Washington representatives to meet with staff associates during the final weeks of March. Fifteen lobbyists also confronted Paul Thomson of the VA-HUD staff, who, in one of his rare sessions with outside advocates, peppered the group with questions about HOME.

Yet running even this relatively small coalition proved difficult, and the lobbyists spent countless hours bickering about who would represent the subgroup as a public witness before appropriators. They argued heatedly over a dozen draft testimonies, only to hear their selected witness, James Rouse, noted for his waterfront and downtown developments, speak on the plight of low-income housing in an account that bore no resemblance to the negotiated statement.

By the time of the House markup even the HOME Alone subgroup had disintegrated. When the VA-HUD bill came to the House floor, only one coalition member lobbied lawmakers outside the chamber. Individual housing advocates, however, continued to press their own agendas, a few with substantial success.

The Environmental Protection Agency's budget had been rising dramatically, the result of competition between President Bush, who wanted to be perceived as the "environmental president," and congressional Democrats, who refused to cede that role to him. Despite such gains, appropriators and other lobbyists view environmentalists as the least effective advocates before the VA-HUD subcommittee. Most conservation groups—such as the Sierra Club, Greenpeace, or the Environmental Defense Fund—virtually ignore Appropriations, preferring to concentrate on the more accessible authorizing committees. The tactic produces shortsighted disconnects; environmentalists, for instance, lobbied aggressively to win strict regulations within the

Clean Air Act, but they paid little attention to whether the EPA has the financial resources needed to implement those regulations.

Leading environmentalists explain their inaction by complaining that the appropriations process is too technical and complex, that lobbying for federal money can't be explained easily in a fund-raising letter used to attract contributors, and that the congressional funding process is controlled by a few entrenched politicians who aren't susceptible to grass-roots lobbying by membership groups. More telling, environmentalists can't develop a unified budget; clean-air advocates disagree with clean-water specialists, who argue with recyclers, and each camp usually wants far more money than can be provided. A clerk offered the groups some advice: "Environmentalists must learn to start earlier in the budget process, offer more realistic requests, and get their hands dirty doing the political work necessary to win money."

To be fair, the National Fish and Wildlife Foundation has long focused on funding for the Department of Interior (controlled by another subcommittee), and Friends of the Earth and the Center for Resource Economics had started new projects to concentrate on the EPA's funding. During consideration of the fiscal 1992 budget, in fact, Friends of the Earth actively mobilized opposition to the space station and promoted more money for EPA salaries.

Most scientists also ignore appropriators, but a few have concluded that in the zero-sum game of federal budgeting the space station and other large projects are taking funds from basic research. Both the American Physical Society and the American Astronomical Society weighed in early against Space Station *Freedom,* arguing that it lacks any scientific justification. Throughout the year, however, those groups and others were to miss opportunities, make poor judgments, and find themselves checkmated by the realities of political hardball in the nation's capital.

In addition to the organized lobbies, appropriators receive letters from hundreds of concerned citizens. A veteran, for instance, complained about the lack of physical therapists at his Chicago orthopedic hospital. A schoolteacher from San Diego worried about asbestos dust in his classroom. A Michigan auto worker asked for environmental cleanups that would enable her family to fish again at the inland lake near her home.

"Each year the multitude of entreaties from average Americans reminds me that I'm involved in one of our nation's basic democratic processes," expounded a clerk earnestly. "Appropriations is essentially the story of government trying to meet the needs of its citizens."

A few of the appeals, however, provoked more humor than solemnity. "We get all types," said a key aide. "I took a call one evening from a crazy woman who supported the space station because she believed humans would soon need to escape to it from the polluted Earth."

The Chairman's Mark

During the last days of April, at about the time hearings ended and subcommittee staff closed their door to lobbyists, Dennis Kedzior and his central office team quietly returned to the VA-HUD panel with a specific allocation number: $81.2 billion. Traxler and Malow knew changes were unlikely. The only public display of the chairman's reaction came at the subcommittee's penultimate hearing. "We don't have good vibrations as to what the allocation of this subcommittee is going to be this year," Traxler moaned. "Rumors we hear are quite dismal."

The panel actually would appropriate some $97 billion since it was obliged to nod its approval for almost $16 billion previously incurred when the Federal Savings and Loan Insurance Corporation closed two hundred failed thrifts in 1988. Because no politician liked to talk about the S&L disaster, let alone be identified with paying for it, the White House and Congress had previously agreed that the $16 billion would not be tabulated publicly in the VA-HUD bill's bottom line.

Of the $81.2 billion allocation, $17.3 billion was already mandated by laws specifying veterans' pensions, disability benefits, and educational aid. Another $338 million was for defense expenditures as a

result of the subcommittee's oversight of the Federal Emergency
Management Agency and the Selective Service System. The remaining
$63.6 billion represented, according to a key staff member, "what the
VA-HUD panel really controlled and cared about." For some per-
spective, that enormous figure exceeded the entire state budget for
California or New York and was only slightly less than the national
budget for Australia or China.

The subcommittee's $63.6 billion of domestic discretionary spend-
ing represented a 5.5 percent increase over the previous year's allocation, matching inflation and slightly exceeding the average increase
given to other panels. But Traxler and his colleagues were supremely
disappointed since the number fell a full $1.3 billion below what the
president had requested and $1.9 billion under what Jamie Whitten
admitted was necessary to meet the subcommittee's domestic spending needs. Complained an appropriator: "We got screwed."

Subcommittee members feel obligated to provide benefits and services to the veterans who fought the nation's wars, affordable housing for today's less fortunate, and investments in science to secure
America's economic competitiveness. But significant strife lay be-
neath this rhetorical claim to the past, present, and future.

"All subcommittees face controversies," said a senior OMB official, "but the VA-HUD panel confronts the most." What was once a
small catchall subcommittee has come to control more domestic
discretionary spending than any other panel, and demands on its
funds are expanding geometrically. The Cranston-Gonzalez National
Affordable Housing Act of 1990, for instance, authorized $4 billion
more than had been appropriated that year. The Reagan and Bush
administrations wanted to double the National Science Foundation's
budget over the course of five years, and they sought double-digit
annual growth for NASA's accounts. Meanwhile, soaring medical
costs and the war in the Persian Gulf promised increased requests
from veterans, while the reauthorized Clean Air Act and expensive
toxic cleanups required additional funds for the Environmental Protection Agency.

Before the subcommittee staff took any decisive steps to settle the conflicting demands, it met with Traxler in late April to review the "big picture" for dividing $63.6 billion. After the clerk and his colleagues had described the budget dilemma in painful clarity, the chairman conditionally decided—pending any last-minute change to his allocation—that the panel could no longer afford the space station. He also expressed his preference for the block-grant HOME program, a Democratic alternative to the housing secretary's HOPE initiative, and he declared that the EPA's funding should be increased.

Traxler, while acknowledging he would face a major fight, was comfortable with the fiscal merits of his decision to kill the space station. But other, less tangible factors also encouraged his choice. By starkly demonstrating the consequence of a tight allocation on the president's pet project, Traxler figured he might help convince the White House to loosen the caps on domestic discretionary spending. "The decision was not coldly calculated to obtain a larger allocation in future years," said a colleague, "but we clearly discussed the outcome as a possible and welcome by-product."

The cardinal also thought that the Bush administration was sending subtle messages that it wanted to distance itself from the space station. For instance, the vice president, a space booster and director of the National Space Council, had recently—for the first time—questioned *Freedom*'s design and progress, and several of Quayle's key staffers were known to be quietly urging him to support cancellation of the project. President Bush, meanwhile, recently declared his top space priority to be an extended and expensive mission to the moon and Mars, an initiative Traxler reasoned could not be afforded if the station was built. "We had a sense that the White House was looking for an executioner," explained an associate. (Several months later the associate admitted, "Clearly we were reading tea leaves, and we read them wrong.")

Among the subcommittee staff Malow manages the overall numbers and tries to produce a balanced bill that factors in both political and technical considerations. He also concentrates on the National Aeronautics and Space Administration and the National Science Foundation; Paul Thomson covers the departments of Veterans Affairs and Housing and Urban Development, the panel's largest accounts; and Michelle Burkett manages the Environmental Protection Agency and the Consumer Product Safety Commission. They split the remaining eighteen small bureaus.

Even those who have been on the receiving end of a Dick Malow diatribe admit that the fifty-four-year-old clerk is a creative thinker and a talented strategist. "Malow's one of the most significant, adroit, quick staff members on Capitol Hill," declared a lobbyist. "He plays the tensions among the agencies and members very well," commented an associate. "He keeps his eye on future negotiations, always improving his position at each stage of the legislative process," said another.

Paul Thomson also has worked on the VA-HUD panel for more than two decades. Lobbyists, although few meet with him, described him as "solid," "straightforward," "thorough," and "detail-oriented." While Malow develops the creative strategies, Thomson provides the subcommittee with quality control.

Michelle Burkett served as a presidential management intern at the Senate VA-HUD subcommittee before spending the fiscal 1991 cycle as a detailee with the House panel from the Department of Housing and Urban Development. Although not trained as a budget analyst, she proved her mettle and became a professional staff member in early 1991, one of the few women to be so elevated. More accessible than her two colleagues, Burkett spends considerable time talking with administration officials and lobbyists about agency operations. Associates described her as "a quick study" and "one of the few Appropriations staffers willing to help." At Burkett's first hearing Traxler began the session by declaring, "I should indicate for the record, this is a very historic day for this subcommittee, indeed for the full Appropriations Committee, because never in the history of this subcommittee have we had a staff person as lovely as Michelle sitting at the table."

An administrative detailee rounded out the subcommittee staff. During the fiscal 1992 cycle Marissa Smith handled logistics, answered the one phone line, and logged member requests on the troublesome computer. A federal employee with the Department of Veterans Affairs, she was paid by the subcommittee for a one-year,

December-to-December stint. Several years ago, when the Appropriations Committee was totally dominated by men, Malow broke the mold by hiring the first female administrative detailee. According to colleagues, he felt proud of allowing a "skirt" into the office, and the position was long referred to as "the girl."

For each agency, the designated staff person looks at two key numbers: last year's appropriation and the president's new request. The panel, as a result, tends to follow precedent and respond to administration priorities. A lot of accounting gamesmanship, however, arises between the White House and the subcommittee. President Bush, for instance, consistently sought zero funding for the EPA's asbestos removal program, but Burkett knew she had to set aside about $47.5 million since a majority of lawmakers just as consistently supported the program.

Thomson and Burkett, as advocates for their programs, essentially lobbied Malow for a share of the $63.6 billion. Constant tension sparked in the two-office suite, but the three professionals believed they were honest with one another about budgetary fat within their jurisdiction. Malow kept a small reserve fund, which Thomson and Burkett periodically tapped for an extra $10 million. But there clearly wasn't enough money to satisfy all demands.

The House staffers knew from past experience that their marks had to be strong for some programs, such as veterans, because senators regularly tried to cut them. "Perhaps we subconsciously factor in what the Senate will do, but it's not a major concern," said Burkett. "Usually it works in the opposite fashion, with senators taking things out of the House bill so they can later negotiate them back to us."

As bargaining progressed among Malow, Thomson, and Burkett, the team periodically met with Traxler to have him understand and possibly amend their more detailed planning. "We present the options and prioritize the funding," explained Thomson, "but it's the chairman's mark. It has his name on it."

Reporters were to focus on the "big fights" associated with the VA-HUD panel's spending decisions—the space station and HOPE—but the vast majority of the subcommittee's actions went unchallenged and virtually unnoticed. Commented a senior staff member:

"Drama is the exception rather than the rule within the Appropriations Committee."

Appropriators include thousands of directives in their bills and accompanying reports about the basic operations of government. The VA-HUD report, for instance, ordered NASA to launch the latest tracking and data relay satellite from the space shuttle rather than purchase a new launch vehicle. It demanded that the Consumer Product Safety Commission prepare a strategic plan addressing its reorganizational problems. It directed the Environmental Protection Agency to expand its definition of pollution prevention beyond industrial toxics to include household and commercial wastes.

Appropriators also make policy by increasing or reducing scores of funding accounts. Concerned about the continuing decline of high-quality science and mathematics education at the nation's secondary schools, the VA-HUD panel added $45 million for science teachers and equipment. It expanded by $3 million the EPA's campaign against lead paint poisoning. And to provide more economic opportunities for low-income people, it targeted $345 million more than Bush requested to community development block grants.

Despite such extensive adjustments, the professional staff and the cardinal simply adopted the administration's recommendations or the previous year's appropriation for many accounts. "You'd be surprised how much we don't change," revealed Malow. "We rarely alter the base."

Yet staffers do spend considerable time responding to the parochial requests of their panel members. Such pork barreling is not new; nineteenth-century political pundits coined the term by comparing lawmakers stampeding for local spending projects to pre–Civil War slaves crowding around a barrel to grab as much salt pork as possible. The media have long portrayed appropriators as entrenched politicians secretly and greedily funding questionable projects. In *Mr. Smith Goes to Washington,* the 1939 Frank Capra classic, Jimmy Stewart plays Senator Jefferson Smith, a naïve freshman who inadvertently learns of a huge dam that the bosses are trying to hide within an appropriations bill. At the film's climax Smith filibusters passionately for twenty-four straight hours to block the project and protect truth, justice, and the American way.

Despite such criticism, most appropriators remain attuned to local interests. Federal projects scattered throughout Bob Traxler's district testify to the diligence of his parochial attentions. When another congressional committee held a field hearing in Saginaw, the cardinal boarded the group's bus and proceeded to point out proudly the earmarked initiatives he had helped deliver: A community center had been financed by the Economic Development Administration; a research laboratory had been supported by the Department of Agriculture; a new dock was to be paid for by the Environmental Protection Agency. Even the bus had been acquired through federal funds targeted by the cardinal.

Parochial earmarks in the VA-HUD report became far more prevalent after Traxler took control of the panel in 1989. Former Chairman Edward Boland, a veteran Democrat from Massachusetts, disliked "directed funding," the term preferred by appropriators to "earmarks" or "pork." Labeled by some as "Dr. No," Boland repeatedly told petitioning lawmakers, "If a single project is so important to your political career, you don't belong in Congress."

Shortly after his ascension to the "college of cardinals," Traxler joked frequently about his fresh assignment and the increasingly tight budgets that limited his flexibility. One standard lead in speeches was: "I was so happy to have my hands on the cash register . . . until I learned that it was empty." Added a colleague: "Traxler's goal in life has been to give away money. His only disappointment is that there's not more to distribute." As a relatively junior cardinal Traxler, although well liked by his colleagues, did not yet possess Boland's level of respect. To get his bill approved, he thought key lawmakers needed to feel a personal stake in his legislation. More important, Traxler believed firmly that representatives and senators should direct government spending. As elected officials, he argued, they are far better qualified to select worthy projects than some "green-eye–shaded bureaucrat holed up within one of the federal agencies." The administration, Traxler maintained, "has no monopoly on wisdom."

These convictions led him to request that his panel members inform him by May 8, about one week before markup, of three deserving projects for which they wanted funding. The unwritten assumption was that each behest be "reasonable," usually $1 million or less. While these petitions could be for programs such as an increase for the EPA's Pollution Prevention Office, one lawmaker explained, "You don't want to waste your chits on anything but parochial priorities." The chairman and the professional staff met individually with each of the eight panel members to review specific requests. Although Traxler appeared supportive during these sessions, appropriators left not knowing which, if any, earmarks would be included in the chairman's mark. They learned just the day before markup when Malow called their associates, often the first and only time during the year that the clerk spoke to these legislative assistants.

Reporters and some authorizers may mock pork barrel projects, but most politicians crave some concrete evidence of their efforts in Washington. Although no one interviewed would defend the appropriation for a Lawrence Welk museum, one representative declared flatly, "Members rarely get burned by pork. I'd relish my political opponent's challenging me on a grant to my district. I'd proudly say that it is my job to represent the district and the grant is more than justified."

Pork barreling is a nonpartisan habit, embraced by members of both political parties. Conservative Senator Phil Gramm, who before becoming an appropriator bashed most government spending as wasteful, developed a series of radio commercials for his reelection campaign that described proudly the projects he had directed to each Texas county. Even Representative Robert Walker, considered by one journal the "archenemy of pork," was caught with a special request in the fiscal 1990 supplemental bill. As debate on the measure began, the Pennsylvania Republican rose on the House floor and roundly attacked Traxler's funding of thirty-seven community development projects the Department of Housing and Urban Development didn't want. "These [projects] were not picked because they are the most meritorious projects in the country," Walker complained. "They were picked because people who were sitting in the room had the political clout to get something in that they wanted, and that is all that it is."

Traxler, ever prepared for such attacks, responded sarcastically,

"Is my good friend suggesting that I ought not to put the language in a bill this year that he has requested to forgive the indebtedness of that urban renewal project?"

A red-faced Walker protested that his request "does not cost the government a dime and the gentleman knows that." But Bill Green, a fellow Republican, noted that forgiveness of repayments did, in fact, cost the government. In a subsequent interview with *Congressional Quarterly,* Walker commented on this encounter: "It's uncomfortable because I do think I carry an important message about keeping this process clean. So they're having fun at my expense." A cardinal reflected on the incident: "See, everyone wants a little pork."

To keep track of which members sought what, the VA-HUD staff developed a computerized system that logged almost six hundred requests in addition to the pleas from panel members, which were given priority consideration. To ensure that proposed earmarks had merit and would not later embarrass the chairman or the subcommittee, Malow, Thomson, or Burkett discussed each project with agency officials, often learning that the venture had been proposed repeatedly but could not be justified. Playing the heavies in this process, staff members objected if a particular earmark set an unwelcome precedent, such as having politicians rather than scientists select National Science Foundation awards. They frequently briefed Traxler about problems with specific requests so the cardinal wouldn't be ambushed by some representative on the House floor seeking to gain a quick commitment from the congenial chairman.

Malow, Thomson, and Burkett offered their opinions of each earmark request. "But it's the chairman's call," asserted Thomson. "And he decides according to what he thinks is needed to get his bill through the House." Most representatives interviewed, including those who failed to obtain local funding, described Traxler as careful. "He spends the time to understand the merits of his selected earmarks so he can defend them if necessary," explained a colleague.

Although Traxler accepted only a small percentage of the requests made to his panel, several representatives remarked on the ease with which earmarked funds could be obtained. "I used to plead endlessly for grants from the agencies," said one, "but I've since learned that it's far quicker and less complicated to approach a cardinal directly."

There is, of course, a catch to easy earmarks. "Although the cardinal hasn't yet asked for anything in exchange," explained a lawmaker, "there's an implicit understanding that one day he'll seek a hand on some vote or with something I can do for him on my committees."

Political campaigns also influence the pace and direction of pork barreling. Even Traxler worried about his political future since Michigan was losing two congressional seats because its population growth throughout the 1980s was slower than that of the rest of the nation. In 1991, it became increasingly clear that Republicans in charge of the Michigan Senate would block any redistricting effort by the Democrat-dominated House. The key player, therefore, became newly elected Governor John Engler, a conservative Republican who was slashing state programs and alienating Democratic politicians. Even if Engler didn't personally sketch the new districts, he could appoint a Republican-dominated set of judges who would. Another Michigan Democratic representative concluded: "A Republican or a court-ordered plan could hurt us all, even Traxler." Some political analysts suggested that Traxler crafted the VA-HUD bill with Michigan's redistricting in mind. The cardinal, they argued, earmarked special projects throughout the state in order to endear himself to influential state officials who could help ensure his political safety.

In addition to weighing such political factors, clerks must consider complex technicalities associated with the federal government's two parallel budgets. The first, budget authority, tracks the amount of money an agency can obligate each year from the Treasury. The second, outlays, defines the actual amount of checks to be disbursed by the Treasury. Differences between the two budget numbers can be confusing but critical.

For example, imagine that Congress wants to build a satellite costing $1 billion. Appropriators might provide $1 billion of new budget authority for the satellite in this year's VA-HUD appropriations bill. NASA, as a result, could legally enter into contracts or obligations totaling $1 billion. But the budget authority would translate into outlays only when the Treasury issued checks to the aerospace contractors. If actual expenditures for the satellite's construction were spread evenly over five years, $200 million of outlays would be accounted for in each of the next five years.

Outlay rates vary dramatically. Budget authority for salary accounts tends to be spent in the year it is appropriated, so accountants say salaries "outlay at close to one hundred percent." Research activity, in contrast, usually has a 50 percent spend-out rate, while construction projects are even lower. After considering past trends and new assumptions, computer analysts at the OMB and the Congressional Budget Office calculate such percentages for virtually every federal program. Yet in the end they are only guessing. The Treasury Department must wait at least a month after a fiscal year ends before government checks have cleared and outlays can be tabulated.

With Washington periodically fixated on the deficit, appropriators have concentrated increasingly on outlays, since the annual deficit is defined as the difference between what the government actually spends and what it receives from taxes and other sources. With an allocation that provided slightly more budget authority than outlays, Malow faced peculiar pressures. Regardless of merit or policy implications, the clerk was inclined to cut salaries and other accounts that outlay quickly before he would trim slowly outlaid construction projects.

A fixation with current-year outlays also induces appropriators to tinker with accounting gimmicks. In Traxler's first season as subcommittee chairman he shifted a federal pay day into the next fiscal year in order to save $850 million in current-year outlays. For fiscal 1992 several subcommittees, notably the labor-HHS panel, delayed substantial budget authority to the last day of the fiscal year, effectively pushing outlays into the following budget cycle. Even the Bush administration proposed postponing an obligation for veterans' medical care equipment in order to reduce outlays in the current year. Such accounting tactics may resolve present crises, but they represent nothing more than a shell game that places enormous pressure on future outlay caps. "Gimmickry is the sad phenomenon we've come to," commented a clerk. "We stay awake nights dreaming up accounting tricks that just a few years ago we would have thrown others out of the office for even suggesting." This tyranny of outlays also forces a short-term focus. "We should be looking at the deficit as a long-haul problem," said another staff director, "but we've become like the corporate executives we criticize for thinking only of their current financial statements."

This obsession with outlays, moreover, has expanded dramatically the power of scorekeepers at the OMB and Congressional Budget Office who calculate spend-out rates for each appropriations account, much to the frustration of the cardinals. "It is a threat to representative government," complained a clerk. "It allows nameless, faceless computer dweebs at OMB and CBO to make policy by deciding which amendments from elected members of Congress will be considered to be within the spending caps."

Well before markup, Malow secretly asked the Congressional Budget Office for an initial scoring of the staff's alternative spending plans. With a disappointingly low allocation and few gimmicks available, the clerk came to appreciate Traxler's inclination to cancel NASA's expensive space station.

Malow prepared two summary tables for his twenty-four departments and agencies, one with the space station in and the other with the station out of the panel's budget. If NASA's pet project received full funding in fiscal 1992, he outlined an array of corresponding cuts, including $1 billion from other space agency initiatives, $327 million from environmental cleanup, $250 million from National Science Foundation research, $142 million from assistance to veterans, and $134 million from homeless aid. The reductions, of course, could have been adjusted a thousand different ways depending upon one's priorities. Part of the clerk's enormous power results from his ability to craft this initial budget presentation, juxtaposing selected accounts, creating certain conflicts. Malow wasn't beyond making the display bolster Traxler's position. "I made it grim for the station in category," the clerk admitted later. "I could have improved it some."

After discussing more and more detailed plans with the chairman, the subcommittee staff prepared the final markup notes, a twenty-seven-page document that listed funding for each program account, making comparisons with last year's appropriation and the president's request. The notes also highlighted the earmarked projects and presented a general sense of the directives that Traxler's report, to be prepared by the staff after the markup, would give to the agencies. Panel members used to receive the markup notes a day before the meeting, but despite strict instructions that the papers be embargoed from public release, representatives regularly passed the document on to agency officials and lobbyists, who would immediately complain to the subcommittee staff. Now only Traxler saw the completed notes in advance of the markup. Malow, Thomson, and Burkett, always closemouthed about their intentions, became increasingly concerned with security as the markup approached. They locked the two doors to their offices, restricted anyone from entering for fear he or she might see "secret" papers lying about, and asked the U.S. Capitol police to make more frequent rounds. "Lots of people at the agencies and lobbying firms desperately want to know what we're going to do," said Burkett. "They'd go to great lengths to get early information."

A few subcommittee observers sensed a critical decision was about to be made. Mark Albrecht with the White House's National Space Council called Malow two days before the markup to inquire about the space station's fate. "I couldn't give him a straight answer," said the clerk, "but I stated quite clearly that the subcommittee had serious funding problems." The day before the markup leaders of the American Astronomical Society, the association of space scientists, began faxing letters to Traxler encouraging the funding of space science over the space station. From the chairman's perspective, these faxes demonstrated that NASA's traditional political partnership between space scientists and astronauts had split, perhaps reducing the agency's lobbying might and thus making it easier to kill the expensive project.

Knowing the space station decision would startle most of his colleagues and mortify those with large NASA contractors in their districts, Traxler covered a lot of bases on markup morning. He first met with House Speaker Thomas Foley to explain his panel's financial

71

predicament and to express his willingness for a lively floor debate on an amendment to restore the station's funding. He also assured Jamie Whitten that the bill contained more than $400 million for the Mississippi-based advanced solid rocket motor project, even though most space experts believe the new motor's only real purpose is to lift components of the threatened station into orbit.

Ever the gentleman, Traxler even tried to alert NASA Administrator Richard Truly to the fundamental change that was about to affect his agency. Truly, however, was in Europe and unavailable. NASA's congressional affairs staff, knowing only that the cardinal wanted to talk with the administrator on markup day, frantically tried to find the deputy administrator, J. R. Thompson, but he, too, was unreachable, flying on a commercial plane back from California. By the time Thompson landed at Dulles Airport outside Washington, the markup had begun. So the only formal communication Traxler was able to give to a NASA official was his passing comment in the hallway to Marty Kress: "We'll do our best."

FULL COMMITTEE MARKUP

Reflecting the cardinal's control of spending decisions, the subcommittee made virtually no changes to the markup notes on May 15. Now Traxler and the professional staff had one week to craft the actual bill and an accompanying report for a markup before the full House Appropriations Committee. "Those were long days and nights," remembered Paul Thomson. "We refused to see anyone, ignored phone messages, and spent the day drafting report language. Each afternoon at five P.M., we'd meet to debate each other's edits." An associate staffer called Michelle Burkett during this period at 10:00 P.M., only to learn that she had gone out for a quick bite and would be right back.

Appropriators tend to place few directives in their bill, believing that the administration usually should be allowed flexibility to adapt to changing circumstances, such as economic recessions, natural disasters, or new authorizations. Cardinals also want to avoid the hassle of amending their own legislation throughout the coming year, so they insert detailed instructions mainly in their "reports." While such narratives are not legally binding since they aren't endorsed by the full House or Senate, appropriators believe strongly that federal agencies must follow report language without deviation—or face their wrath.

The VA-HUD bill specified funding for some 140 accounts, including only 5 for NASA: research and development, space flight and control, construction, salaries and wages, and the inspector general's office. To give some sense of the difference between the legislation and the report, consider that the space station was not even mentioned in the bill; it fell under the general obligation for the space-flight and control account. Traxler's hundred-page single-spaced report, however, spelled out the project's fate: "The Committee deeply regrets that, owing to the overall budget constraints, it has been forced to suspend funding for the space station program."

On May 22, one week after Bob Traxler's dramatic markup, the fifty-nine members of the House Committee on Appropriations reflexively endorsed Whitten's allocations to the thirteen subcommittees and then turned their attentions to spending bills from the energy and water and VA-HUD panels. Full committee markups are usually rubber-stamp events since appropriators rarely challenge their colleagues, believing the subcommittee with expertise knows best and fearing other appropriators might retaliate.

Space station supporters, however, flexed their substantial political muscle before the meeting. OMB Director Darman threatened a presidential veto of the VA-HUD spending bill unless appropriators restored money for the $40 billion project. "If a program, which has been supported by a bipartisan national consensus for the last seven years, is now canceled, it would call into question our ability to execute any large, complex science and technology program," Darman wrote to committee members. "Other nations would rightly question our reliability as a partner in such ventures." Aerospace lobbyists who had not visited some congressional offices in years suddenly descended in force. They paid particular attention to members of the VA-HUD panel who had voted against the station in the subcommittee's straw poll, believing that any conversion before the full committee meeting would be politically valuable. Marcy Kaptur felt special pressure from Jim Chapman, who, two years before, had delivered the swing vote electing her to Appropriations. In the "tit-for-tat" culture on Capitol Hill, Kaptur owed Chapman a favor, and now the Texas Democrat wanted it. But caring more about housing and environmental programs than about NASA, Kaptur stuck with Traxler.

Chapman and Lowery soon realized the folly of challenging a cardinal within his own lodge. Moreover, Chapman and other Texas appropriators knew they'd be busy at full committee markup protecting their state's controversial superconducting super collider, funded within the energy and water bill. They decided to wage their space station fight on the House floor.

Still, Traxler received a surprising blow from the full committee. The cardinal, believing he was doing Maryland-based Senator Barbara Mikulski a favor, had refused to provide any money for the National Science Foundation to relocate from Washington to suburban Virginia. Representative Frank Wolf, a Republican from Virginia, made a pitch for the new location with little fanfare, and his anticipated amendment was going nowhere until Representative Steny Hoyer spoke. The senior Democrat from Maryland explained the long history of Virginia and Maryland battling over the NSF site. The previous year Mikulski had delayed the planned move to Virginia so that another Maryland location could be examined. Subsequently administration experts again identified Ballston, Virginia, as the best spot for the agency.

To Traxler's dismay, Hoyer offered an impassioned plea to follow through on the process and move the NSF's headquarters to Virginia. Few appropriators could object to the Marylander's unselfish entreaty, and the money Traxler had cut was reinstated. More than one associate staffer worried that the cardinal's unexpected defeat might be an omen.

4

THE HOUSE FLOOR

A SPACE STATION is an old idea. In the late 1800s novelists Jules Verne
and H. G. Wells foresaw its role in space travel. In the 1920s theoreti-
cal scientist Hermann Oberth predicted a refueling depot orbiting the
Earth that "would constitute a sort of miniature moon." And in 1968
filmmaker Stanley Kubrick popularized the concept with his movie
2001: A Space Odyssey, which began with a massive space station
rotating to the graceful sounds of "The Blue Danube."

The idea, despite its age and beauty, initially engendered little
political or public support. Although the National Aeronautics and
Space Administration saw the station as a critical step toward its
"ultimate objective [of] manned travel to and from other planets,"
the Kennedy administration, anxious to provide a dramatic response
to Yuri Gagarin's 1961 orbit around the globe, rejected the notion of
a way station on America's sprint to the moon. The Nixon White
House, sensitive to public opinion surveys showing that 50 percent of
Americans wanted to "do less" in space, slashed NASA's budget and
approved construction of the shuttle but not the station. President
Jimmy Carter issued an even more restrictive space policy: "It is
neither feasible nor necessary at this time to commit the United States
to a high-challenge space engineering initiative."

NASA, however, never abandoned the idea. For nearly a quarter
century the space agency devised design after design for a perma-

nently manned orbiter. Virtually ignoring appropriators, it siphoned money from diverse accounts to have McDonnell Douglas, Rockwell, and other aerospace contractors draft construction plans. Congress in 1967 did approve funds for a twenty-two-foot-diameter space can christened *Skylab*, but the modest orbiting laboratory, too small for a permanent base, generated little enthusiasm among NASA astronauts. The space agency deserted *Skylab* after only three missions, including a well-publicized linkage with a similar Soviet craft, *Salyut 1*.

The U.S. Air Force experimented in the 1960s with a not-so-secret effort to build a man-tended spy station that would orbit high above the Soviet Union and China, but the military abandoned the project in 1969 because of advances in less expensive automated satellites. With some fear that a civilian space station might siphon funds from other military space projects, the commander of the Air Force System Control declared, "We know that we can put people into space, but to put military people in space just because it's something we can do is not my idea of a judicious expenditure of our scarce resources."

NASA persisted, more for bureaucratic than pragmatic reasons. After serving as NASA's administrator in the early 1980s James Beggs conceded, "The feeling was that unless we could get a station, the manned activities would truncate and we'd run out of mission." William Proxmire, Barbara Mikulski's predecessor as chairman of the Senate Appropriations subcommittee overseeing NASA's budget, sensed the agency's underlying, if unspoken, goal. "I am concerned that [the space station] will proceed regardless of the real need for such a program because your agency needs it more than the country needs it," the senator complained to NASA officials. "I have long believed that your agency has a strong bias toward huge, very expensive projects because they keep your centers open and your people employed."

Beggs and NASA sought a broad coalition of support by promising a station design that would do virtually everything for everyone. The manned orbiter was to be a research laboratory for scientists; a manufacturing facility for industrialists; a permanent observatory for astronomers; and a transportation node, servicing facility, assembly facility, storage depot, and staging base for astronauts on ambitious future missions. (By 1991 each of these eight initial justifications had been abandoned; one wag described the station's changing mission as "a revolution of declining expectations.")

The space agency, while overestimating the station's uses, intentionally underestimated its cost. Edwin Meese, a NASA supporter and counselor to President Ronald Reagan, revealed this "lowball strategy" when he declared, "Let's get our foot in the water so that we have a commitment and then we can worry about the long-range costs later." In 1983 NASA claimed that an eight-astronaut station could be assembled in space by 1991 for a total cost of $8 billion. (By early 1991 NASA had spent $5.6 billion and had constructed nothing.)

NASA also cleverly lined up international partners to strengthen its coalition of supporters. American officials approached the European Space Agency, Japan, and Canada in 1982, well before the president had made any commitment to the project. According to NASA's deputy director for advanced programs, "We knew that if we found ourselves locking in with international agreements, it would be awfully hard to say no to the program." (By 1991 the three foreign partners had contributed close to $2 billion, and they planned to devote four times that amount.)

The key player in Beggs's plan was the new president, Ronald Reagan. The former governor of California understood the economic benefits of a strong aerospace industry, and as an advocate of private industry he appreciated NASA's vision of American businesses producing sophisticated products in a zero-gravity environment. Beggs scheduled corporate executives to lobby the president for strong commercial participation in a space station.

Still, opposition to the project, even within the Reagan administration, remained substantial. Budget Director David Stockman called the facility an example of "high-tech socialism." The conservative critic of government spending argued that technological progress resulted not from expensive federal science ventures but from lower taxes that reward private inventors, entrepreneurs, and investors. Reagan's science adviser, George Keyworth, questioned the very purpose of a manned space program. "I would support additional funding if I were shown something that I have not yet been shown—a single well-defined application of a space station," he told appropriators. "For the nation that is the world's leader in automation technologies and in microprocessors and the underlying technologies, to take a step backwards to emphasize man in space at the very time when we are best equipped to use our automation technologies is a most unfortunate step."

Scientists at the distinguished National Research Council also expressed skepticism. While praising NASA for consulting with the research community, the council's Space Science Board in September 1983 wrote, "On the issue of meeting the needs of space science, our recommendation would be to use the space shuttle." Other prominent scientists and engineers also concluded that the station would be overweight, consume too much power, and require extensive maintenance.

Overlooking these complaints, President Reagan endorsed the idea of a space station in his 1984 State of the Union address. Twenty-three years after President John Kennedy had stood at the same podium in the House of Representatives and proposed that Americans travel to the moon, Reagan directed NASA "to develop a permanently manned space station and to do it within a decade." The president, who later called the project Space Station *Freedom*, cited the potential for "research in science, communications, in metals, and in lifesaving medicines which could be manufactured only in space."

Despite Reagan's declaration, battles over funding persisted. Beggs sought $63 million for the space station in fiscal 1984, but Stockman cut the request down to $14 million. Appropriators approved that amount with little debate, but they grew increasingly skeptical of the project. Edward Boland, then chairman of the House Appropriations space subcommittee, worried aloud that NASA was designing a station "that we can neither afford to operate nor effectively use." Ranking Republican Bill Green, even more dubious of NASA's grand plan, argued that if an automated space station visited infrequently by astronauts could "do the job as well and less expensively, we should take that path." Although NASA supporters on Capitol Hill rejected proposals to redesign *Freedom* as a man-tended unit that relied mostly on automation and robots, Congress over the next several years approved only 40 percent of the funds Reagan requested, forcing NASA to stretch out the station's planning and construction.

Bickering within NASA further stalled the project. "People studying the earth wanted to be in polar orbit; people studying the heavens preferred an orbit near the equator," explained space historian Howard McCurdy. "Space explorers wanted artificial gravity, while space manufacturers wanted no noticeable gravity at all."

NASA also kept changing the station's mission, bending to catch the political winds. It initially claimed that the orbiter would observe the Earth and stars, but that need lost credence with the advent of sophisticated satellites. Administrator Beggs sold President Reagan on the notion of a zero-gravity manufacturing center, but industrialists quickly declared the operation costly and unnecessary. When President George Bush declared his long-term space goal to be a manned mission to Mars, NASA again reinterpreted the station as a biomedical laboratory that would examine the effects of weightlessness on space travelers.

Ironically, it was the House VA-HUD subcommittee that championed *Freedom* in fiscal 1991 with a substantial $2.25 billion appropriation. Yet Traxler issued strict instructions that NASA redesign the project within ninety days to trim $6 billion in total costs and to ensure that each major phase create a self-sufficient enterprise. The House and Senate cardinals jointly declared: "The Committees on Appropriations have warned since the outset of this program that future budget constraints would render it virtually impossible to design, test, and build the space station envisioned in 1984." NASA, recognizing the station's growing cost and controversy, proceeded to redesign in earnest. But as if to warn appropriators of the consequences of cutbacks, agency officials ended a $24 million space station contract at the Goddard Space Flight Center in Mikulski's home state of Maryland. The cancellation eliminated 240 jobs.

Dan Quayle, named by President Bush to be chairman of the National Space Council, which coordinates the government's military and civilian space activities, considered redesigning NASA's entire operation after *Challenger* exploded and the Hubble telescope malfunctioned. To review the agency's future, the vice president assembled in mid-1990 a twelve-person blue-ribbon panel that became known as the Augustine Commission after its chairman, Norman Augustine, chief executive officer of the Martin Marietta Corporation, a major aerospace contractor. Commission members, after five months of study and discussion, offered their recommendations to Quayle at a dinner at the vice president's residence in early December 1990. According to *Washington Post* reporters David Broder and Bob Woodward, Augustine explained the group's five priorities over salad. First, he said, was space science. Fifth and last was the space station. Richard Darman, an acknowledged "space freak" and station advocate, groaned. Knowing that the final item on a list of budget priorities would be targeted for extinction, by dessert the White House budget director had convinced the group to highlight space science but to lump the other items together, abandoning any priority listing.

Despite Darman's success at toning down the commission's skepticism toward the space station, Quayle emerged from the dinner suspicious of NASA's pet project, and he soon joined appropriators in calling for "a complete redesign of the space station to reduce cost and complexity." But several months later and just a few weeks before Bob Traxler's panel marked up its bill, Darman again confronted Quayle. While the vice president's senior advisers asserted that the station should be killed, the OMB director argued fervently about the public relations disaster that would result for the Bush administration if *Freedom* were canceled. After a half hour meeting Quayle emerged a strong station advocate. "I'm not rolled," said the vice president in response to the reporters' questions. "People present me the facts, and I make up my mind."

The Augustine Report, unlike those from many similar government commissions, excited substantial attention from lawmakers, scientists, and journalists. Despite an unrealistic appeal for annual budget increases of 10 percent above inflation, the paper proposed a cogent and dramatic refocusing of America's civilian space effort.

Specifically, it said NASA should build an unmanned rocket booster to eliminate its total reliance on a fleet of space shuttles. It clearly stated that space science "ranks above space stations, aerospace planes, manned missions to the planets and many other major pursuits which often receive greater visibility." Moreover, it recommended a major redesign and simplification of the space station.

NASA presented its redesign plans to the National Space Council in early February 1991, arguing that it had met requirements of both the Augustine Commission and the Appropriations Committees. Agency insiders referred to the slimmed-down project as "Kohrs lite," after Richard Kohrs, director of the space station program. Most scientists didn't see the humor. The Space Studies Board of the National Research Council, chaired by Louis Lanzerotti of AT&T Bell Laboratories and including former astronaut Sally Ride, issued a scathing seven-page statement in March arguing that the reconfigured station failed to meet the basic requirements of the two disciplines for which it was intended: life science and microgravity research. The board concluded, "Neither the quantity nor the quality of research that can be conducted on the proposed station merits the projected investment."

Traxler's panel, meanwhile, called a special hearing to talk with Norman Augustine. As he did with many witnesses, the cardinal asked for assistance in setting spending priorities. But the aerospace executive waffled when pressed to choose between the station and a new launch vehicle. "Had the space station not been started, had we not made a major investment and major commitment of talent to it, we may have made a different recommendation," said Augustine. "We think the space station is essential. We think that in the ideal world, we would probably give higher priority to the new launch vehicle. But in the world we live in, we think it is necessary to pursue both as best we can."

Across the Capitol, also on March 20, the administration began its campaign to defend the redesigned station. At a closed-door luncheon within the vice president's Senate suite, Quayle met with NASA Administrator Truly and leaders of the congressional science and space committees. In a letter to NASA that he subsequently released to the media, the vice president asserted that manned exploration of space is "man's destiny." Using patriotic, if vague, language, Quayle declared, "Science is but one reason for building a space station. The ultimate mission of the space station is . . . the reaffirmation of the leadership in space of the United States of America, the world's only superpower."

Space station critics soon responded with a General Accounting Office report that calculated construction at $40 billion, $10 billion more than NASA had admitted. Since total expenses, including operational charges, would reach at least $118 billion, the space station would cost $500,000 for every hour of its useful life.

On May 2 the House science committee, long a space station cheerleader, brought forth its NASA reauthorization bill. So deep was the panel's support for *Freedom* that a subcommittee chairman ignored skepticism from leading scientists and predicted, "We are going to find some cures for the dreaded diseases, cancer and diabetes, [on the station] because we can't find them on Earth." With little debate the full House of Representatives approved the legislation, which authorized the administration's full $2.03 billion for *Freedom*. But Representative Howard Wolpe warned space station supporters, "These same NASA programs will be reviewed again on the floor within the next two months as part of the HUD/independent agencies appropriations bill. . . . If we are not confident that NASA's programs are scientifically strong and financially credible, then they will not survive intact in an appropriations process which pits space against other pressing national needs."

CRAFTING AN AMENDMENT

After appropriators endorsed Traxler's bill on May 22, space station advocates spent countless hours arguing about how to redirect some $2 billion within a tight budget. Few believed they could vanquish the cardinal on the House floor, especially since they had only two weeks to plan and organize a defense. Options abounded, but all seemed unappealing. Some NASA officials wanted to ignore the House and concentrate on the Senate; others reasoned that the conference committee would simply split the difference, leaving the space station program without enough money to build anything. Several aerospace industry lobbyists proposed an amendment to cut environmental, science, housing, and veterans' programs, yet this strategy would alienate large groups of lawmakers who supported these initiatives.

Even space station opponents got into the act—to a limited degree. Lobbyists from the American Federation of State, County, and Municipal Employees (AFSCME) met with Representative Jim Chapman's chief staffer to request that an amendment not harm public housing subsidies, wastewater treatment loans, community development grants, and asbestos abatement funds that are critical to local governments. The congressman's aide, in the words of a union lobbyist, "became quite exercised that we were getting involved."

Representative George Brown used his Science, Space, and Technology Committee to organize the initial series of strategy meetings among station supporters, including Vice President Dan Quayle. Although the new authorizing chairman had previously questioned the station's value, particularly compared with space science, he took an institutional view toward the current funding battle. After years of setting unrealistic targets and letting appropriators define NASA's agenda, the science committee wanted to regain control, and its new leader had worked hard earlier in the year to promote reauthorizing legislation that uncharacteristically cut the space agency's overall funding request by $488 million. From Brown's perspective, the pending floor debate became a test of his leadership, a contest between authorizers and appropriators, a struggle for political turf. Brown wanted to offer the amendment to restore *Freedom*'s funding, but Jim Chapman and Bill Lowery demanded control. They argued convincingly that the vote should not be viewed as a jurisdictional fight between congressional panels and that the station's prospects would improve if representatives voted on the project's merits rather than intercommittee politics.

While authorizers debated strategy, the aerospace industry formed a space station working group and began aggressive lobbying. Press reports in late May and early June suggested, with some exaggeration, that contractors arrived in Washington by the planeload to lobby Congress. Still, industry executives met with more lawmakers than did NASA, White House, or science committee officials combined. Several contractors even put in all-nighters preparing reports and charts to bolster their case.

When it came to crafting the actual amendment, however, both authorizers and lobbyists found themselves out of the loop. Officials at the OMB and NASA later admitted that they, rather than the amendment's cosponsors, devised the final approach. "When Chapman and Lowery read our legislative language," said a senior administration official, "they saw its genius." This core group of strategists included Robert E. Grady, the OMB's associate director in charge of science and environmental programs, and Charles Kieffer, its liaison to appropriators; Mark Albrecht, from the vice president's National Space Council; and Marty Kress, NASA's assistant administrator in charge of congressional affairs.

About ten days before the vote these experienced politicos concluded that the space station couldn't win if it competed directly against popular housing, veterans, environmental, and science projects. Most cuts, they reasoned after lengthy discussions, had to come from within NASA itself, largely from space science. To counter Traxler's argument that funding the space station required slashing popular programs in other agencies, the group decided to sweeten its proposal with an extra $33 million for veterans' medical care, a fashionable priority after Operation Desert Storm. Needing more money, the administration's team clipped $250 million from a housing initiative that Kemp disliked and that Traxler and Green could have a hard time defending. As usual, the appropriators had increased operating subsidies that help 3.6 million low-income residents pay their utility and maintenance costs, and they had fenced, or reserved, those funds until the last days of the fiscal year, when such housing contracts are normally renewed. Space station supporters concluded that such delayed funding, although common and legal, could be portrayed to other representatives as shady accounting.

NASA's Kress agreed with the strategy of taking most cuts from space projects, but he dreaded informing his bosses, who were nervous about "self-immolation." Administrator Truly worried that space scientists, "running loose and angry about budget cuts to their programs," would prompt a damaging debate. His worst-case scenario was first to admit in an amendment that many NASA projects could be trimmed and then still lose the space station vote on the House floor. The OMB's Grady and Kieffer had to sell the proposal to the vice president and president, and they weren't sure the White House would "go to the mat for the station." Bush and Quayle, of course, also favored many funded projects at other agencies, and a veto threat could provoke the cardinal to place those initiatives in jeopardy.

The core group had to convince aerospace contractors to go along as well. Since many of the companies worked on NASA projects that the amendment would shave, that task became unpleasant. "Some lobbyists didn't like our cuts, most disagreed with our strategy, and all thought we didn't have a prayer," acknowledged an OMB official. But according to an industry lobbyist, "the contractors were in no position to object. The 'powers that be' said this was going to be the amendment, and no one in the aerospace industry had the nerve to oppose it." NASA officials and aerospace contractors took solace in the hope that Barbara Mikulski would restore the space science funding in the Senate. "We had feelers that the senator would be supportive," said a lobbyist. "We therefore viewed the amendment as an interim step, something that the Senate would improve." According to another industry executive, "If Chapman-Lowery had been the final and only option, I would have looked at it differently, but we had faith—perhaps blind faith—that the Senate and the conference committee would provide balance."

Although OMB and NASA executives consulted with many other players, they did so quietly, hoping the element of surprise would knock Traxler off-balance. Said an aerospace lobbyist: "We learned what was up a few days before the vote, but we were counseled not to talk about it." In fact, the core group conducted an effective campaign of disinformation, encouraging authorizers to tell journalists that the final amendment would propose across-the-board cuts at other agencies.

The cardinal believed these reports, and his staff spent considerable time preparing charts and tables showing the damaging impact of such reductions on popular programs. "If they exempted veterans' medical care because of its popularity," said an aide, "the cuts everywhere else to save the space station would have been substantial, on the order of six to eight percent. We were confident of defeating such an amendment."

LOBBYING

The wild card, at least from Traxler's perspective, was the White House. As the cardinal and Bill Green discussed strategy over lunch before the subcommittee markup, they couldn't forecast how aggressively the president and vice president would press for the space station. President Bush's recent speech favoring a NASA mission to Mars and the vice president's call for a complete redesign of *Freedom* led the appropriators to bet that the administration's commitment would be halfhearted. They bet wrong.

Bush had supported space programs since he briefly represented Texas in Congress and learned the importance of the Johnson Space Flight Center to the Lone Star State's economy. To counter criticism for lacking "the vision thing," the president also grew to enjoy waxing on about how Space Station *Freedom* prepared the United States for the twenty-first century. Bush's stance was bolstered by an unlikely but aggressive associate, Budget Director Darman. Since the Kennedy administration OMB leaders had complained that the space station cost too much money and provided too little benefit. But Darman, no fan of most government programs, was a ardent NASA advocate; some labeled him "Rocket Richard." Two days before the House vote, testifying before the House space committee, Darman proclaimed, "The decision whether or not to commit to Freedom may be seen as a defining test of our civilization."

Reflecting on the White House lobbying effort, Bill Green later commented, "I got the impression that no cabinet secretary or agency head did anything else for several days before the vote but call representatives on behalf of the station." Several administration officials said the ranking Republican exaggerated his assessment, but there's no doubt the Bush team orchestrated an assertive lobbying campaign.

Particularly effective were phone calls from Housing Secretary Jack Kemp and Veterans Secretary Edward Derwinski, who could easily support an amendment that provided an additional $33 million to veterans' medical care. Kemp, a former member of the House Appropriations Committee, had a more complicated agenda. The Chapman-Lowery amendment, at least on its face, should have troubled the housing secretary since it proposed cutting $250 million from public housing maintenance. But Kemp cared little about traditional housing programs, and he hoped that representatives supporting Chapman-Lowery would later feel obligated to vote for a Kemp-backed amendment that supplemented HOPE, his favorite initiative to help low-income people purchase their homes.

The State Department got into the act with a letter alerting members of the House Foreign Affairs Committee to the negative diplomatic consequences of canceling space station contracts with the European Space Agency, Japan, and Canada. With encouragement from the Bush administration, Japanese, Canadian, and European officials also lobbied Congress on the project's behalf. Japan's foreign minister, commenting on the possible cancellation, wrote, "I fear that the credibility of the United States as a partner in any major big science effort would inevitably be damaged." Less diplomatically, other irate Japanese officials threatened to withhold billions of dollars in contributions to U.S.-sponsored science and technology projects, including the Texas-based superconducting super collider.

The president even introduced his trump card, declaring that he would veto the VA-HUD bill if the space station were not fully funded. The warning carried substantial weight on Capitol Hill since Congress had failed to override any of Bush's previous vetoes.

Space station opponents, meanwhile, mobilized most of the 602(b) Coalition, which had been formed to seek higher allocations for the VA-HUD panel. Two days after Traxler's markup Friends of the Earth (FOE), an environmental advocacy group, sent a letter praising the subcommittee's action to all representatives. Its Ralph DeGennaro argued that the VA-HUD panel wisely killed an expensive project that would have wrested funds from the Environmental Protection Agency. FOE also convinced the League of Conservation Voters to declare that a vote for the Chapman-Lowery amendment would be considered a vote against the environment in the group's annual rating of lawmakers' records.

Moreover, Friends of the Earth initiated a joint letter to the entire House that DeGennaro hoped would be endorsed by environmental, veterans, housing, and science groups. His first draft called for outright opposition to the space station, a stance rejected by several coalition members who feared antagonizing Mikulski and her clerk, Kevin Kelly. The final letter, dated May 24 and supported by twenty-one organizations ranging from the Veterans of Foreign Wars to the Council of Large Public Housing Authorities, sidestepped outright opposition by asking that money to restore the space station not be taken from programs that Traxler had funded.

DeGennaro, however, took an additional step that antagonized his own allies and the Senate clerk. On the morning after the groups had agreed to the final draft, *The Washington Post* printed a strong editorial against restoring money to the space station. Without consulting others, the FOE activist included that editorial in his packet to representatives. Housing and science advocates were furious, believing that the enclosure made them appear to be against the station. (DeGennaro later apologized.) Kevin Kelly did not take the dispatch lightly, and he phoned most of the signatories to express his feelings. Douglas Vollmer of the Paralyzed Veterans of America remembered having a "less than cheerful conversation" with the Senate clerk. Another lobbyist recounted his reaction to Kelly's animated and angry phone call by holding his telephone receiver far away from his ear.

Traxler conducted his own lobbying campaign. In the words of an associate, "The chairman really worked the House." The ebullient cardinal, a consummate inside player, frequently wrapped his arm around the shoulders of colleagues, a lobbying stance perfected by Lyndon Johnson, or he was off in a corner of the House floor endearing himself to other lawmakers with a series of jokes or banter.

Although Traxler usually shuns the media, he met with scores of reporters to make the case for fiscal responsibility and against the space station. Yet the cardinal had his limits. When an NBC News television crew encouraged Traxler to smash NASA's $6,000 model of the space station, which he kept in his office, in order to demonstrate the VA-HUD subcommittee's recent action, the chairman concluded that such theatrics were inappropriate.

Two days before the House vote Traxler and Green sent a three-page "Dear Colleague" letter to all representatives, urging a no vote on any amendment to restore the space station's funding. At that point the senior appropriators weren't sure what Chapman and Lowery would introduce, so they argued that their own VA-HUD bill "represents the best balance that could be achieved within the resources allocated to our subcommittee." The senior appropriators explained that their bill, relative to the president's request, provided full funding for the National Science Foundation, virtually full funding for NASA's science projects, and $265 million more for veterans' medical care. "If space station funding is restored at the expense of these programs," Traxler and Green asserted, "we will be continuing the policy of trying to be all things to all people while not having sufficient resources to allow any of our subcommittee's agencies to perform particularly well."

House Democratic leaders rejected a visible role on the space station amendment, arguing that the issue was a jurisdictional fight between science committee authorizers and appropriators. Behind the scenes, however, Majority Leader Gephardt actively promoted *Freedom* to wavering Democrats, largely because his Missouri district abuts the headquarters of McDonnell Douglas, a major space station contractor. Speaker Foley, moreover, was pressured by Boeing, a key corporation in his home state of Washington, to avoid any appearance of support for Traxler's action. By standing on the sidelines, Foley and Gephardt signaled that the Chapman-Lowery measure would be a free vote, one on which a Democrat could oppose the Appropriations Committee and not be punished by the leadership. Although Traxler never sought the Speaker's endorsement, cardinals frequently complained about Foley's lack of support. The leader of House Democrats, they grumbled, views appropriations as too technical and complex to condense into politically potent press releases. At the end of 1990, for instance, the Speaker's summary of accomplishments failed even to mention how William Natcher used his power on the Labor, Health and Human Services and Education Subcommittee to push through a 35 percent $1.6 billion increase in education funding for disadvantaged youth, a significant Democratic success. Foley also lacks the camaraderie that Tip O'Neill shared with Jamie Whitten, who played golf regularly with the former Speaker. When he was majority leader, moreover, Foley challenged one of Whitten's supplemental spending bills, something the chairman did not forget or forgive.

Representative Mary Rose Oakar demonstrated the maxim that "all politics is local" when she arranged for Ohio's House delegation to be lobbied on June 4 by NASA's Richard Truly and the director of the Cleveland-based Lewis Research Center. Although the Democrat from Cleveland had long supported the housing and environmental programs that the space station threatened, her district included the NASA facility that was producing *Freedom*'s power systems. Arguing strenuously that NASA-Lewis advanced the state's economy, Oakar placed considerable pressure on Louis Stokes and Marcy Kaptur, Buckeyes on the VA-HUD panel who voted against the station. (Traxler later commended his subcommittee members for their bravery in withstanding such coercion.)

After accepting the political judgment that an amendment cutting space science was the only means to save the station, NASA's political machine swung into action. Playing up the notion that *Freedom* meant money and jobs throughout the country, the agency's lobbyists distributed to lawmakers a brochure titled "Business Getting Buck$" and a thick briefing book with maps showing the states and congressional districts benefiting from space station contracts.

NASA also arranged for Truly and his five associate administrators to send separate letters to every representative explaining how the station aids all aspects of the space agency. William Lenoir, a former astronaut who oversaw the shuttle and station programs, had no problem declaring that "the recommendation by the House Appropriations Committee to terminate the Space Station *Freedom* would put the United States on a downhill slide out of manned space operations." But Robert Fisk, who supervised NASA's space science programs, faced severe cutbacks to his programs from the Chapman-Lowery amendment; his endorsement was obtained, according to a NASA official, "after much weeping and gnashing of teeth."

Administrator Truly made more than a dozen trips to sway Capitol Hill's uncommitted. Perhaps his most effective outing, however, was to the annual White House picnic, which coincidentally fell on the day before the House vote. With help from Representative Bill Lowery, the former astronaut worked the crowd, confronting uncommitted members of Congress as they stood in line for food or drinks. According to the amendment's cosponsor, "I think we picked up a dozen votes that evening."

Space scientists, despite their opposition to cuts proposed by the Chapman-Lowery amendment, failed to organize any significant lobbying effort. The University of Maryland's Robert Park later admitted that researchers miscalculated the political effectiveness of advocates of the manned space program and mistakenly trusted the conventional wisdom, which held that Traxler would prevail on the House floor.

Rather than lobby, the university research community became the focus of lobbying by White House and NASA officials who feared that space scientists could kill Chapman-Lowery's prospects. Astronomers, for instance, had sent scores of faxes opposing the space station to Traxler before his subcommittee markup, but they backed down after the administration offered a deal: less vocal opposition to *Freedom* in exchange for more money to the National Science Foundation's astronomy program, particularly for the rehabilitation of observatories.

"NASA really cracked the whip on us," complained a space physicist with a government contract. "If we valued our grants, we were told to keep quiet." Another university official remarked that administration officials threatened to cut federal reimbursements for indirect costs associated with membership dues paid by scientists to the

American Physical Society or other space station opponents. "Richard Darman never called to say I'd lose my government funding if I opposed the space station," Professor Park observed. "But friends and colleagues did call to warn that they had overheard such threats. It was an intimidation campaign of whispers."

Jockeying for Position

The Rules Committee sets the format for most debate on the House floor. This task may not seem important, but the committee's nine Democrats and four Republicans often determine the fate of legislation by deciding which bills will be considered when, which amendments will be offered and which will not, and whether a point of order raised by an individual lawmaker can or cannot strike certain sections of bills. Since appropriations bills are considered privileged, cardinals can bypass the Rules Committee and bring their measures directly to the floor at a time of their own choosing. Such an approach exposes appropriators to a myriad of amendments and points of order, but several veteran cardinals, particularly William Natcher and Jamie Whitten, take the risk because they don't want to be beholden to any other committee.

House rules declare that spending bills can't legislate or fund projects not previously authorized. Representatives break this rule routinely since authorizers often fail to update policies affecting basic government functions. "What are we to do when the authorization for many Department of Energy programs lapsed a decade ago?" asked a frustrated appropriator. "Our colleagues certainly don't want us to close down the agency, so we devise ways to fund unauthorized initiatives." To minimize objections to such forbidden funding, clerks frequently consult with legislative committee staffs and make minor changes to satisfy key authorizers. Most cardinals also ask the Rules Committee to exempt certain sections of their bills from this House rule, making it impossible for a disgruntled lawmaker to raise a point of order that strips unauthorized funding or legislative provisions.

Not quite two weeks after representatives had debated Traxler's bill, the House Appropriations Committee confronted an awkward point-of-order challenge. The controversy began when James Trafi-cant asked the Rules Committee to allow an amendment to the Treasury–Postal Service spending bill that would protect taxpayers from Internal Revenue Service harassment. The flamboyant Ohio Democrat had previously claimed to be a victim of such abuse when a federal tax court ordered him to pay back taxes, interest, and penalties associated with $108,000 in alleged bribes from organized crime that Traficant accepted while sheriff of Mahoning County; he was later acquitted after claiming he had pocketed those payments as part of his own sting operation.

Ironically, the Treasury–Postal Service cardinal, Edward Roybal, encouraged the Rules Committee to allow Traficant's amendment, but the Ways and Means Committee chairman wanted the IRS mea-sure considered by his panel rather than be inserted into a spending bill. Traficant took out his frustration on appropriators, raising points of order against substantial portions of the Treasury bill that had not been protected from House rules. Hour after hour the maver-ick legislator objected to whole sections that contained unauthorized provisions, and Roybal was forced to concede. "Traficant destroyed our bill, embarrassed the House Appropriations Committee, and made us subject to the Senate's actions," complained a cardinal. "We work very hard to protect ourselves from such challenges by the legislative committees, but I guess we can't shield ourselves from a rogue."

Few people could attend the session on June 5 when the Rules Committee considered the VA-HUD spending bill. A cordial staffer explained to the waiting group that Rules occupies the smallest com-mittee room in the Capitol and that outside observers would be limited to one each from the White House, NASA, and the Depart-ment of Housing and Urban Development. Still, a dozen lobbyists and aides lined the wall outside the panel's third-floor room. NASA brought a team of five, one of whom talked regularly with his head-quarters on a portable Panasonic telephone. (When an observer asked why the U.S. space agency had purchased a Japanese phone, the NASA lobbyist replied with a smile that it symbolized international cooperation on the space station.) Others in line included congressional staff members (who couldn't enter unless their bosses were testifying), a National Science Foundation lobbyist, and the Washington representative for New York City's mayor, who worried about cuts to public housing projects.

Traxler had read the actual Chapman-Lowery amendment only the previous afternoon, when the junior appropriators announced it proudly in a press release. "No doubt we were staggered," admitted a professional staff member. "We had prepared for an across-the-board cut, and suddenly we learned that NASA was going to swallow most of the cut. More troubling from a strategic standpoint, they even added thirty-three million above our mark for popular veterans' programs. For the first time I realized that space station advocates could win." Traxler, left scrambling for a response, weighed alternative tactics with colleagues and staff well into the evening.

Inside the Rules Committee hearing room on June 5 the cardinal began by explaining the provisions of his bill that needed protection from points of order. He was specific, asking for waivers "beginning on page 8, line 15 through page 9, line 25; beginning on page 10, line 5 through page 11, line 24. . . ." With Chapman and Lowery present, Traxler also outlined an arrangement for consideration of the space station amendment. To counter Chapman-Lowery's additional money for veterans, the chairman proposed that he initially offer his own amendment to transfer $33 million from among three agencies to veterans' medical care. "What we're doing is leveling the playing field," Traxler explained. Chapman and Lowery objected, arguing that such an amendment would eliminate one of their tactical advantages, but the Rules Committee sided with the cardinal.

Chapman and Lowery then described their "strikingly simple" amendment, which added $1.9 billion for the space station and $33 million to veterans' medical care, while it cut almost $1.7 billion from other NASA projects and $250 million from public housing operating subsidies. The Rules Committee declared that the measure would be considered after Traxler's tactical move.

When it came to possible housing amendments, Marge Roukema of New Jersey, a Republican supporter of HOME and HOPE, asked that representatives be allowed to vote on a measure adding $150 million for HOME block grants and another $100 million for public housing tenants wanting to buy the units they live in. The Democratic majority on the Rules Committee rejected this plea, allowing instead for Jim Kolbe (R-Ariz.) and Mike Espy (D-Miss.) to seek $151 million more for HOPE. The Kolbe-Espy amendment, Democrats reasoned, offered a starker and less appealing referendum on Republican Jack Kemp's favorite project.

Shortly after the Rules Committee deliberated, Richard Darman delivered to Capitol Hill his "Statement of Administration Policy" regarding the VA-HUD bill, numbered H.R. (for House of Representatives) 2519. This customary report evaluated the subcommittee's provisions and provided presidential guidance to congressional Republicans. The OMB director minced no words: "The administration objects in the strongest terms to the termination of the space station and the funding of excessive public housing subsidies instead of HOPE." Calling *Freedom* "a major contributor to long-term U.S. economic health," Darman described Traxler's cut as "tantamount to an abandonment of America's manned space program."

On housing issues Darman complained that the VA-HUD panel added $1.4 billion above the president's request for "the costly and ineffective housing construction programs that have been tried in the past," and he criticized appropriators for slashing the president's HOPE request by 76 percent. Without mentioning the specific amendments, the Bush administration clearly went on record favoring Chapman-Lowery and Kolbe-Espy.

Darman also jabbed at several subcommittee actions the House could not alter under the approved rules of debate. Tweaking Traxler personally, he protested the $20 million earmarked for construction of an ecology center and dock facilities in the cardinal's district at Bay City, Michigan.

Finally, the OMB statement questioned the subcommittee's scoring of accounts and suggested the panel had exceeded its allocation by

$310 million. Darman, for instance, objected to Traxler's classification of $14 million as emergency spending, and thus outside the budget caps, for the Department of Veterans Affairs to process claims and provide transition assistance to individuals returning from Operation Desert Storm. At this stage in the annual budget drama, the Congressional Budget Office has more relevance on such scoring matters than the OMB, since the Budget Committee uses only the CBO's estimates to determine if appropriators can be challenged by a point of order on the House floor for exceeding their spending limits. (Contradicting the OMB's comment, the CBO ruled that the VA-HUD panel had complied with its allocation.) Later in the year, however, the OMB's scoring would be crucial for the bill's ultimate enactment.

At 4:00 P.M. on June 5 Robert Byrd called a hastily arranged meeting of the Senate Committee on Appropriations to review his own spending allocations to the thirteen subcommittees. Barbara Mikulski, while publicly supporting her chairman, groused about an allocation only $50 million above Traxler's. Since the Senate VA-HUD panel suddenly seemed to lack sufficient resources to guarantee funding for the space station, the pending House vote became even more crucial to the project's promoters.

Space station supporters and its critics conducted daily "whip counts" to determine how lawmakers would line up. Bill Green had been confident of the subcommittee's strength since markup, but he sensed support slipping slowly: "Friends who had promised commitments began to back away." NASA officials and authorizers knew they were gaining ground, but they had little confidence of victory. Mary Dee Kerwin of NASA's Congressional Affairs Office said that as of the Rules Committee meeting, space station advocates were far from a majority.

CHAPMAN-LOWERY

Space station champions read their morning newspapers on June 6 and groaned. *The New York Times,* long a critic of NASA's enterprise, editorialized: "The grandiose project, designed to be the next centerpiece of the ailing space program, has become ever more pinched in scope and vision, yet it remains dreadfully costly. Termination is probably the only cure."

President Bush took to the phones early, calling a short list of uncommitted Republicans to discuss his view of the space station's importance. Personal calls from the Oval Office proved to be effective, as with Republican Representative Jim Saxton of New Jersey, who ended up endorsing Chapman-Lowery despite his concerns about the project's cost and the criticisms of space scientists.

Aerospace lobbyists met for breakfast at the Capitol Hill Club, the Republican restaurant and bar catty-corner to the Cannon House Office Building. Bill Green, hoping to demonstrate cordial relations, accepted their invitation and spoke for a few minutes about how Chapman-Lowery would destroy valuable NASA projects.

Vice President Quayle, as chairman of the National Space Council, had a lot riding on the vote. Some commentators even tagged the Chapman-Lowery amendment as a test of his leadership. Yet on June 6 Quayle was forced to be out of town, meeting in Czechoslovakia with President Václav Havel; still, he placed about a dozen international calls to wavering lawmakers.

White House lobbyists, who had arrived at the Capitol before Congress convened, were suggesting to anyone who would listen that they had the votes to win on Chapman-Lowery. Legislative veterans remained skeptical since the lobbyists were known as "bad counters." Majority Leader Gephardt, considered a more realistic source, told a few colleagues outside the members' dining room that the vote was too close to call.

Not everyone, of course, focused on the space station vote that morning. Even NASA's own astronauts were busy studying the biological effects of space travel aboard the shuttle *Columbia,* and lawmakers were recovering from the previous night's cantankerous debate on a civil rights bill. Meanwhile, most Americans were gossiping about the latest tabloid scandal, the alleged rape of a woman by Senator Edward Kennedy's nephew at the family's estate in Florida.

The House of Representatives formally began its day on Thursday, June 6, 1991, in typical fashion: The chaplain delivered a short prayer, and a member of Congress recited the pledge of allegiance. For the next half hour lawmakers offered "one minutes," or short speeches to a virtually empty chamber about sundry topics for which they wanted publicity on C-SPAN, the cable television network. Nita Lowey complained about the Supreme Court's recent decision to restrict "a woman's right to comprehensive family planning advice." William Clinger warned against "ecoterrorists" who drove metal spikes into trees in order to discourage lumber companies from logging.

At 10:30 A.M. the Rules Committee called up its resolution outlining the terms for debate on H.R. 2519, the VA-HUD spending bill. With support from both Democrats and Republicans, discussion was limited, and the rule allowing three amendments was approved, 404–14.

Bob Traxler rose and requested that the House resolve itself into the Committee of the Whole House, a procedure that allows more efficient consideration of complex legislation; when in the Committee of the Whole House, for instance, only 100 (rather than 218) representatives are needed for a quorum. Dick Malow and Paul Thomson sat to the chairman's right at the table reserved for the floor manager of bills; Michelle Burkett and Marissa Smith settled in behind the men. Traxler and Bill Green, who sat at a similar table on the minority side of the main aisle, delivered their initial statements. "We had to make tough, hard choices," the cardinal began. "The subcommittee had to prioritize between funding major new initiatives such as the space station versus funding for other ongoing program requirements both within NASA and the other agencies in the bill. Not fun, not easy."

Traxler and Green had decided to stress the "tough choices" theme, believing that representatives, increasingly troubled by the budget deficit, would vote for fiscal responsibility rather than an orbiting platform. The cardinal explained his panel's predicament succinctly: "How can we expect to provide ten to fifteen percent increases in NASA, eight to nine percent increases in the VA medical care, an eighteen percent increase in the National Science Foundation, and eight to ten percent increases in environmental programs, and do all that when the allocation will go up within a range of three to four and one-half percent? It don't work. That dog don't hunt. The turkey don't fly."

Other subcommittee members bolstered Traxler's arguments before critics took their opening shots. By 1 P.M., after "general debate," the chairman introduced his $33 million amendment for veterans' medical care, which was approved by a voice vote with little objection.

Then a bit of parliamentary maneuvering ensued as Chapman tried to restore his tactical advantage with a new amendment that would add another $33 million to the VA medical account, to be funded by the same $33 million of cuts that Traxler proposed from the Environmental Protection Agency, Department of Housing and Urban Development, and National Science Foundation. The Texas Democrat needed unanimous consent to offer a motion that the Rules Committee hadn't endorsed, and Traxler objected.

Chapman tried a different tack. Since the House had just approved Traxler's call for another $33 million to veterans, the Texas Democrat believed his amendment no longer needed to increase that account. Instead, Chapman reasoned, he should reduce by $33 million the amount his amendment would take from housing accounts to help pay for the space station. On that item Traxler assented.

The real debate then began. Science committee chairman George Brown, perched behind the rail at the back of the chamber with a cigar in his mouth, interrupted his colleagues repeatedly throughout the afternoon to score debating points in favor of the space station. When Leon Panetta, chairman of the Budget Committee, was commending Traxler for making difficult spending decisions, Brown lurched forward and asked rhetorically if Panetta's panel earlier in the year hadn't endorsed spending for the station. Irritated at being challenged, Panetta answered that the VA-HUD subcommittee had to set different priorities since it received a smaller allocation than the Budget Committee recommended.

Traxler was cornered, to some degree, by his own actions. He couldn't attack the station directly since NASA had reconfigured the project in ways that satisfied most of the demands he had put forth only a few months before. The cardinal and most of his allies, therefore, made a straightforward financial argument: The United States government could not afford the space station. Station advocates, in contrast, waxed eloquent about America's technological leadership in the twenty-first century. While the VA-HUD subcommittee chairman spoke as an accountant of balance sheets, they presented a patriotic vision of the nation's future.

Traxler assumed that the key issue before the House was simply whether the space station should be funded, but station supporters effectively linked *Freedom* to America's manned space program, conjuring up proud visions of astronauts walking on the moon and Mars. Robert Walker perhaps provided the turning point when he heatedly asserted, "Make no mistake about it. If the station is canceled this year, the appropriators will be back next year with a suggestion that shuttle flights be curtailed, and with further cuts to an already too-small exploration program. The U.S. manned space program will come to an end." Walker's argument was a time-honored tool of demagoguery; the shuttle *Columbia* circled the Earth during the debate, and Traxler proposed no cuts in the spaceflight program, yet speaker after speaker suggested that the vote was about "whether the United States will have a manned space program."

By late afternoon a frustrated Traxler had to rise and declare, "Let me put this question to rest. The manned space flight program is not in jeopardy. The space station is in jeopardy with this amendment."

Amid the fervent debate Traxler tried to hold the higher ground. He went out of his way to praise Chapman and Lowery, even though these junior panel members had dared challenge him. "They have conducted themselves in the finest manner," the cardinal said publicly, acknowledging a code of honor among appropriators. "They have absolutely kept their word on every issue that we talked about." Traxler argued that an item as important as the future of the space station should be considered by the full House rather than by only nine members of his subcommittee. One lawmaker commented that "this openness to a wide-ranging debate is a most unusual procedure on an appropriations bill, and the chairman should be commended."

Each side, however, asserted that the other played hardball.

Traxler, according to several representatives, threatened to eliminate funding to the districts of lawmakers who voted for Chapman-Lowery. One congressman, who would benefit from a provision within the cardinal's report, informed Traxler that he was under substantial pressure from aerospace contractors in his district to support the space station. "Tough!" was the reply attributed to the cardinal, who denied the charges, saying he exercised no undue pressure. Indeed, the final bill's earmarks for Bill Lowery's San Diego district suggest the cardinal practiced little, if any, retribution. Despite Lowery's challenge, he obtained $49 million for an international sewage treatment facility across the border in Tijuana, Mexico, $40 million for a waste-water treatment plant in San Diego, and smaller grants for local drug and homeless projects.

Space station supporters offered threats of their own. Several lawmakers said Robert Walker warned that the Science, Space, and Technology Committee would not authorize projects favored by representatives voting against the station. "You're going to have to deal with the science committee as well as the Appropriations Committee if you want funding," Walker was reported to have told representatives bluntly.

As the debate lengthened, so did the line of lobbyists in the short hallway leading onto the House floor. An odd ritual is performed along this so-called lobbyists' corridor: Police ensure a pathway remains clear while advocates try to pass out pamphlets to passing representatives, to wave to their friends, and to lobby swing votes. Several wear buttons advertising their positions, hoping that any last-minute influence, however subliminal, will sway opinions. Two advocates from Friends of the Earth arrived early. Joining them for this last-minute exercise to block Chapman-Lowery were staff members from the National Low Income Housing Coalition and the American Federation of State, County and Municipal Employees. Veterans' groups, although they had signed the FOE letter, decided not to make an appearance since the original Chapman-Lowery amendment added $33 million for their constituents. Interspersed in the small crowd were aerospace lobbyists and other space station supporters, including Bob Grady, the OMB's top lieutenant in charge of science, space, and environmental programs. To ensure that AFSCME's presence didn't suggest that organized labor opposed *Freedom*, a representative from the machinists' union, whose members were to build the project, made a brief appearance.

After almost four hours of polemics on the Chapman-Lowery amendment and seven hours on the entire bill, Lawrence Smith, a junior appropriator known for his flashy ties and self-promotional style, offered to broker a compromise that would leave housing programs alone and force NASA to fund the space station entirely from its own budget. Neither side wanted such mediation. Traxler thought it muddied the waters. Space station supporter Robert Walker concluded, "I believe [Smith] is trying to be helpful, and I think he could end up hurting us badly." Despite pleas from both camps to withdraw his amendment to Chapman-Lowery, Smith persisted and demanded a time-consuming roll call vote.

As Smith's motion failed, 122–296, many lawmakers grew testy. At 5:15 P.M. Traxler asked to limit the remaining speakers to three, rather than five, minutes, but Robert Roe objected fervently, complaining that he and fifteen other lawmakers still wanted to speak. Traxler withdrew his suggestion, and when Roe got his turn several minutes later, he declared, "Hosanna, hosanna, hosanna, Mr. Chairman. After four hours I get a chance to talk with my colleagues." What Roe offered, three days before the planned national celebration of Operation Desert Storm, was the questionable proclamation that America would not have been able to fight the Middle East war without the advanced technology provided by projects like the space station.

Numerous other Chapman-Lowery proponents also got carried away with flowery praise for the project and their own polemics. Jan Meyers, a Kansas Republican, declared, "This vote here will prove to be one of those defining moments in history." Jack Brooks, a Texas Democrat, observed, "If we want to continue to exacerbate the decline of the United States, if we aim to become a second-class nation, then we should go ahead and kill the space station, kill the space program, kill it all." Jim Chapman suggested that research on the space station would combat cardiovascular diseases, hypertension, osteoporosis, AIDS, and cancer. Don Ritter, a Pennsylvania Republican, implied that the station's technology represented "the pinnacle of America's national achievement." But Jim Bacchus, a Florida Democrat, took perhaps the greatest rhetorical leap by declaring, "The space station will be useful to the advance of democracy."

No space station critic matched such passion, and few attacked the project directly. Perhaps the most forceful was Richard Durbin. "If we are to fund this space station, then it clearly is not for scientific reasons," argued the Illinois Democrat. "It is for the reason that we wish to fund and somehow continue to subsidize the contractors who are involved in this project. This has in fact become a WPA [Work Projects Administration] project for the aerospace industry." Some conservative lawmakers, who usually object to federal jobs programs, ironically turned Durbin's criticism around and unabashedly praised the station for providing employment. Ron Packard, a California Republican, went so far as to say, "I think every member would do well to find out how much the space station and the space program benefit their state. In fact, it would be a poor vote to vote against the economy of their own states."

Only late in the debate did space station opponents criticize the Chapman-Lowery amendment for chopping NASA. "What this amendment will do is force NASA to eat its own," declared New York's Charles Schumer. "Every new program in space science, in satellites, in everything else, will be squeezed out by the space station." In fact, despite Chapman's argument that canceling the station would reduce U.S. preeminence in the aerospace industry, his own amendment cut $79 million from Traxler's mark for aeronautical research and technology. Despite Chapman's argument that eliminating the station would destroy America's manned space program, his own amendment cut $187 million from space shuttle production funds and another $225 million from shuttle operations. Despite Chapman's argument that killing the station would harm space science, his own amendment cut $465 million from the space agency's science account.

Bill Green tried to demonstrate the existence of a broad coalition against the Chapman-Lowery amendment by reading aloud letters from the League of Conservation Voters and the American Legion. "Although this proposal would not reduce the level of VA appropriations," wrote the veterans' group, "its approval could seriously endanger veterans program funding as H.R. 2519 moves though the legislative process."

As debate dragged on into the early evening, a couple of younger lawmakers picked up their children from the House day-care center and brought them into the chamber. Several went downstairs for dinner. Most called home to say it would be another late night.

Many representatives made up their minds on the amendment at the last minute, but few were swayed by the debate. Some bent to pressure from administration and aerospace lobbyists, who threatened the loss of jobs in congressional districts if Chapman-Lowery failed. Others, angry that appropriators again ignored the authorizing legislation, sided with the authorizers. One politician was so torn by the measure that he went to the members' dining room, drank a cup of coffee, and flipped a coin that landed in favor of the space station. The mood on the House floor slowly reflected these swings toward Chapman-Lowery. "In the morning I didn't think we had the margin to win," said Lowery. "But as people talked, it became clear. By early evening we grew increasingly confident that the Republicans would hold, and when the Democrats started endorsing our amendment, we felt the win would be big."

Traxler and Green seemed to concede their forthcoming defeat. While Chapman, Lowery, and science committee members scurried about to confront wavering representatives, the senior appropriators sat at their desks. Traxler even acknowledged that the fight would carry on: "If the cost of the station continues to escalate, we will be back down here in another year on another day and we will be drawing this line and this fight will be held all over again."

When a recorded vote on the Chapman-Lowery amendment was finally ordered at 7:15 P.M., the wall above and behind the Speaker's chair lit up with the alphabetized names of 435 representatives. Two bells rang throughout all House buildings, alerting members to the vote. Traxler joined Chapman and Brown at one door to greet and appeal to their colleagues as they walked onto the floor; Green and

Walker headed to the other main entrance. Lawmakers milled about, placed their arms around one another to share news, and finally proceeded to the back of the House benches, where they inserted voting cards, similar to credit cards, into boxes and punched the green button for aye or the red for nay. The chamber's south wall reflected their color-coded votes. Green lights quickly dominated the board. Chapman emitted a brief cheer when the tabulator passed the 218 votes needed for a clear majority.

As they filed out of the chamber after voting, several representatives labeled the Chapman-Lowery amendment "an easy vote," arguing that they expected little political criticism for supporting the station, particularly since NASA had endorsed the cuts to the space science and since congressional leaders didn't actively back the appropriators; in contrast, voting against the station promised condemnations from the administration and the aerospace industry. One representative said he would have opposed the space station if the tally had been closer, but he decided not to hurt himself politically on a position that wasn't going to win. Another congressman commented, "By voting for Chapman-Lowery, I could appear to be a supporter of space, and it didn't cost me anything." Of course, it cost low-income housing tenants $217 million and the rest of NASA almost $1.9 billion.

After the fifteen-minute voting period had been extended to allow for stragglers, despite catcalls of "Vote!" from weary legislators, the tabulator announced that the Chapman-Lowery amendment was approved, 240–173. The station had been saved, and a cardinal had suffered a rare defeat.

Chapman, a short man with a shiny bald head, beamed with pride as he strutted around the House floor, accepting the backslapping congratulations of his colleagues. After basking for several minutes, he headed outside to trumpet his victory to reporters. On the Capitol lawn, in an area known as the triangle, some thirty journalists and six television crews had been waiting impatiently as the debate dragged on past most of their deadlines. Chapman and Lowery strode across the parking lot and shook hands briskly with NASA chief Richard Truly, who had just arrived from the space agency's headquarters near the bottom of Capitol Hill. The congressmen proclaimed it a great day for America and the nation's technological leadership. Truly, despite enthusiasm for the come-from-behind victory, was less sanguine. The successful amendment might have saved the space station, but it cannibalized most other NASA projects. "Much work needs to be done to restore balance to the agency's budget," admitted the administrator.

Appropriators are not used to such a public defeat, and *Congressional Quarterly* and *The Washington Post* soon wrote similar articles about how the committee was losing its clout. "The tide is turning," agreed the minority staff director of a legislative committee. "Authorizers are standing up to the Appropriations Committee and winning." Appropriators and OMB officials scoffed at such notions. "You never like to puncture the image of invincibility," said a clerk, "but we still control hundreds of billions of dollars. Who else in Washington has that power?"

Traxler suggested he had been the victim of a "Goliath" lobbying effort by the White House, aerospace lobbyists, and authorizers. No doubt the president's activism surprised the cardinal, and it demonstrated an administration's ample ability to sway uncommitted lawmakers. Aerospace contractors, hoping to profit from an expensive space project during an era of military cutbacks, had also mounted a full-court press, lining up most of the large congressional delegations from Texas, California, and Florida that benefited from substantial NASA contracts. The cardinal had suffered as well from latent antiappropriator sentiment in the House, ignited because representatives had only recently approved a NASA reauthorization bill that endorsed the space station. The combination of these forces, argued a clerk, was too much for even a cardinal to overcome.

Space station advocates offered two different explanations for their victory. One lobbyist said, "Traxler seriously miscalculated the breadth of congressional support, particularly among Democrats, for the manned space program." Another suggested that Chapman-

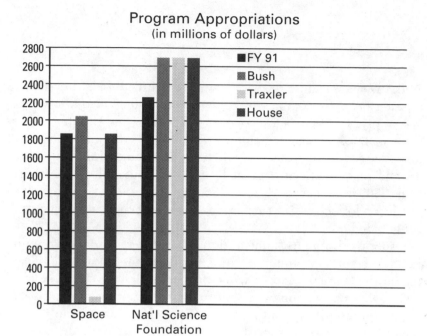

Program Appropriations
(in millions of dollars)

Lowery had benefited considerably from tactical surprise. The core group of strategists at the OMB and NASA dispensed enough disinformation so that the cardinal was ill prepared to counterattack a measure having NASA assume most of the cuts.

The vote reflects the constant struggle for power between authorizers and appropriators within Congress and between appropriators and the administration. It also attests to the historic changes that have occurred within Congress and the Appropriations Committee; thirty years ago junior members would never have considered challenging a cardinal on the House floor. Perhaps most important, the amendment's victory reveals the real problem of reducing the deficit; said one frustrated representative, "If we can't eliminate a boondoggle project opposed by most scientists and appropriators, I don't know when we'll ever cut federal spending."

HOPE

With the space station rescued, lawmakers turned their attentions to housing policy, a complex topic that often baffles even knowledgeable appropriators. The Department of Housing and Urban Development manages a far-flung empire that oversees 4.5 million units of public and federally subsidized housing, distributes 5 million vouchers and rental certificates annually to poor households, and insures some $300 billion of mortgages. "So many programs, so many different forms of subsidy, so much confusion over account balances," complained a clerk.

Under the Reagan administration HUD suffered from corruption, political favoritism, and fraud. Secretary Kemp won kudos for cleaning up the scandals, and he worked to have HUD become the focal point for a new war on poverty. After a decade of inaction in Washington, Kemp convinced the White House and Congress in 1990 to approve major housing legislation that targeted more federal aid to the poor and encouraged more local control of housing developments. The National Affordable Housing Act (often referred to as the Cranston-Gonzalez Affordable Housing Act after its chief congressional sponsors) authorized a whopping $57 billion for housing initiatives over two years, far more than appropriators could realistically spend.

The legislation's cornerstone, from Kemp's perspective, was the new HOPE (Homeownership and Opportunity for People Everywhere) program designed to convert public housing units to tenant-owned homes. The housing secretary and his conservative colleagues viewed HOPE as the best means by which poor people could control their own properties, a move designed to stabilize neighborhoods and reduce housing costs. If fully funded, HOPE was to upgrade and sell some twenty thousand public housing units. According to the Heritage Foundation, it would "transform HUD from an open cash register for the housing industry into an agency to help poor Americans obtain decent homes." A zealous Kemp suggested in congressional testimony that tenant ownership "is going to save babies, save children, save families, and save America."

Democrats and moderate Republicans wanted to lay a different cornerstone to the housing legislation. Their version, the HOME Investment Partnerships program, was designed to provide a flexible source of funding for state and local governments to expand the supply of decent and affordable housing. While HOPE transfers ownership of existing public housing, HOME's block grants encourage new construction and thus are popular with developers as well as budget-strapped governors and mayors.

Three months before Traxler's panel marked up its fiscal 1992 bill, Kemp had asked Congress to shift within the previous year's appropriation, almost $500 million of public housing funds, to the HOPE program. A fire storm of opposition erupted from a coalition of forty-six disparate organizations, including the National Association

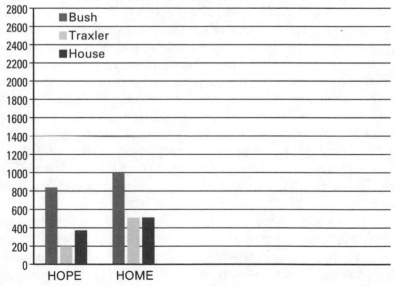

Program Appropriations
(in millions of dollars)

of Home Builders, U.S. Conference of Mayors, National Puerto Rican Coalition, and Union of American Hebrew Congregations. The housing secretary tried to soften the protests by promising that additional reprogrammings would benefit the popular HOME program, too, but Traxler's panel rejected any transfer. Kemp's amendment to the "supplemental" spending bill lost on the House floor, but it garnered a respectable 177 votes, provoking a promise from Traxler to seek more HOPE funding in the fiscal 1992 budget.

The House cardinal didn't deliver, however, providing only $210 million of the requested $865 million. So when HUD's fiscal 1992 appropriation approached the House floor, Kemp teamed up with Jim Kolbe, the Arizona Republican, and Mike Espy, the Mississippi Democrat, to introduce an amendment that would transfer $151 million from conventional housing subsidies to HOPE.

Traxler, weary from the space station fight, asked that floor discussion on the Kolbe-Espy amendment be limited to one hour. Yet the time constraint did little to curtail the debate's passion. Kolbe set the tone by declaring that the $151 million "is for a program that has been authorized, has strong bipartisan support, and the money that we are taking this from is for a program that the authorizing committee has never had hearings on, never authorized. It stinks."

Bill Green, the subcommittee's ranking Republican and Traxler's ally, tried to defend the targeted flexible subsidy program, announcing that the Bush administration had requested that it serve as a financing conduit for a new housing repair program. He also branded Kemp's empowerment plans as risky and unproved. Back in 1974 HUD had initiated a 2,000-unit demonstration program for the sale of public housing to tenants; the VA-HUD subcommittee subsequently provided $30,000 per unit for repairs and remodeling. But as of mid-1991 the agency had sold only 343 of the dwellings. Green observed dryly, "So, obviously, this has not been a fast-developing program."

Bill Clay offered a harsher indictment of HOPE and Kolbe-Espy. "The amendment," asserted the Missouri Democrat, "is based on an ill-conceived, politically driven plot devised to relieve the federal government of its responsibility to provide decent, low-income housing for the poor. It is a cruel scheme backed by those promoting the discredited notion of supply-side economics. For supporters of this amendment to suggest that the poorest element in our society—those who subsist primarily on welfare, food stamps, old-age assistance—who can barely afford clothing, medical care, transportation, and other basic necessities—to suggest that this government will make home ownership for them a reality is a farce. It's unadulterated hypocrisy."

Most lobbyists left after the space station vote. Clare Doyle, a representative of the nonprofit National Coalition for Low Income Housing and a critic of the HOPE amendment, had lobbyists' corridor to herself until Jack Kemp bounded up the steps around 8:30 P.M. with five of his aides. His shirtsleeves rolled up, the congenial and boisterous housing secretary shook hands with any representative he could spot, attracting a pack of both Democrats and Republicans. From inside the chamber a few lawmakers called to have Kemp come onto the floor and give a speech. "Not ethical," he said demurely. Doyle, who had introduced herself just a few minutes before, jokingly asked why the housing secretary's lobbying in the hallway was any more ethical. Laughing, Kemp responded, "Give me a break, Clare."

Doyle tried to peel lawmakers away from the small crowd surrounding Kemp, informing them that housing advocates opposed the Kolbe-Espy amendment. One Democrat responded with surprise, "That's not what Jack just said." The hallway, in Doyle's word, became a "circus." One of Kemp's associates kept shouting, "Tenants want it!" Kemp himself repeatedly cried, "Vote with me on HOPE!"

Within the House chamber Republican Whip Newt Gingrich eulogized the housing secretary: "He cares about children who live in violence, he cares about a welfare program that has failed, and he cares about public housing projects that have failed." Traxler responded by listing some of the many organizations opposed to Kemp's expensive experiment, including the Catholic Conference, AFL-CIO, and Partnership for the Homeless. But the cardinal, sensing the mood of the House again turning against him, concluded the debate with a weak plea: "We would appreciate it very much if the members would reject this amendment."

Representatives, however, sided with the housing secretary rather than the cardinal, approving the Kolbe-Espy motion, 216–183. The subcommittee staffers, not having expected this defeat, slumped in their seats. Outside in the hallway Kemp's aides jumped about jubilantly, giving one another high fives.

AUDITORS

By 10 P.M., after having dealt with several less controversial issues, tired representatives began to grumble audibly about the incessant debate. Several authorizers, however, had a bone to pick with Jamie Whitten. The Appropriations Committee chairman, who had begun serving in Congress shortly before the Japanese bombed Pearl Harbor, shuffled onto the House floor, appearing frail and dull-witted. Capitol Hill veterans understood that these signs of age mask a crafty politician who gets his way with remarkable consistency. Not well known outside Washington, the chairman is considered within the Beltway to be a "skilled legislator," a "talented negotiator," and a "shrewd fox." A few observers are less kind. Former lawmaker Phil Burton, for instance, once referred to Whitten as "one big puddle of sneak." A current colleague suggested that he "mumbles to advantage," slipping into an inaudible southern drawl to conceal his Machiavellian schemes.

Whitten considers himself of the "old school," and he fondly recalls the era when committee chairmen, rather than upstart politicians, exercised control over federal policy. In today's era of omnipresent congressional staff, Whitten is one of the few politicians who still writes some of his own legislation; the chairman's flurry of non sequiturs and free-floating exchanges make it easy to determine his contributions. And in this age of the media sound bite, Whitten's Appropriations Committee never issues a press release, and the chairman avoids television cameras. "You have to remember," said an associate, "Whitten began his political career in the Mississippi legislature before television was invented, and he still doesn't trust the media. Perhaps more significant, he doesn't really need the media." The chairman and other veterans occasionally joke about some of the

112

younger, publicity-hungry appropriators, particularly Vic Fazio, who, they say, "can hear the clicking of television klieg lights from a hundred yards."

Conventional political labels don't conform to Whitten. The chairman is virtually the last of the New Deal liberals still in Congress, but his voting record is quite moderate. At heart a pragmatist, he described his outlook simply: "My political philosophy is to get the job done." Whitten's staff keeps a file folder of pithy quotations from the chairman, one of which demonstrates a preference for economic vitality over balanced budgets. "Ethiopia has a balanced budget—it doesn't owe a dollar. In fact, it doesn't have a dollar," Whitten announced periodically. "Ethiopia is poor because it lacks the highways, bridges, sewers, and other government-financed infrastructure that support a vibrant economy." Such items, of course, are what the Appropriations chairman wants to build across the United States.

No doubt Whitten, at age eighty-one in 1991, was slowing down. He walked stiffly, relied on hearing aids, and suffered an odd twitch that made him appear to be chewing tobacco constantly. Sensitive about his age and tenure, particularly in light of growing public support for term limitations, the chairman became enraged when Vice President Dan Quayle mentioned Whitten personally as an example of why representatives should not become entrenched. (This pope of the cardinals, as was his way, retaliated by cutting funds for the vice president's mansion.) Although Whitten's mind remained agile, colleagues on the Appropriations Committee spent considerable time discussing the chairman's inevitable retirement and the ascendancy of a new generation of leaders.

Authorizers rarely challenge Whitten for fear their congressional districts will face the same fate as the vice president's mansion. Still, when it came to the issue of federal accounting reform, many thought the Appropriations chairman had crossed the line. The dispute focused on the Chief Financial Officers Act, which Congress had passed in 1990 in response to mismanagement and corruption at the Department of Housing and Urban Development. HUD's accounting system had been so lax under Secretary Samuel Pierce, Jr., that agency officials allegedly placed, without detection, some $6 million into the pockets of Reagan administration officials and other prominent Republicans. The new law, for which the Bush administration sought a $105 million appropriation in fiscal 1992, calls for chief financial officers (CFOs) and a uniform system of financial accountability at cabinet departments and major federal agencies. It also empowers the Office of Management and Budget to oversee the CFOs, to hire a deputy director of management, and to create an Office of Federal Financial Management.

Whitten, distracted by budget summit negotiations in the autumn of 1990, failed to object to the bill when the House approved it by voice vote. "I do not know how many folks heard the debate," he said during consideration of the fiscal 1992 VA-HUD spending bill. "I did not know anything about it until a few weeks ago." Now the chairman was trying to kill the measure by blocking money to implement it. "I have great fear that this [law] will constitute one more impediment to the operations of our Committee on Appropriations and the Congress," Whitten warned. Reminding his colleagues, once again, that his panel since 1945 had suppressed total appropriations more than $180 billion below the budget requests of presidents, the chairman argued that CFOs would interfere with the efforts of cardinals to obtain reliable information from the federal agencies. By funding the CFO provisions, he said, lawmakers would "squeeze us where we cannot look after the country."

Whitten's stance provides insights into the chief appropriator's mind-set and exposes Washington's proclivity for turf battles, but it shocked CFO supporters since their bipartisan "good government" measure had been approved overwhelmingly. Trying to determine Whitten's motivation, in fact, consumed countless hours of the proponents' time. A few quietly hypothesized about the aging chairman's mental health. Some assumed Whitten would do anything to block increased authority for the OMB, especially after Richard Darman's recent sequester that required an across-the-board cut equal to a dime each month for every federal employee; irked by such "small-mindedness," Whitten declared, "I object to turning over the operations of the legislative branch to a representative of an executive department." Others speculated that Whitten was swayed by the

Agricultural Department's budget officer, with whom the chairman enjoyed a long and close relationship and who feared a loss of clout with the arrival of a chief financial officer.

CFO supporters met with the stubborn country lawyer in the morning of June 6 to seek a compromise but made little progress. Facing an obstinate Whitten again during floor debate later that evening, they agreed to postpone, at least temporarily, a real showdown. Almost two weeks later, lawmakers dealt Whitten a major defeat, 341–52, by deleting his anti-CFO language from the Treasury–Postal Service spending bill. In the end, however, the chairman won a partial victory by restricting CFO funding within the thirteen appropriations bills to less than half the president's request. "Another Whitten adage in the staff file," observed a frustrated OMB official, "is that there are lots of ways to win in Washington."

By almost 11 P.M., with all amendments settled, Traxler rose to request that the Committee of the Whole report the VA-HUD legislation to the House. To mark the formal transition, the staff transferred the mace, symbolizing the authority of the Speaker, to its regular position atop a pedestal near the American flag. Majority Leader Gephardt assumed the Speaker's chair and read from a prepared script about the parliamentary procedures for having the bill "engrossed and read a third time." The vote on the final bill, as amended, was yeas 363, nays 39, not voting 29.

Debate on H.R. 2519 had lasted almost twelve full hours. Although the subcommittee lost two major items—the space station and HOPE—Traxler, Green, and Malow displayed no sign of disappointment, accepting handshakes and gentlemanly slaps on the back. The cardinal and his colleagues took solace knowing that most spending decisions within their bill had not been challenged. Moreover, they understood better than anyone that the annual budget drama was far from over and that they would enjoy more opportunities to shape federal spending.

5

THE SENATE RESPONSE

No ONE COULD have predicted at the beginning of 1991 how Barbara Mikulski would deal with the space station. The previous year the senator sheared almost 30 percent from the House mark, and her interest in the project should have fallen even further after NASA's redesign had eliminated several station contracts from Maryland's Goddard Space Flight Center. Yet the Senate VA-HUD chairman experienced a space station conversion after seeing NASA's latest blueprint. "We told the space agency to do the station incrementally, and they came back with a decent plan," she remarked. "They deserve to go ahead."

Mikulski's resolve was heightened on May 23, the day after the House Appropriations Committee markup and a week before the House floor vote, when President George Bush asked the cardinal to visit the White House, her first invitation since she entered Congress fourteen years before. Understanding the effectiveness of personal appeals and political symbolism, Bush ushered Mikulski into the Oval Office and had her sit in the armchair usually reserved for heads of state. The experience had a lasting impact on the junior senator from Maryland. Time and again throughout her subcommittee's deliberations, Mikulski recalled proudly how the president of the United States had asked her to save the space station, his highest funding priority. Joining forces with a Republican president may not have been a Democratic senator's natural instinct, but it provided enormous benefits to Mikulski, the most obvious being that the White House would pressure Senate Republicans to support her bill as long as it funded the space station. By sitting down with the president, moreover, Mikulski reasoned that the OMB would help identify "scoring gimmicks" that might free up more money for her panel to distribute.

The cardinal's actions also were framed by her 1992 reelection campaign. Senators, who stand before the voters only every six years, seem totally absorbed by the process of raising money, lining up constituency groups, and warding off political opponents. By the summer of 1991 Mikulski had banked a substantial $750,000 war chest, but she still felt vulnerable to attacks from conservatives, particularly after she had voted against sending troops to fight in Kuwait and Iraq. A poll taken by Mason-Dixon Opinion Research found 65 percent of Maryland respondents disapproved of her opposition to Operation Desert Storm. By making league with President Bush, Mikulski hoped she could avoid having the White House and the National Republican Senatorial Committee promote a conservative challenger.

Congressional observers offered numerous other theories for the cardinal's conversion. An aerospace lobbyist suggested that she simply wanted to soak political action committees for campaign contributions. Another appropriator speculated that she cut a deal in which the Bush administration, desperate to fund the space station, would support, or at least not oppose, her $20 million earmark for construction of the Christopher Columbus Center of Marine Research and Exploration in Baltimore, NASA's first, and some suggested questionable, entry into the undersea world. The chairman denied such charges strenuously.

The stout, aggressive, four-foot-eleven-inch lawmaker doesn't fit the mold of the telegenic politician, but this granddaughter of Polish immigrants appeals to Maryland's middle-class and ethnic communities. Mikulski made a name for herself fighting highway developers who tried to level several Baltimore neighborhoods. She won a seat on the Baltimore City Council in 1971 and then in 1974 ran a shoe-string campaign against veteran Republican Senator Charles McC. Mathias that surprised the skeptics with a respectable 43 percent of the vote. In 1976 she won a seat in the House of Representatives, where she stayed for ten years. When Mathias retired in 1986, a better-funded and better-known Mikulski beat back a slew of challengers to become the first Democratic woman not a former senator's widow or daughter elected to the United States Senate.

Upon moving from the House to the Senate, Mikulski maneuvered aggressively to obtain a seat on Appropriations. She argued that Maryland deserved a presence on the committee, particularly since Mathias had been a senior Republican there, and she made her case at length to John Stennis, then chairman, and Robert Byrd, the panel's ranking Democrat. Although the pugnacious activist appeared to be a stark contrast with Stennis, the reserved southern gentleman admired her energy and fiery advocacy. Byrd, whose life story matched Mikulski's rapid rise from meager beginnings, developed a special bond with the Maryland lawmaker. Once accepted on the committee, Mikulski targeted the VA-HUD panel, which represents a microcosm of Maryland's interests. There she could help manage community development programs affecting Baltimore's ethnic neighborhoods, space initiatives important to the Goddard Space Flight Center, science projects critical to Johns Hopkins and the University of Maryland, and environmental funds needed to clean up the Chesapeake Bay. Maryland also is home to 527,000 veterans, accounting for 1 in 9 of the state's population.

If Mikulski's initial placement on the panel was an anomaly, her meteoric rise to cardinal was unique. Two years after she joined the Senate and the VA-HUD subcommittee, Chairman William Proxmire and senior Democrat Lawton Chiles decided to retire. Patrick Leahy and Bennett Johnston stood next in line, but they didn't want to abandon their respective control of the foreign operations and energy and water panels. Most committee observers thought Frank Lautenberg would switch from the Transportation Subcommittee to manage VA-HUD's significantly larger budget, but he remained the highway and mass transit cardinal in order to assist New Jersey's aging systems. That unusual sequence meant the gavel passed to Barbara Mikulski, the subcommittee's most junior member, and she reveled in her unexpectedly early assumption of power.

The relatively unknown chairman initially aroused substantial anxiety within several of the agencies she managed. NASA and National Science Foundation officials worried that this unabashed liberal would trash science projects to provide more money for housing and community development. Mikulski, however, spent considerable time meeting with department personnel and learning the programs, and she took what many lobbyists later described as a measured approach.

NASA supporters expressed particular relief when the cardinal, rather than divert the agency's money, began to promote space initiatives as an integral part of a southern strategy for the Democratic party. Mikulski, for instance, escorted Texas Governor Ann Richards on a tour of the Johnson Space Center near Houston, explaining to the Democratic executive what NASA spending meant to her state. Talking with reporters after that tour, the senator tried to build upon the popular appeal John Kennedy first tapped when he sent astronauts to the moon.

HEARINGS

The Senate cardinal did not reveal her space station strategy early. In fact, she initially ordered her clerk to locate and delete controversial items that federal agencies—particularly NASA—had hidden deep within their fiscal 1992 justification books, often obfuscated by technical language. Kevin Kelly focused special scrutiny on the space agency's disguised application for a $13 million private jet to be used by NASA executives. During the previous funding cycle appropriators had rejected NASA's plea to purchase the plane, but the clerk knew the astronauts would try again. After finding no mention of an aircraft in the headquarters budget, he spent hours scouring the fine print of the space agency's request and finally discovered money for the plane in an obscure line item within the research and program management account for the Marshall Space Flight Center. "It took me awhile, but I shot it down," bragged the clerk.

Unlike Dick Malow, his House counterpart, Kelly is no budget-analyzing professional. House staffers may consider themselves independent of politics, but Kelly straightforwardly admits to being a political junkie who loves partisan polemics. He is Barbara Mikulski's biggest proponent, having begun his professional career with her in 1985, when she served in the House. Associates who knew him said that the twenty-seven-year-old was even then pugnacious and driven.

When Mikulski assumed the Senate VA-HUD chairmanship in 1989, several appropriators and senior staff members urged the new cardinal and chairman Byrd to retain Tom van der Voort, the popular clerk who had worked with retiring Senator Proxmire. But as an appropriator observed, "Mikulski wanted her boy in there, and Byrd was willing to satisfy her wishes." Kelly impressed observers early with his quick mastery of the government's Byzantine budget procedures as well as the labyrinth of programs contained within twenty-four federal departments and agencies. After he met his official obligations, the clerk spent his evenings finishing the final year of law school at Georgetown University. To top it off, he also got married.

Born in Butler, a small town of seventeen thousand in rural western Pennsylvania, Kelly, like Mikulski, was reared a Catholic; in fact, the clerk studied eleven years for the priesthood but never took his vows. Religious references remain part of Kelly's vocabulary. In a talk before housing advocates, for instance, the clerk used the ancient biblical term *an aween* to describe the dispossessed and demonstrate his commitment to antipoverty programs. While meeting with reporters after the markup, he jokingly referred to his Catholic roots as the justification for a funding earmark to the Wheeling Jesuit College in West Virginia.

Colleagues and lobbyists hold strong opinions about Kelly. No one questions the clerk's aptitude, and he was variously described as "quite bright," "a quick learner," "perceptive and most energetic," and "awesomely intelligent." But such compliments were tempered by complaints about his arrogance, ambition, and stubbornness. Kelly constantly pushes agency officials and lobbyists for information. "He's robust and two-fisted about it," protested a budget officer. "He drives me nuts." Moaned another weary agency official: "Kelly has put a lot of age on a lot of us." Recalling that the clerk was even more demanding during his early days on the subcommittee, the bureaucrat added, "Thank God Kevin got married because his wife actually calmed him down a bit. I've meant to send a dozen roses just to commemorate her efforts." The stocky staffer tries to appear controlled—wearing starched white shirts, keeping his suit coat buttoned, and trimming his hair short—but he can't keep his body still. Before public events with the VA-HUD subcommittee, Kelly paces about nervously. Even at one-on-one meetings, he frequently jumps from his chair to find some report and make a point.

Although staffers scrutinize the president's budget intensely, senators spend far less time than House appropriators on investigatory hearings. Mikulski serves on a total of eleven different subcommittees—on and off Appropriations—and she simply doesn't have time to review an agency's operations and budget request thoroughly. While Traxler interrogated NASA officials for a day and a half, Mikulski devoted only one hour and a half. The House prepared eight volumes of hearing records, compared with the Senate's two. Traxler dwelt on each agency's justification books, asking detailed questions about personnel needs and construction cost overruns; Mikulski, in contrast, focused on broad themes. "We don't want to admit it," admitted a Senate clerk, "but our hearings have become pro forma. The real action is done by staff behind the scenes. The public show is necessary as part of our democracy, but the hearings rarely alert staff or senators to anything new that needs to be addressed."

The Senate VA-HUD panel launched its hearings in early February, only two days after President Bush had submitted his budget, and continued until June 5, about a month before the markup. The subcommittee started with the small agencies, such as the Office of Consumer Affairs within the Department of Health and Human Services, and moved to the larger departments, ending with Housing and Urban Development. The cardinal often managed the hearings all by herself since busy senators tended to attend other meetings. When most of her subcommittee showed up to greet Jack Kemp, Mikulski remarked, "It is really something to have so many of my subcommittee members here. Usually when I hold these hearings I feel like either the Lone Ranger, or Lonesome Dove, or somewhere in between."

In mid-May the panel opened its doors to the public, but Mikulski again favored a more succinct approach than Traxler. While the House panel's outside witnesses dragged on for four days, the Senate chairman provided only two hours. She ran the session, moreover, like a town council meeting at which no one had an assigned time to speak. Testifiers simply showed up at 7:00 A.M., signed in, and were taken in order. Finding most presentations boring, Mikulski cut each individual's time to only two and one-half minutes.

As some compensation for the scanty hearings, the subcommittee submitted a host of questions for agency officials to answer in writing. During consideration of the fiscal 1992 budget Mikulski's staff alone issued fifty-nine queries to NASA. Other panel members added more, and the space agency's responses filled sixty-seven pages.

Senate VA-HUD hearings provoke speeches rather than discussions. Even the hearing room sets a formal tone, with Mikulski sitting on a raised dais in a large chamber made somber by dark brown paneling and brown-gray linoleum. The senator uses a puffy blue pillow to boost her small frame, yet her head barely appears over the platform. Senatorial courtesies prompt elected officials to spend much of each hearing paying flowery tribute to one another and to administration leaders. At Jack Kemp's defense of HUD's budget, for instance, Jake Garn made a passing reference to his planned retirement from the Senate, moving the assembled senators and housing secretary to praise his tenure on the panel. Mikulski declared, "You have been a terrific chairman of this subcommittee when it was your opportunity to do so and just an extraordinary ranking minority to work with." Alfonse D'Amato chimed in, "I, too, would like to join you in paying tribute." Christopher Bond, Frank Lautenberg, and Patrick Leahy added to the chorus, joking about how the Utah senator would improve his skiing upon retirement. Even Kemp got into the act, announcing, "To Jake Garn, may I say with great respect and admiration that the country and both sides of the political aisle will miss your integrity and tenacity, and your perspicacity as well. That means vision of the future."

Before questioning could begin, senators felt the need to praise the housing secretary, too. Republican D'Amato exulted, "His enthusiasm is important. It is contagious. It is good." Even Democrat Lautenberg added, "To Secretary Kemp, who I see on many good occasions and with whom I have some disagreements and some agreements: He is a man of principles. He sticks up for what he believes in." And before Kemp could deliver his testimony, he had to applaud Mikulski. "We have had our differences," the housing secretary said, "but I particularly appreciate you, your integrity, your commitment to people, to their empowerment, and to their equality of opportunity which all too often is a dream, not a reality."

As in the House, most junior panel members focus on parochial issues. Missouri's Bond pleaded with the housing secretary to forgive the St. Louis housing authority for having submitted part of its funding application five days late. New Jersey's Lautenberg probed HUD's investigation of management abuses at several of his state's housing authorities. Nebraska's Bob Kerrey pushed a grant for the Omaha Tribal Housing Authority.

Time and again at the hearings Mikulski complained about the tight budget and tough choices facing appropriators. Commenting on rumors about her subcommittee's allocation, the cardinal said simply, "It looks bleak."

THE ALLOCATION

Within a week of the president's budget submission, each Senate clerk prepared a summary analysis for Robert Byrd and his central office staff. "In this first pitch we focus on the big items and ask for a big allocation," admitted a subcommittee staff director. As in the House, a team of central office staff members meets individually with each clerk. The Senate interrogators included James English, the staff director; Terrence Sauvain, whose title is deputy staff director but whose primary duty is to ensure that West Virginia obtains ear-marked projects; and John J. ("Jack") Conway, the numbers specialist.

Jim English, fifty years old and a certified public accountant, usually plays the heavy, as a clerk explained, "Mao-Maoing us, accusing our estimates of being filled with fat, declaring that we could live with a lower allocation." Over and over again the staff director asked, "What do you really need to obtain enough votes to get your bill through the Senate?"—the same question that dominated House discussions. Terry Sauvain, a longtime Byrd associate who prominently displays his title beside the door to his office on the first floor of the Dirksen Senate Office Building, posed a different question, but he also repeated it many times: "What have you done recently for West Virginia?" Jack Conway, whose unmarked office is known as Numbers Central, prepares detailed budget tables, offers advice on scoring, and ensures that subcommittees keep their expenditures within their allocations. "Everyone else but Jack could disappear and the appropriations process would still run," declared a former senior staffer. "God forbid if the KGB ever enlisted Jack Conway as a secret agent."

Clerks tend to be coy about their strategies with the central office team. "I don't beg for my allocation," claimed W. Proctor Jones of the Energy and Water Development Subcommittee. "As a professional staff member I can write a tight budget or I can write one having excess money." Another clerk said his discussions focused on the subcommittee's specific legal and contractual needs. "My job is to present detailed information on what I'm required to spend," he said. "Most of my basic costs for salaries and ongoing activities don't change, and I tend to know when construction outlays for specific projects will come due." Others outright lobby English, Sauvain, and Conway. Kevin Kelly, for instance, argued long and hard that the VA-HUD panel needed even more money than the administration proposed. "No one believed him," said a central office staffer. "We assume most clerks are trying to take us." About an hour or two into each initial meeting, English suggested an allocation number to each clerk. Then the appeals began. Said a subcommittee staff director:

"We have some three or four weeks to make our arguments within the bosom of the lodge."

Outside the lodge George Bush trekked to Capitol Hill in late May to ask Byrd personally for special attention to the space station and Mikulski's VA-HUD panel. Members of the 602(b) Coalition also sought to influence the allocation, but Byrd dislikes Washington-based influence peddlers. Coalition lobbyists, as a result, approached West Virginia University President Neil Bucklew, who wanted increased funding from the National Science Foundation. Bucklew refused to sign a coalition letter, but he did talk with Byrd at a West Virginia barbecue and later sent his own note pressing the case for Mikulski's subcommittee. When asked about the impact of presidents or lobbyists, several Senate clerks asserted that the allocation is an internal decision. Outsiders not only don't affect the outcome, declared these insiders, but aren't encouraged to try.

The central office staff returned several times to the thirteen subcommittees for more discussions, more appeals, more Mao-Maoing. "This is not a consultative process," moaned a clerk. "There's lots of talk back and forth, but in the end the central office makes the decisions."

By late May English and his team had developed a set of recommendations for Byrd. Meeting alone, the chairman and the staff director reviewed the proposed allocations. Byrd, who had memorized last year's allocation and the president's request for each of the thirteen panels, played a more active role in setting priorities than did Whitten, but he made only minor changes to the staff draft.

Byrd is an intensely private and driven man. He prefers to spend his free time reading histories, the classics, or the Bible. Over one summer vacation the chairman finished a multivolume chronicle of Great Britain and then tried to impress other senators with his ability to recite in order all of Albion's monarchs. He's also writing his own multivolume history of the United States Senate; in June 1991 the Government Printing Office released his 682-page second segment, described by the *Almanac of American Politics* as "based on impressive research, gracefully written, full of arresting anecdotes and sound insights; it surpasses any previous work on the subject."

Appropriations staffers quietly hope Byrd will take up something other than writing the history of the Senate, a hobby that keeps him around and them busy. The chairman, according to an aide, "is not a laugh riot. He simply works harder than anyone else." Hard work, in fact, seems to be one of Byrd's favorite qualities—in himself and others. A box in the chairman's office is labeled "Secrets of Success"; inside, it reads, "Work." A clerk added that Byrd's ultimate compliment to a staffer is "He works late." The chairman, however, was supremely embarrassed in 1990 when forced to admit publicly that he hadn't taken the time to read an amendment offered in his name. "At the core," said an associate, "Byrd wants the facts so he'll not be made a fool of." Concluded another lawmaker: "Despite his pomposity, the chairman is insecure."

Byrd's drive for self-improvement has consumed him since his early days as a virtual orphan in West Virginia's coalfields. The senator was born in 1917 in North Carolina as Cornelius Calvin Sale, Jr. His mother died shortly after his first birthday, and his father sent the infant off to live in southern West Virginia with an aunt and uncle, Vlurma and Titus Byrd. The chairman infrequently but emotionally describes the poverty and privation of that part of Appalachia.

Byrd showed academic promise early but couldn't afford college. He worked almost a dozen years as a welder and butcher before being elected to the West Virginia legislature in 1946. During that first campaign Byrd joined the Ku Klux Klan and even urged a Klan rebirth "in every state of the Union." He later expressed regret for this affiliation, calling it an ill-conceived way to gain votes in rural West Virginia. More a pragmatist than a dogmatic ideologue, Byrd slowly adapted to his state's changing racial mood.

The West Virginia senator never lost an election and rose quickly through the leadership ranks. He entered the House of Representatives in 1952, served three terms, and soundly defeated a veteran Republican senator in 1958. For his strong support of Majority Leader Lyndon Johnson, he was rewarded during his first year with a seat on Appropriations. At the same time, he studied law at night and earned his degree from American University, having the diploma presented to him by President John Kennedy. Byrd challenged Edward Kennedy in 1971 for the position of majority whip; with

Kennedy's attentions diverted by Chappaquiddick, he won by the deathbed vote of Richard Russell. When Majority Leader Mike Mansfield retired in 1976, the West Virginian assumed the Senate's key leadership post.

Byrd's twelve-year tenure as Democratic boss of the Senate proved frustrating, particularly during the half dozen years Republicans controlled the chamber. The role of minority leader, he declared, was a "purgatory if not worse." But even when he managed Senate actions, Byrd failed to endear himself to his Democratic colleagues, many of whom complained that the West Virginian appeared too forbidding and stuffy, especially compared with the master of the televised image, President Ronald Reagan. In 1988 Byrd announced he'd leave the majority leader post up for grabs, in a fight won by George Mitchell of Maine, and he inherited the plum assignments of Appropriations chairman and president pro tempore, a largely ceremonial job given to the most senior member of the Senate majority. The latter task entitles Byrd, a master of parliamentary procedure, to preside over the Senate whenever he chooses; it also puts him in the line of succession to the presidency, behind the Speaker of the House. As chief appropriator Byrd quickly doubled the president pro tempore's budget, claiming that funding had not kept pace with inflation or the office's responsibilities.

When he became Appropriations chairman, Byrd felt he had to compensate for having been away from the committee and its issues for the dozen years he was Democratic leader and spent countless hours studying the details of each bill, memorizing scores of allocation and funding levels. Many consider Byrd, after only a few years on the job, to be the most effective Senate Appropriations Committee chairman in a generation. His willingness to assume leadership is one factor in this, as are the ages and ill health of his predecessors, including the eighty-seven-year-old John Stennis, who retired in 1988 after a single term directing the committee. "Byrd is certainly a strong chairman," said an appropriator. "He is forceful and ensures the committee follows procedures." Another more bluntly summarized the chairman's leadership style: "If you cross Byrd, he'll cut your nuts off."

***

Beginning at noon on June 4, Byrd and English met separately with each cardinal and his or her clerk. The West Virginia senator, a skilled negotiator and acknowledged "arm twister," excels in these small-group sessions. Most cardinals quietly accepted the chairman's mark, knowing it could be worse if they antagonized Byrd. Said Quentin Burdick of the agriculture panel, who faced a substantial $434 million cut from the president's request: "If that's what you need to make the thing work, Mr. Chairman, I'll do my part."

Byrd went out of his way to assure Mikulski that he had tried to raise her VA-HUD allocation above the House mark by more than $50 million. The Maryland senator didn't protest, even though congressional insiders assumed she needed an extra $300 to $400 million to fund the space station as well as popular science and social programs. "I know the chairman has done his best to give fair allocations," she said stoically. Cardinals who sit on four or five Appropriations subcommittees can't be too assertive for the panels they chair. Mikulski, for instance, wants the Labor-HHS subcommittee to receive enough to provide some $9 billion to the National Institutes of Health, headquartered in her state. Similarly she craves substantial mass transit funding for Baltimore and the Washington suburbs.

Only after his series of meetings had evoked endorsements from the cardinals did Byrd telephone his Republican counterpart, Mark Hatfield, to discuss the proposed allocations. Since it was late, Hatfield agreed to meet the chairman in his office the following morning at nine-thirty. Joining the senior senators on June 5 were Jim English and Keith Kennedy, the majority and minority staff directors. The foursome quickly reviewed the numbers for the thirteen subcommittees, Byrd asked for Hatfield's support, and the chairman announced that the full committee would meet at 4:00 P.M. to endorse the allocations.

At 10:30 A.M. Kennedy assembled Republican staffers in Hatfield's office and distributed Byrd's table. He also faxed a copy to OMB officials, asking for the Bush administration's immediate reactions and suggestions. By noon Hatfield had spoken with the ranking minority members for each subcommittee. Most upset was Pennsylvania's Arlen Specter, who complained that Byrd should have matched the Budget Resolution's higher mark for education and health. The senior Republican on the Labor-HHS subcommittee decided to offer an amendment that would move $2.7 billion from other panels to Labor-HHS, and he worked throughout the early afternoon with OMB strategists to craft an alternate allocation table.

At ten minutes past four, Byrd hammered his gavel loudly to quiet the senators assembled in the committee's elaborate conference room on the first floor of the U.S. Capitol. The West Virginian's face appeared strikingly red against his bright white hair, and his head twitched slightly as he read an opening statement about how he had wanted to give more money to each subcommittee. Expressing the need for compromise and tough choices, Byrd distributed his table and briefly explained the line items. Ironically, it was Democratic appropriators who were seeing the complete allocations for the first time. The day before, Byrd had informed each cardinal of his or her number, and his or her number only. The Republicans, in contrast, had received the full table from Hatfield earlier that morning.

Compared with the House's, Byrd's largest increase—$490 million or 2.3 percent—went to America's dams, roads, and other physical infrastructure funded by the Energy and Water Development Subcommittee. Continuing his commitment to antidrug initiatives, he increased spending available for the Commerce, Justice, State, the Judiciary, and Related Agencies Subcommittee by $310 million. The VA-HUD panel, said the chairman, would receive a "microscopic" increase of $52 million over the House mark. When Byrd proclaimed that he had made a personal sacrifice by allocating $705 million less than the House to his own Interior Subcommittee, a journalist who happened to hear of the unpublicized meeting chuckled and murmured that Byrd had employed the same ploy before, only to retrieve the money in subsequent negotiations with Jamie Whitten.

His businesslike introduction completed, Byrd thanked Hatfield for his help, even though Republican staffers later complained they had "precious little" to do with the allocation process. The ranking minority member explained that he had learned of the numbers only that morning, he noted Jake Garn's concern that the VA-HUD panel might be unable to support the space station, and he advocated adequate funding for the Internal Revenue Service. These concerns raised, however, Hatfield moved the adoption of Byrd's allocation.

Specter tried to introduce his alternate proposal, but Byrd, ever the stickler for parliamentary procedure, briskly ruled the motion to be an amendment to, rather than a substitute for, the Hatfield-Byrd motion. Jim English then stood and read the roll; only Specter, Garn, and Phil Gramm objected to considering the chairman's proposal. Byrd, pulling proxies for the five missing senators from his coat pocket, announced that the vote was 26–3.

The Pennsylvania senator then offered his amendment, but he garnered little support. Republican Warren Rudman complained that Specter would reduce funding for justice and crime programs. Mikulski argued that he would destroy the space station and restrict money for HOPE and HOME. Democrat Frank Lautenberg described the

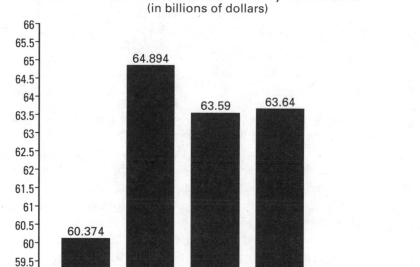

VA-HUD Domestic Discretionary Allocation
(in billions of dollars)

131

motion as "shocking and surprising" and stated that Byrd's allocation looked eminently fair in comparison. Specter, recognizing he
wouldn't win, criticized Byrd's allocation procedures and argued that
he could have developed a better amendment if given more time. He
challenged the chairman to improve consultations with the minority.

Obviously irritated and growing even more red in the face, Byrd
began a controlled response. "Someone has to make the hard decisions, to do the hard work," he explained slowly. "My credo has been
to be fair. Any senator can offer an amendment." Outlining his
procedures, Byrd continued, "I feel that I must be clear first with my
subcommittee chairmen. That's West Virginia common sense. Then
I spoke with the ranking member." Explaining the obvious, the chairman pointed out that since the Democrats held the majority of seats,
they presided over the Senate and the Appropriations panel. Staring
intently at Specter, he concluded, "When you are chairman, you can
run this committee as you want—and you won't find me grumbling."
The Pennsylvania Republican withdrew his amendment.

Outside in the committee's antechamber after the session, Garn
complained that the VA-HUD allocation was "totally inadequate."
Mikulski, responding to a question about the feasibility of funding
the space station, said wearily, "I don't know."

NEW MONEY

For almost two weeks after Byrd had formally announced the Senate
allocations, Kevin Kelly walked about gloomily. "He was extremely
tense," observed a colleague. "He felt the pressure of having to do the
impossible: fund both the space station and HOME." By late June,
however, the clerk displayed a bounce in his step and a determined
smile on his face. "Something was up," said a lobbyist later, "but I
didn't realize at the time that Kevin had found more money."

"It's not like we discovered cash lying around on the street,"
explained Stephen Kohashi, the chain-smoking Republican staff director and assistant to Senator Garn. "But we did exploit every
opportunity." Said Kelly: "We had been pulling our hair out trying

to find enough resources to do all we had to do, and suddenly, *voilà*, there was new money." Kelly's and Kohashi's sudden break came when lobbyists for senior citizens suggested that the Cranston-Gonzalez Affordable Housing Act changed financing rules in ways that could free up funds from housing subsidies for the elderly and disabled. In the past the Department of Housing and Urban Development had offered loans to organizations building housing for the elderly and disabled and then had provided those organizations with rental assistance to pay off those loans. The new rules, approved in 1990, had converted the loan program to a grant program, perhaps allowing appropriators to provide less rental assistance.

Scorekeepers at the Congressional Budget Office and the Office of Management and Budget had to be convinced of the scheme's legitimacy and had to determine how much the plan would provide in budget authority and how much in outlays. Kelly approached them secretly, wanting to maintain personal control of the potentially larger funding pot and to avoid alerting lobbyists and senators. OMB officials had been aware of the possible windfall and had quietly hoped no one else would notice so that the administration and HUD could enjoy a bit of financial slack throughout the fiscal year. CBO statisticians couldn't make up their minds how to score the scheme, changing positions three times before offering a confidential ruling that the change allowed the VA-HUD panel to play with an extra $1.2 billion in budget authority.

So clandestine were Kelly's tactics that the clerk didn't even discuss the deal with the Budget Committee, which had to declare formally to the full Senate that the panel's total spending—even after adding an extra $1.2 billion—didn't exceed its allocation. Without the Budget Committee's endorsement, a single lawmaker could have prevented consideration of the entire VA-HUD bill with a simple point of order on the Senate floor. Although the Budget Committee usually follows the Congressional Budget Office's advice, Kelly's was a risky move. "Up here we play by high wire," commented the clerk.

Once he had realized the fluidity within HUD's complex accounts, Kelly began a dogged search for even more money, paying particular attention to funds that appropriators had previously provided but

HUD had not spent. After several days of digging, the clerk found an unused $565 million, which he decided to take back from the agency, allowing Barbara Mikulski rather than Jack Kemp to determine how it would be spent. Kelly discussed this particular maneuver with HUD officials only the day before his subcommittee markup. Kemp, as an associate put it, "went ballistic" and again pleaded with White House officials to threaten a presidential veto unless the money was restored to HUD's control. The clerk, after the markup, admitted with irony in his voice that "Kemp was not a willing coconspirator in this deal."

The two accounting gimmicks—rental assistance and HUD's unobligated funds—totaled $1.76 billion. Mikulski decided to recycle most of this fresh funding within HUD, appeasing mayors by adding $1.5 billion above the House mark for the HOME Investment Partnerships program. As a reward to the senior citizen lobbyists who only a few weeks before had clued Kelly and Kohashi to available HUD funds, the cardinal set aside enough money to construct ten thousand residences for the elderly, far more than the thousand housing units requested by the administration or the six thousand units proposed by the House.

The challenge of funding HOME might have been solved, but the space station's prospects remained bleak. Kelly appealed again to the central office staff for a larger allocation, but Jim English, aware of the scorekeeping tricks within HUD, rejected the taking of funds from other subcommittees. The clerk needed more gimmicks.

With the Soviet military threat reduced, many politicians, particularly Democrats, wanted to cut defense spending sharply and transfer the savings to domestic discretionary projects. The spending caps approved in the 1990 budget deal, of course, restricted such transfers, but that didn't stop lawmakers from seeking a back door to defense funds. One door proved to lead to Antarctica. Because the National Security Agency had long proclaimed the military importance of the South Pole, America's scientific projects there were managed initially by the Department of Defense. But as a senior Pentagon official admitted, "The navy fucked up the program so badly—dumping tons of litter and toxics indiscriminately on the pristine environment—that Congress transferred control to the National Science Foundation." Appropriators, as a result, provided some $105 million annually to special NSF accounts that the navy drew upon to clean up its pollution and to cover the logistical costs associated with Antarctica research.

In early 1991 Dick Malow called OMB officials to explain his funding predicament, describe the vulnerability of the president's beloved space station, and suggest that Antarctica expenses be pushed onto the navy. But the Bush administration wanted no backdoor tricks, claiming that Defense Secretary Richard Cheney wouldn't countenance a raid on his funds. Later when Traxler decided that the space station must go, the cardinal and his clerk lost interest in accounting gimmicks; the pain from any amendment to restore funds for the station, they reasoned, had to be severe.

Kelly, in contrast, desperately needed money to satisfy Mikulski's newfound support for NASA's orbiting platform. Navy funds looked particularly attractive to the clerk after senior NSF officials forwarded a "secret white paper" that calculated Antarctica's logistical costs over the next decade at $1.5 billion. Unloading those substantial costs onto the Defense Department would enable Kelly's VA-HUD subcommittee to fund many more domestic programs. The clerk convinced Jim English, who knew Byrd wanted increased domestic spending, to present the case to Bob Grady, the OMB associate director in charge of environmental and science programs. Grady knew President Bush had gone out on a limb to advocate full funding for the space station, and the OMB staffer had received less-than-subtle encouragement to cooperate with Mikulski's efforts in that regard. From a personal perspective, Grady also could make a dispassionate case that the navy's work in Antarctica should be considered a defense expenditure. Moreover, he didn't mind the thought of expanding his own portfolio at the OMB with the transfer.

While Grady and English negotiated, Kelly talked with his counterpart on the Defense Subcommittee, Richard Collins, about how Mikulski and Garn needed help to cover some of the space station's costs. Kelly knew that the OMB, despite Grady's sympathies, wouldn't accept a military item within the VA-HUD bill, so he asked Collins to find $105 million in his legislation. Mikulski reinforced the appeal by discussing the matter with Collins's boss, Senator Daniel Inouye of Hawaii. On the surface, it seemed unlikely that Inouye would give up any money, but there were deeper currents influencing the defense cardinal. Said one clerk: "Good Lord, Inouye has two hundred and seventy billion to play with, and it's amazing the amount of money sloshing around in the defense bill." Another argued that Inouye was willing to do Mikulski a favor in exchange for Hawaii-based earmarks in the VA-HUD bill. Still another claimed that Byrd, who wanted a VA-HUD bill flush enough to fund West Virginia projects, also made known his sentiments for the transfer.

Meanwhile, this scorekeeping scheme sparked heated debates within the OMB, particularly between Bob Grady and Robert Howard, the associate director responsible for defense matters. Howard argued assertively against focusing just on the VA-HUD subcommittee or the space station, warning that any transfer from the defense budget could open the floodgates to further appeals and become untenable for the Republican administration. Kelly and English, however, continued to get the sense that the administration wanted to be accommodating. Budget Director Darman even agreed formally that at least $30 million—the amount related to cleanup and health care costs associated with the navy's pollution—would be classified as defense spending. Yet the fate of the remaining $75 million remained uncertain by the time of Mikulski's markup.

Kelly concocted one last scorekeeping gimmick, this one involving NASA's services for the Department of Defense (DoD). For years the space agency had financed the Tracking and Data Relay Satellite System (TDRSS), an international communications network about 22,300 miles above the Earth that relays signals between ground controllers and low-orbiting satellites. Although the Pentagon had long used TDRSS, it had never compensated NASA. The clerk decided the time had come to adjust that arrangement.

Since military satellites are funded within DoD's "black," or secret, budget, Kelly and Mikulski again contacted Collins and Inouye about a $384 million transfer to NASA. Again, the Defense appropriators agreed. And again, Grady and other OMB officials suggested that Defense money could be used to help finance TDRSS, yet they

136

put nothing in writing nor offered an opinion from Budget Director Darman or Defense Secretary Cheney.

Faced with such uncertainties over his newfound money, Kelly fell back on a tenet of appropriators: "If a problem develops, we fix it later in the process." For the moment, however, Kelly walked with a bounce and a smile.

CRAFTING A BILL

Mikulski became the center of attention among space station supporters immediately after the June 6 House vote. Agency officials pleaded with the cardinal to "fix the wound in NASA's science programs." Representative Bill Lowery declared hopefully, "We're not done yet." And House Science, Space, and Technology Committee Chairman George Brown urged the senator to identify "creative solutions" that would fund both science and manned space programs. Yet Mikulski didn't want to be held to a specific number for science or the space station, so the watchword for space advocates became "balance."

On June 16 four senators from states with large space station contracts—Texas's Lloyd Bentsen, California's Alan Cranston, Utah's Jake Garn, and Alabama's Howell Heflin—met with Mikulski to plot a Senate strategy. Cornered by a reporter as he left the committee's conference room, Garn, a fervent space advocate who had ridden aboard the shuttle *Discovery* in 1985, said a plan "has not yet been formulated, but we need votes—that sums up the whole strategy." Similar sessions, held weekly, turned into pep rallies for the five senators and staffers from about twenty other Senate offices. "Mikulski learned early in her career how to build coalitions," commented a colleague. "The campaign to save the space station was just another example of her ability to organize diverse constituencies."

On July 8, two days before the Senate VA-HUD markup, this campaign obtained signatures from sixty-five senators, a clear majority of the chamber, on a letter to Mikulski declaring, "We wish to express our support for Space Station Freedom." On the same day space station foes admitted they were still searching for someone to champion their cause.

Outside the Senate, in contrast, the station faced a rising chorus of criticism from space scientists, most of whom had been rudely awakened to the funding peril facing their projects by the Chapman-Lowery vote. The amended House bill provided only 44 percent of the resources researchers wanted for the comet rendezvous asteroid flyby, only 48 percent for the advanced X-ray–astrophysics facility, and only 57 percent for the Earth observing system. It cut the inquiry into climate change by $145 million, and it curtailed microgravity and life science experiments scheduled for the shuttle. Frightened scientists drew ominous parallels between the space station battle and the one fought a decade before over the space shuttle. To divert funds then, NASA had slashed spending for most science missions; between mid-1978 and mid-1989, for instance, the United States had launched no planetary probes.

James Van Allen, the University of Iowa physicist known for discovering the radiation belts that ring the Earth, called the space station "a monster that will kill off a lot of space science." John Bahcall, an astrophysicist at Princeton University, puzzled over NASA's willingness to sacrifice science projects: "If NASA were a mental patient instead of an agency, you'd say it has schizophrenia." Critics also wondered aloud why the United States should invest so much money doing what the Soviet Union had already done; the Soviets had launched their first small orbiting lab, named *Salyut,* in 1971, and their first module with a multiple docking port, named *Mir,* in 1986.

The largest, if late, challenge came from Robert Park, the University of Maryland physicist, who organized a coalition of fourteen leading scientific and engineering organizations—including the American Physical Society, American Chemical Society, American Geophysical Union, and American Mathematical Society—to question the "scientific, technological and educational merit of the currently planned station." While not calling for the project's demise, the coalition's letter to every senator declared that scientists were "especially disturbed" by the possibility that the station's current outlays

138

and "escalating costs in subsequent years" would drain funds from the National Science Foundation and other research centers.

The scientists' letter, released at a well-orchestrated press conference the day before Mikulski's markup, drew substantial media attention. Yet it also prompted sharp public responses from Budget Director Darman, who derided scientific protests as "factional cannibalism" from selfish researchers wanting to protect their own grants rather than advance a program that would profit the entire nation.

Kevin Kelly complained privately, but vociferously, to the chancellor of the University of Maryland System, for whom Park nominally worked, hinting that the NSF would cut its grants to any college whose scientists opposed the station. The clerk also telephoned Park directly to demand a retraction for the researcher's article in an American Physical Society newsletter that suggested Mikulski had cut political deals with the White House to craft her bill. He even screamed at NASA's scientific officials, "Why can't you get your Indians back on the reservation?"

"The pressure caused a few coalition members to get sweaty palms and peel off," admitted Park. "For myself, however, tenure protects me from such abuse." The physicist knew his last-minute challenge would not change Mikulski's or the Senate's predisposition toward the space station, but he promised to continue fighting what he labeled "an outmoded and unnecessary project."

Mikulski, a tough urban pol, frequently stands up to such lobbying pressure whether from Washington's most aggressive lawyers or from cabinet secretaries. Edward Derwinski of the Department of Veterans Affairs, for instance, pressed the chairman for money to replace an acute care hospital in Palo Alto, California, damaged by the 1989 Loma Prieta earthquake. Mikulski snapped that the $250 million tower, to be associated with the Stanford University Medical Center, would be overbedded and gold-plated and that "Gucci universities should not drive the train." Over objections from the powerful veterans' lobby, Mikulski also ordered Veterans Affairs laboratories to comply with quality standards developed by the Department of Health and Human Services.

The cardinal often displays a prodigious temper, which she unleashed on environmentalists and space scientists for using "her 602(b) Coalition" to lobby against "her space station." Particularly troubling to this senator, who deeply values her relationship with Senator Robert Byrd, were the vocal protests by some coalition members against the disappointing allocation the chairman gave to the Senate VA-HUD panel. As a Mikulski associate explained, "She simply can't tolerate anyone who gets between her and Chairman Byrd."

Kelly usually doesn't bend to the demands of lobbyists either. In fact, he frequently directs their actions. An early promoter of the 602(b) Coalition, the clerk met with its steering committee shortly after the House floor vote to complain about member groups opposing the space station. He blasted Friends of the Earth for sending its letter and a critical editorial to representatives, asserting that those actions reduced his Senate allocation and hurt his efforts to craft a balanced bill. According to one participant at the meeting, "Kevin demanded that the groups stay in line and support whatever Mikulski comes up with."

Some lobbyists believe Mikulski and Kelly perform an effective good-guy, bad-guy routine. "My boss gets along well with Mikulski, but then Kevin does his own thing and screws us," said an agency official. "It's not clear if she wants Kevin to play the bad ass or if she just doesn't know what's going on."

Others complain that the clerk focuses more attention on the cardinal's interests than on the government's business. "For Kevin, doing the right thing is very low on his list," said an associate. "Doing what's best for Mikulski's reelection is his highest concern." Kelly, however, stresses his subcommittee's substantive endeavors: the development of farsighted strategies to revitalize NASA and combat lead paint poisoning, the organization of a pioneering hearing on the readiness of Veterans Affairs to help returning Operation Desert Storm troops, and the two-volume report on mathematics and science education that remains the key study on the subject. The clerk's admirers say his cleverness and hard driving benefit the Committee on Appropriations. "Sure he can be rough and selfish," commented one appropriator, "but no one's going to pull something over on Kevin."

In the collegial environment of the U.S. Senate, members frequently and informally confront Mikulski on the chamber floor and in caucus meetings with funding requests. To organize their chaotic lobbying input, Kelly and his assistant, Carolyn ("Carrie") Apostolou, logged and tracked on the subcommittee's computer each of the approximately fourteen hundred spending requests from senators.

Like Traxler in the House, Mikulski changed dramatically how the Senate VA-HUD panel directs appropriations toward the preferred projects of favored lawmakers. Her predecessor, William Proxmire, not only disliked earmarks but with great fanfare spotlighted the more outrageous pork barreling with his "Golden Fleece Awards." The Maryland senator, in contrast, considered congressional appropriators better able than administration bureaucrats to identify worthy projects, and she labeled "pork busting" as simply a political ploy by Republicans who controlled the administration but not the Congress.

To imbue other senators with a personal commitment to her bill, Mikulski, an astute deal maker, ordered her staff "to take care of the members." While she couldn't satisfy all fourteen hundred requests (totaling some $41 billion), the cardinal, despite a tight allocation, virtually doubled earmarks from the previous year. The Maryland senator first made sure that her own state was well provided for, to the point that an embarrassed colleague declared, "Mikulski is pigging out." Among the bill's largest earmarks were $40 million for improvements at the Back River Wastewater Treatment plant in the cardinal's hometown and $20 million for construction of Baltimore's Christopher Columbus Center of Marine Research and Exploration.

Following one of her tenets—"to be deferential to the full committee chairman"—Mikulski gave priority to requests from Robert Byrd. Within the NASA budget she virtually endowed the Wheeling Jesuit College in Wheeling, West Virginia, awarding $22.5 million for its National Technology Transfer Center, $6 million to construct and equip its "classroom of the future," and another $1.5 million to develop academic programs for the classroom's videos and space

141

simulators. Before being showered with federal money, the small college in the Allegheny foothills had an annual budget of just $14 million.

To ensure bipartisan support, Mikulski also took care of Jake Garn, her ranking Republican member, by providing $10 million to construct and equip a space dynamics lab at Utah State University, which presumably will be named after the state's retiring senator and onetime astronaut. Stretching HUD's defined mission, she even set aside $500,000 to buy land outside Provo, Utah, on which a well-connected developer could build an alternate route to the municipal airport. Phil Gramm, another subcommittee Republican, obtained $750,000 for drug elimination efforts by the Fort Worth, Texas, Housing Authority. Some of the largess flowed beyond appropriators. Alaskan senators appreciated the $2 million for a wastewater treatment plant in the city of Homer. Georgia's senators welcomed the $750,000 for the cleanup of Allatoona and Lanier lakes. Lawmakers from northern California valued the $2 million for San Mateo County's employee homeownership program.

Senator Daniel Inouye, the cooperative cardinal of the Defense Appropriations Subcommittee, obtained numerous earmarks for Hawaii, including $1.2 million for "infrastructure development of Hawaiian home lands," $1.3 million for training of agricultural workers at two sugarcane mills, $2 million to establish the Pacific Center for Posttraumatic Stress Disorder and War-Related Disorders, and $500,000 for a new National Commission on Native American, Alaska Native, and Native Hawaiian Housing.

To guarantee that lawmakers appreciated her generosity, Mikulski informed each senator of the funded projects in his or her state. Personalized letters concluded with a less-than-subtle plea: "I hope I can count on your support to preserve this well-balanced bill."

As part of the annual negotiating minuet with the House panel, Mikulski deleted virtually all of Traxler's earmarks. Not touched, of course, were House-earmarked projects that senators also wanted. "We can't tell a senator that we won't include an item because the House will take care of it in conference," a professional staff member explained. "The senator must be able to take credit for that item's

142

being in the Senate bill." All the key players, however, understood that House earmarks would be reinstated during conference committee negotiations.

Mikulski's hearing records might have been thinner than Traxler's, but not the report accompanying her bill. The Senate cardinal and clerk went out of their way to deliver lengthy policy directives. Recognizing that a leaner budget would require NASA to redefine its basic goals and missions, they ordered the space agency to submit a strategic plan with its fiscal 1993 budget, and they outlined eight restrictive assumptions. Provision 4, as an example, insisted: "The plan should assume the continued historical balance between manned and unmanned programs, wherein space science receives no less than 20 percent of the total amounts provided in NASA's 'research and development' and 'space flight' accounts."

The cardinal's decrees demonstrate anew the willingness of appropriators to tackle problems others don't. While House and Senate authorizers endlessly debated measures to abate lead poisoning, Mikulski outlined a set of federal requirements to tackle this significant environmental threat to children. The subcommittee's guidelines were quite detailed, declaring that "the training curricula shall address at a minimum: the health effect of lead and sources of exposure; worker protection practices and procedures; medical monitoring; abatement methods and practices including encapsulation and maintenance; testing and monitoring; prohibited abatement methods; cleanup procedures; and disposal requirements." Mikulski knew that House authorizers, particularly John Dingell, the aggressive chairman of the Energy and Commerce Committee, would complain about appropriators imposing on their turf. But on the Senate side Mikulski simply devised legislative language acceptable to Harry Reid, a fellow appropriator as well as chairman of the relevant Senate authorizing subcommittee. "We told the authorizers that when they pass something, we'll make changes," snapped the cardinal. "But until then we can't wait. Something needs to be done."

Mikulski, Kelly, and Apostolou wrote their report and bill with one eye toward upcoming conference negotiations with Traxler,

Malow, Thomson, and Burkett. Knowing they would compromise later, the Senate team issued an array of strong statements, sometimes for the sole purpose of scaring the agencies into action. Consider the case of pollution prevention. The previous year's VA-HUD report instructed the EPA to move the twenty-six-person pollution prevention division to the administrator's office in order to highlight the importance of this new approach to environmental management. Without conferring with appropriators, however, agency officials had transferred the personnel to the Office of Toxic Substances. Mikulski, Kelly, and Apostolou expressed their anger at being ignored by placing a similar directive within the fiscal 1992 bill itself, making the EPA liable for lawsuits if it failed to comply. "We knew our legislative language would cause a real stink at EPA," said Apostolou. In fact, the agency's response made this relatively small matter—involving only twenty-six out of a seventeen-thousand-person agency—one of the most volatile environmental issues before the conference committee.

Mikulski and her staff also knowingly opened themselves to controversy by stripping from the House bill $300 million of earmarked projects for sewage and wastewater treatment facilities. The earmarks first surfaced when Bush, in his effort to be the "environmental president," sought special funds to clean up Boston Harbor, a focus of significant rhetoric during his 1988 presidential campaign against Massachusetts Governor Michael Dukakis. Since White House advisers believed that targeting a single city would be perceived as a blatant political ploy, the administration added earmarks for Los Angeles, New York, Seattle, and San Diego, even though Congress had not authorized funds for those sites. Traxler, wanting to appease his Michigan colleague John Dingell, inserted a Rouge River project. Mikulski killed them all, arguing, at least in this instance, that congressional earmarks were not fair to other communities across the country that had to compete within EPA guidelines for sewage treatment grants. "We caught hell from several senators who had expected earmarked projects in their states," admitted a Senate staffer. "We knew some compromise in conference was inevitable, but we wanted to be able to have an example of our opposition to pork."

The subcommittee, moreover, tried to beat back the EPA's growing bureaucracy in order to save money and protest the agency's chronic delays. The Bush administration requested a substantial 12 percent increase for EPA salaries and wages to provide a cost of living increase and to implement the reauthorized Clean Air Act. Mikulski, a former community organizer bred to distrust bureaucracies and large salary accounts, decided to trim the president's request by $61 million, the equivalent of more than a thousand staff members. EPA officials protested vehemently, blaming Kevin Kelly and complaining that he disliked environmental issues. The clerk countered that the agency was bloated with staff, that it supported thirty-three hundred more employees than the Department of Housing and Urban Development but oversaw only one-fourth the budget.

Kelly lives in Frederick, about fifty miles north of Washington, and commutes daily by train, using the valued free time away from the phones to perform much of his written work on the committee's laptop computer. In fact, he drafted most of the panel's report while passing through Maryland suburbs and farmlands.

Carrie Apostolou supplements Kelly's efforts. Bright, thoughtful, and friendly, she pays particular attention to the Environmental Protection Agency, Department of Veterans Affairs, and Consumer Product Safety Commission. She worked several years for Tom van der Voort in an administrative-clerical position. When van der Voort and the assistant clerk left after Proxmire retired, the central office staff wanted some continuity at VA-HUD, and Apostolou was in the right place at the right time. Lobbyists praise her intuition and tenacity, but Kelly seems to call the shots. According to one agency official, "My negotiations with Carrie often don't stick after Kevin gets involved."

Rounding out the VA-HUD staff in 1991 were three federal agency detailees: Thomas Spence from the National Science Foundation, Sarah Linstead from NASA, and Paul Bryant from the General Accounting Office. Spence and Linstead served for a single year, while Bryant spent two years helping the panel wade through both the savings and loan and disaster relief issues.

Stephen Kohashi managed the subcommittee when Republicans

controlled the Senate in the early 1980s. Throughout the fiscal 1992 budget cycle he served as the panel's minority clerk and assistant to Senator Garn, working closely with Kelly to identify and promote scoring gimmicks that made additional funds available to the VA-HUD unit. Although Kohashi didn't write the actual legislation or report, a lobbyist commented, "Compared with his House Republican counterparts, Stephen is a real force on the panel." Associates described Kohashi as "an experienced professional," "shrewd," and "a brilliant technician concerned with the beauty and power of report language."

"After staff crunch the numbers and craft the bill, the cardinal plays the politics of selling it," explained a senior appropriator. Kelly and Apostolou finished most of their work about two weeks before the markup. Only then did Mikulski discuss the bill's basic provisions with Jake Garn, the panel's ranking Republican. The two lawmakers reviewed major issues, such as full funding for the space station and increases for HOME and HOPE, but many important spending details, including the $61 million cut for salaries at the EPA, were not discussed. The cardinal also made sure Byrd and her other panel members supported the bill's outline.

The afternoon before the markup Kelly and Apostolou briefed associate staffers and unveiled the embargoed report. Attendance was restricted, and associates felt the threat of serious retribution if they leaked any information. Although Kelly reviewed the programmatic particulars within the bill, legislative assistants spent most of their time determining the status of their bosses' earmarks. Leaving little to chance, the clerk told associates for the Democratic senators not able to attend the following day's markup to provide Mikulski with proxies of support in case something upset the fragile compromises crafted within the bill.

Kelly couldn't control everything, however. Later that evening Jack Kemp called Barbara Mikulski to say he needed an extra $1.1 billion because HUD's primitive computer initially provided an inaccurate estimate of the subsidies needed to renew contracts for landlords of low-income housing. Unless appropriators corrected the administration's mistake, some twenty-four thousand families could be put on the street the following year, an unpleasant prospect for politicians during an election.

"We goofed," Kemp admitted. Outside Washington, it's hard to imagine how anyone could make a $1.1 billion "goof," but HUD's sloppy records couldn't even show what federal housing contracts were expiring or which units needed substantial repair; a 1990 report from the department's inspector general found an error rate of 95 percent. This accounting problem had begun in the mid-1970s, when the young agency virtually ignored record keeping in order to concentrate on housing construction. HUD also suffered from constant reorganizations, and bureaucrats simply lost records in their many moves. Considerable information was never computerized, and contracts and other records still lay scattered in boxes throughout the department.

It's equally astonishing that Kelly could be expected to locate $1.1 billion overnight, but late in the evening on July 9 the clerk devised an innovative plan. Rather than slash other programs, he decided to shorten the landlord's contracts from five years to three, freeing up the funds in fiscal 1992. Like most accounting gimmicks, the scheme provided only a short-term fix and the $1.1 billion would come due eventually. (House-Senate conferees later concocted a slightly different solution to the shortfall.)

HUD's last-minute glitch, its second in three years, further strained the already tense relations between the housing secretary and the cardinal. The following morning Mikulski demanded and received a commitment from OMB Director Darman that an administration "SWAT team" would immediately investigate the Housing Department's latest screwup.

MARKUP

By 1:30 P.M. on July 10, a full half hour before Mikulski was to convene the VA-HUD panel, some three hundred anxious lobbyists and agency officials snaked their way down one long hallway and around the corner. The session was "open," but no more than half a dozen of these "outsiders" would be allowed in the conference room. One lawyer-lobbyist near the end of the queue tried to calculate how much he and his colleagues would bill their clients for a meeting they never attended. If we assume that 250 of those on line were lawyers, that each charged at least $150 per hour, that each took a half hour to get to the session, a half hour to return, and at least an hour to stand in line (the senators were late), the legal bill alone for the half hour markup approximated $75,000.

The appropriators' conference room on the first floor of the Dirksen Senate Office Building lacks any of the ornate trappings of the committee's suite in the Capitol. In staid but formal 1950s architecture, the rectangular room features fluorescent lights, purple carpeting, and a long dark wood table. Black-and-white pictures of previous Appropriations Committee chairmen hang on the short north wall, beginning with William Pitt Fessenden (a Republican from Maine), who directed the panel from March to September 1869. The long west wall, behind where the chairman presides, is bare except for a color photograph of Robert Byrd. Twenty reporters were directed to couches along the south wall, and associate staffers squeezed into the front row of chairs along the east wall. The second row was reserved for representatives from some of the affected federal agencies. The first six lobbyists in line obtained the remaining seats.

Senator Robert Kerrey, the Medal of Honor winner who was soon to run for president, arrived before his colleagues. As the newest Democratic member of the subcommittee he took his place farthest right of the chairman's chair. Kevin Kelly, who had been pacing anxiously, huddled with the Nebraska Democrat and complained about how Jack Kemp "threw a $1 billion bomb on us last night."

Mikulski arrived at 2:15 P.M., inquired loudly where everyone was, and promptly left with Kerrey to vote on the crime bill being considered on the Senate floor. She returned at 2:30 P.M. with Jake Garn, gaveled the meeting to order, and read her three-page prepared statement, a copy of which had been delivered to the assembled reporters.

"This has been, without a doubt, the toughest year I have faced as a subcommittee chair," intoned the cardinal. "We have faced some of the greatest pressures among the various agencies in the bill, with the skimpiest of allocations."

Six other senators trickled in and sat along one side of the table, facing associate staffers, agency officials, and the half dozen lobbyists. The seating arrangement made it clear that the markup would be a display rather than a discussion. Unlike the House, where appropriators behind closed doors plowed through the chairman's markup notes and offered amendments, senators presented only pleasantries and short speeches for the benefit of assembled reporters and outsiders. All deals had been settled ahead of time. Even the chair's report was already prepared and printed. No amendments were expected.

Garn complimented the cardinal and her staff for being willing to compromise, and he formally moved the adoption of Mikulski's bill. After suggesting he might become a paid advocate for the aerospace industry, the soon-to-retire Garn predicted the VA-HUD chairman would face extremely tight budgets in the future. Mikulski jokingly asked if Garn would supply her with a case of Rolaids. "I'll provide Madam Chair with anything she needs," the future lobbyist responded, and the crowd laughed.

In ranking order, Mikulski called on the assembled senators to offer brief statements. Democrat Patrick Leahy praised the cardinal lavishly and thanked Garn for his service. Phil Gramm, a Texas Republican protecting the interests of his state's Johnson Space Center, declared emphatically that Space Station *Freedom* was "the next logical step for the world's greatest nation." Bob Kerrey, the only senator to express any concern about the measure, commented, "The space station does not pass the excitement test. It does not engage me." Regarding housing, he warned that "the HOPE program could turn into a false hope rather than real homeownership for the poor." Despite these concerns, Kerrey announced his support for the bill and expressed amazement that Mikulski had been able to craft such a compromise.

After the scripted opening statements, Garn asked to make an unexpected point. Mikulski blanched. The ranking member assured

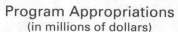

Program Appropriations
(in millions of dollars)

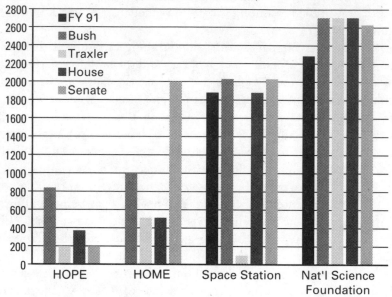

her that he didn't have an amendment, and the cardinal sighed, "Don't do that to me." Garn then noted that every senator had "visitation rights" on the bill when it reached the floor, meaning that each could raise concerns publicly. But he warned with a not-so-subtle reference to the earmarked projects, "Senators should not tear apart the delicate balance, because once the balance is disturbed, other provisions and promises could suffer." With no other requests for comments or amendments, Mikulski obtained unanimous voice approval for Garn's motion to report the bill to the full Appropriations Committee. The actual markup lasted half an hour.

Mikulski mingled with senators and staff for about five minutes before heading to the south end of the table, where she sat down for a "press availability." The staff shooed everyone else out of the room. Yes, she expected a floor amendment attempting to kill the space station. No, she didn't have a firm whip count on such an amendment since many senators would make commitments only after they learned how the subcommittee dealt with the popular HOME and veterans' medical programs. Yes, she anticipated winning on the merits of the space station. No, the letter from Robert Park's science coalition didn't faze her, especially since none of the groups was involved in astronomy. "Does *Freedom* pass Kerrey's 'engagement test'?" a reporter queried. "Lots of things in this bill don't meet that criteria," countered the cardinal.

Asked how she had been able to fund both the station and HOME, Mikulski neglected to mention the accounting gimmicks and said only that she had taken "small bites" from numerous accounts. She highlighted selected cuts to the Department of Veterans Affairs' construction account, including money taken from the Palo Alto acute care hospital. "It's tough munchies for a VA hospital in California that wants to move part of a structure so it won't disturb the ninth hole of an adjacent golf course," barked Mikulski. "I know how to punt and how to putt, and this project passes neither of those tests." Her staff later admitted that the tough-talking cardinal "misspoke" about the golf course's being a factor in the hospital's redesign, which actually was required because of earthquake damage.

After about ten minutes Mikulski's press secretary called it quits, the cardinal left, and Kevin Kelly proceeded to offer a more detailed briefing, clicking off five major differences between the House and Senate bills. First, the clerk noted, senators provided $437 million more for NASA, including the president's full request of $2.03 billion for the space station. Second, they increased HOME by a whopping $1.5 billion. Third, they eliminated all earmarks for sewage and wastewater treatment projects but provided an additional $205 million to the account. Fourth, they trimmed EPA salaries and expenses by $55 million ($61 million compared with the president's request). And fifth, they used $575 million of HUD's previous year's carryover and $1.2 billion from a modified elderly housing program. Not wanting to appear overly generous to the space agency, Kelly emphasized that despite the increase above the House mark, the Senate's total for NASA fell $1.4 billion below the president's request. Moreover, he

151

stressed that the station's costs were capped at $2.25 billion for fiscal year 1993, some $200 million less than NASA had hoped.

In trying to put the best spin on Mikulski's accomplishment, Kelly impressed the assembled scribes with detailed data about the bill and agency operations. He grew testy, however, toward any reporter who asked naïve questions or sought to have information repeated. In response to a question about whether funding for veterans' hospitals in Traxler's state had been cut, the clerk coyly admitted deleting "unauthorized add-ons" from the House bill. To a follow-up question, he smiled and conceded that senators had added some "minor" earmarks to the legislation.

FULL COMMITTEE

Senator Robert Byrd often holds up consideration of subcommittee bills until add-ons of concern to West Virginia have been settled, a habit that moved *Newsweek* to label him "the Prince of Pork." The chairman brought this characterization on himself by declaring proudly on the campaign trail that he'd be "a billion-dollar senator," earmarking that amount of federal projects within five years; he actually accomplished the substantial task in less than two budget cycles.

With his first opportunity as Appropriations chairman—a 1989 supplemental spending bill—Byrd added $75 million for the reconstruction of a telescope at the National Radio Astronomy Observatory in Green Bank, West Virginia. According to his critics, Byrd then kidnapped the FBI's fingerprint processing center from the District of Columbia and brought it and its twenty-six hundred employees to Clarksburg, West Virginia. The Reverend Jesse Jackson labeled the move "economic rape," and *The Washington Post* editorialized against "Sen. Byrd's Federal Job-Heisting," but few lawmakers challenged the chairman in charge of the federal purse. Even the Bush administration, which once attacked the $185 million FBI transfer as a crude example of Congress's adding extraneous items to spending bills, quietly endorsed the move in order to gain Byrd's support for its own controversial $720 million aid package to Central America. Clarksburg residents, thrilled with the economic stimulus that the facility brings to their community, constructed the Robert C. Byrd High School.

The chairman's next major pork barreling transformed a $4.9 million staff training center for the Fish and Wildlife Service into a $60 million "world-class, state-of-the-art" tourist attraction in Harpers Ferry. Then Byrd maneuvered to relocate seven hundred jobs at the Bureau of the Public Debt from Washington to Parkersburg, issuing to West Virginia reporters in March 1991 a press release claiming credit for that transfer. "For the past several years," he wrote, "I have added report language to appropriations bills urging the Bureau of the Public Debt to review the feasibility of consolidating some of the agency's Washington operations in Parkersburg. . . . In response to my efforts, the agency over the past four years has shifted more responsibilities to Parkersburg." West Virginia reporters virtually lionize the senator for such earmarking exploits.

The chairman's biggest, and most contentious, plot involved shifting three thousand Central Intelligence Agency employees to West Virginia. Byrd initially placed the money secretly within a classified annex of the CIA spending bill, but he later claimed it was not there. "Appropriators often hide things," remarked a reporter, "but this is the only incident I've seen when they outright lied." After this minor controversy the cardinal more openly set aside $30 million in the fiscal 1992 budget for what was to be a $1.4 billion CIA structure, but criticism continued.

The chairman's penchant for diverting funds to his own state provokes protests from several quarters. Observed one lawmaker: "Byrd is not just bringing home the bacon. He's carting off the entire pig." Agency officials denounced the chairman for defiling the federal budget by placing his political clout above their professional judgment. Even some Appropriations staff members expressed embarrassment at the chairman's obvious greed, complaining that they don't want to be identified with a committee concerned primarily with pork. A clerk professed, "There's enormous pressure on the subcommittee staffs to deliver on Byrd's home state interests. He expects to be taken care of." Another staffer argued, "We used to discuss national priorities. Now we fear for our jobs if we don't add West Virginia projects or respond to the chairman's whims. It's not a healthy atmosphere."

Byrd's supporters object to such criticism, declaring that lawmakers are expected to help their constituents and that the federal government should send money to a state with high unemployment and a low standard of living. "How are the chairman's actions any different from Virginia Senator John Warner's specifying within the defense authorization bill a shipbuilding contract for Newport News?" argued an appropriator. "Or to Senator Larry Craig's pushing for low grazing fees that subsidize Idaho ranchers?" Byrd's defenders also point out that the chairman obtains no financial gain from his earmarks and that he has never been touched by even a hint of corruption.

Much that Byrd promotes, of course, is not parochial. The chairman has fought hard for money to battle drugs, conduct biomedical research, and construct public works across the country. He has also won accolades for exposing the actions of lobbyists. After a 1989 *Washington Post* article outlined how influence peddlers secure earmarks for their clients, including $18 million for a research center at West Virginia University, Byrd, asserting control over the appropriations process and objecting to outsiders claiming credit for projects in his own state, excised funds for the center and pushed legislation that requires a full accounting by lobbyists pursuing federal funds. Although the chairman's bill was limited in scope, he beat back a thicket of opposition that for two decades had blocked efforts to regulate lobbyists, and the bill passed.

On July 11, the day after the VA-HUD markup, Byrd asked the full Senate Appropriations Committee to consider four spending bills, including Mikulski's. Although no lobbyist gained access to the small conference room on the first floor of the U.S. Capitol, another large crowd assembled. An elderly executive with an aerospace firm, complaining that he had come to these events for years and never entered the conference room, announced that appropriators "would have to do it without me today." A lobbyist for the union representing government employees joked that Disney World had shorter lines. A smartly dressed Saudi Arabian tourist, escorted by an entourage of six men, asked if she could meet "the senators." A young lobbyist for a national group combating illiteracy, on his first visit to the Capitol, remarked repeatedly on the beauty and significance of the surroundings. And a lawyer for a health care organization justified his standing on line for hours on the off chance that a congressional aide would exit the room and offer some valuable bit of information. Senators, usually escorted by two or three staffers toting heavy budget justification books, passed through the fairly narrow hallway while Capitol police fought a losing battle to keep the pathway clear.

Above the main entrance to the committee's suite is a painted portrait of the Roman goddess of war, reflecting the room's use until 1911 by the Senate Military Affairs Committee. A lawyer on line suggested the painting remains fitting since the space now accommodates the most heated controversies on Capitol Hill. Although a military motif pervades the reception area and offices, the conference room is decorated with copies of paintings from the Baths of Titus and the excavations of Pompeii. A cynical reporter, one of the only "outsiders" to obtain access, found these depictions of decadence fitting symbols for America's federal budgeting process.

Inside the conference room Byrd firmly gaveled the meeting to order shortly after 2:00 P.M., with Republicans sitting to his left and staff director Jim English and the Democrats to his right. Following the chairman's short introduction, Bennett Johnston offered several "technical amendments" to his energy and water bill. Byrd, after checking for an endorsement from the subcommittee's ranking Republican, nodded his approval and didn't bother with a vote. Senators floated in and out of the room to take phone calls, meet constituents, or negotiate some last-minute amendment with a colleague. Patrick Leahy arrived an hour late and quietly asked staff members near the door, "Are we having fun yet?" Eighty-three-year-old Quentin Burdick lowered his head and slept through much of the session. Ernest Hollings of South Carolina, chairman of the Commerce, Justice, State, the Judiciary, and Related Agencies Subcommittee, drawled on about provisions within his $22 billion legislation. Several senators offered amendments. Johnston, for instance, obtained the transfer of $1 million from research on global climate change to a study of shrimping in his home state of Louisiana.

Before Mikulski began her description of the VA-HUD bill, the lawmakers took a ten-minute break to vote upstairs on the Senate floor. When the cardinal returned with Jake Garn to find no other appropriators at the table, she jokingly moved that her bill be approved. Staffers laughed. When the committee reconvened, Mikulski began her formal statement by thanking Byrd for his guidance in shaping the bill. She reviewed the major spending provisions and then complained bitterly that the morning's *Washington Post* declared mistakenly that "housing programs for elderly are cut." An agitated Kevin Kelly distributed copies of letters supporting Mikulski's bill from the American Association of Retired Persons and the National Council of Senior Citizens.

Garn lauded Mikulski and her staff, saying they had done a remarkable job developing a balanced bill. Blasting the *Post* reporter for not understanding the bill's complex provisions, the subcommittee's top Republican declared that the $1.2 billion excised from HUD represented unneeded and unspent funds. He then laid into the scientific organizations that criticized the space station, claiming that the same groups had naïvely attacked President John Kennedy for wanting to go to the moon. Senator Inouye, Mikulski's coconspirator on several scoring gimmicks, commended the cardinal for her commitment to Native Hawaiians. And in a rare expression of effusive praise, Byrd said Mikulski had done "an excellent, excellent job."

Dennis DeConcini introduced the only factious amendment, a change in housing rules to exclude closing costs from the eligibility requirements for home mortgages. Jake Garn, also the ranking member of the Banking Committee, said the measure sounded attractive because it would allow more home buyers to qualify for loans, but he warned that it could lead to substantial losses for the Federal Housing Administration, perhaps similar to those suffered by savings and loan institutions. After fifteen minutes of discussion, Byrd softly asked DeConcini if he'd consider withdrawing his amendment and offering it on the Senate floor, enabling the staff to calculate the long-term spending implications. The Arizona Democrat, expressing regret that he wouldn't have the authority of a positive committee vote during floor debate, said he would, of course, abide by the chairman's request.

The assembled appropriators neglected to discuss the space station since Mikulski had crafted enough compromises to silence even the skeptics. (Byrd failed to reveal his own views on NASA's preferred project, but several months later he was quoted describing the super collider and the space station as "exotic luxuries that perhaps ought to be put off or canceled until we can shore up our faltering economy.")

With no amendments, Byrd called for a voice vote and ordered Mikulski's bill to be sent to the full Senate with a unanimous recommendation from appropriators. He asked the cardinal and clerk to be ready to make their floor presentation within a week. Kevin Kelly, winking at reporters, carried his large budget justification books out the door and into the mass of lobbyists desperate for news.

THE SENATE FLOOR

The chaplain began the Senate's day on July 17, 1991, with the following quotation from I Timothy: "For the love of money is the root of all evil." Later that morning OMB Director Darman reported to the Budget Committee that the fiscal 1992 deficit would be $70 billion more than anticipated as a result, in part, of greedy savings and loan executives. That evening, as if lampooning the chaplain's plea to "recognize the peril in the love of money," Robert Byrd pushed through what was described as a "swift, stealthy coup" to raise salaries for U.S. senators.

Lawmakers had been informed that the legislative day would include consideration of the VA-HUD spending bill, but Senate proceedings, governed in comparison with the House less by rules than by the will of individual senators, shifted from one topic to another before Barbara Mikulski got her chance. After the morning prayer,

Bennett Johnston described his comprehensive energy legislation, and Christopher Dodd spoke of refugees from Ethiopia and the Soviet Union. Then Alan Dixon introduced legislation regarding Medicare benefits for low-income elderly, and Larry Craig offered his "freedom of speech on campus act." Robert Dole spoke about Soviet President Mikhail Gorbachev's request for financial assistance from Western industrialized nations. Edward Kennedy paid tribute to the retiring chairman of the International Rescue Committee, and scores of politicians argued about the Supreme Court's recent ruling on pregnancy counseling.

Finally, at about 1:30 P.M., Mikulski rose in a virtually empty chamber to present and defend her bill. Repeating much of her speech given a week before to the VA-HUD panel, she declared, "This has been, without a doubt, the toughest year I have faced as a subcommittee chair." The cardinal took five minutes to describe the legislation's highlights before yielding the floor to Jake Garn, who again expressed his respect and admiration for Mikulski and for the spending bill's balance.

Wanting to complete action quickly, the cardinal and the ranking Republican appealed for other senators to come forth quickly and offer their amendments. "I realize the C-SPAN audience is not as big this time of day as it is in the evening," complained Garn. "But on the other hand, I will be on the floor, as will the distinguished senator from Maryland, and we will not tolerate any complaints about a late-night session tonight. The major reason we stay around here until nine or ten o'clock at night is because our colleagues on this, or other bills, simply will not come to the floor." Seeing no action, Mikulski asked the Senate clerk to provide "filler" by calling the roll. Senators periodically interrupted this boring procedure with unrelated speeches about trade with China as well as more commendations for the International Rescue Committee's retiring chairman.

Some two hours later Dale Bumpers arrived with an amendment that he claimed was "in the final stages of drafting." Knowing that Mikulski already had lined up sufficient votes to approve her bill, the Arkansas Democrat admitted "no illusions" about the prospects of his last-minute attack on Space Station *Freedom*. Still, he recalled fighting a lot of losing battles in the Senate, and he quipped, "It doesn't bother me as long as I am on the side of the angels."

Bumpers asserted that the space station was popular only because it had never been debated. A critical and thorough review, he argued, was needed since NASA's cost estimates had soared 300 percent. The flamboyant debater compared the space station with the Clinch River breeder reactor, which he had opposed for five years before convincing enough senators that the nuclear venture was a turkey. Attacking NASA's jobs argument directly, Bumpers said that the agency may have parceled out the station's contracts across the country but that only five states obtained more money than they paid in taxes for the orbiting project. After aides finished rewriting a few lines, he formally proposed an amendment to transfer most of *Freedom*'s funding to veterans' medical services, the National Science Foundation, and other NASA projects.

Mikulski responded by saying that two years before, she, too, had questioned the station's purpose. "Is it simply going to be a condo in the sky, waiting for someone to occupy it, with not a clear idea of what we would do there?" she reported asking. But after NASA had redesigned the enterprise, Mikulski declared, "This senator is a convert to the space station, and like a lot of converts, I am a true believer."

Garn supported the cardinal's arguments and proceeded to attack the station's critics. "I personally am offended by most of these scientific groups, and particularly Dr. [Robert] Park from the University of Maryland, who wrote an insulting article for *The Washington Post* in his opposition to the space station," said the onetime astronaut. Suggesting that the heart pacemaker and implantable insulin pumps were made possible by space research, if not exactly invented in space or by NASA, Garn claimed, "For every single dollar we invest in the space program, we get eight or nine dollars back in the private sector."

Senators from Texas, California, and Florida, whose states benefited most from space station funding, predictably praised the project profusely. Yet when Senator Ernest Hollings rose, no one knew quite what to expect. As chairman of the committee that authorizes

NASA—thus, the Senate counterpart of Representative George Brown—Hollings had long supported the station and other space projects; moreover, his former staff assistant, Marty Kress, had gone to work for NASA as director of legislative affairs. But the South Carolina Democrat also cared deeply about the massive federal deficit, as evidenced by his association with the Gramm-Rudman-Hollings Act. Earlier that day he had heard Richard Darman acknowledge that the 1992 deficit would total almost $399 billion, and the news troubled him. Hollings said he had planned to vote quietly for the Bumpers amendment, but "somehow the word got around and, ye gads, my office filled up with NASA people." He admitted to having supported the space station's authorization, but he decided that "somehow, somewhere, we are going to have to draw a line and stop this binge of borrowing and spending."

The line for frugality was not drawn that day. Instead Mikulski ended her defense by stating, "Fiscal 1992 will be the five hundredth anniversary of Christopher Columbus discovering America. On that anniversary I do not think we should be chintzy about the space program." The Bumpers amendment, finally voted upon at 8:30 P.M., failed, 35–64.

Several other senators spoke quickly about various segments of the VA-HUD bill. Massachusetts's John Kerry, for instance, urged the Senate conferees to accept the House earmark of special funds for a wastewater treatment project to clean up Boston Harbor.

At 8:47 P.M. Majority Leader George Mitchell, having completed private negotiations with Robert Byrd, interrupted the VA-HUD discussion and called for consideration of the legislative branch's appropriations and an amendment to increase senators' salaries. The ensuing debate demonstrated the power of appropriators, particularly the committee chairman. Observed a colleague: "Byrd's the only one with enough authority and leadership to push such a controversial item through this Senate."

The pay hike issue had generated substantial strife since 1989, when representatives raised their annual pay to $125,100, despite stormy protests from consumer advocate Ralph Nader, the National

Taxpayers Union, and radio talk show hosts across the country. Skittish senators backed away at the last minute from those moves, approving a smaller salary increase and only a gradual phaseout of payments for their speeches to outside groups. Nader and the talk show hosts continued to blast senators for their honoraria, arguing that wealthy corporations and trade associations unfairly influenced elected officials. By mid-1991 several lawmakers had threatened to introduce legislation that would ban the practice, and most observers believed a majority would vote for such a politically charged measure.

That was when Robert Byrd decided to take action, personally meeting with nearly ninety senators, talking to most of them at least twice. The appropriations chairman proposed a simple deal: Ban honoraria in exchange for a salary increase.

The existing system rankled Byrd. This lover of the Senate, who believed that he worked in the "upper house" of Congress, couldn't tolerate representatives' earning more than senators. Even more irritating, eighty-one House staffers received larger paychecks than senators. "It is my belief that members of the Senate should be paid the same as members of the House, and paid by the taxpayers who send them to serve and not by the special interest lobbies in Washington," argued Byrd. "That is my version of good government—have salaries high enough to attract the top talent which the American people deserve, prohibit outside income from special interests, and keep the top levels of government from becoming solely the province of millionaires."

The secretive and orchestrated way Byrd introduced his measure, however, led Nader and others to question the chairman's "good government" intentions. Earlier in the day some two dozen senators had responded to Byrd's summons and assembled quietly in the Appropriations Committee's conference room to share coffee and review the chairman's whip count of fifty-two lawmakers willing to vote for a salary increase. Wanting to avoid drawn-out controversies, the group decided to introduce the amendment that evening before opponents could organize.

The floor debate, particularly for this deliberative body, proved surprisingly brief—only forty-five minutes. The majority and minority leaders announced bipartisan support for Byrd's amendment, and only a few lawmakers worried publicly about the political implications of voting themselves a $23,200 salary increase during a recession when thousands stood in unemployment lines. Liberal Paul Wellstone objected to the pay hike, stating, "I feel very strongly that there is already too great a disparity between the income of those who are elected to office and the people that they represent." Barbara Mikulski, up for reelection in 1992, declared, "This is the wrong time to raise senators' salaries."

Byrd's amendment passed, 53–45. The chairman had underestimated his support by one vote.

The following morning, Thursday, July 18, the Senate reconvened at nine-fifteen. But before continuing with the VA-HUD bill, senators digressed with speeches about the nomination of Judge Clarence Thomas to the Supreme Court and the plight of Lithuania. Then the body considered appropriations for the Treasury Department and Postal Service, as well as amendments by Jesse Helms to restrict child pornography and to test health care workers for the HIV virus.

When the majority leader finally allowed Mikulski's spending bill to reappear in the early afternoon, freshman Robert Smith attacked the measure's many earmarks and introduced an amendment to cut all "special-purpose" housing grants and transfer the $72.8 million saved to veterans' medical care. Why, the New Hampshire Republican asked rhetorically, should $500,000 be set aside for the Newark, New Jersey, Public Library rather than book-lending institutions in any other city? The unspoken answer, of course, was that New Jersey's Frank Lautenberg, a member of the VA-HUD panel, had asked for the money.

Some Appropriations staffers cynically stated that only an inexperienced first termer would introduce a measure that alienated the many senators benefiting from the bill's earmarks. But Smith wanted to make a point. The individual grants, he said, were "put in the bill with no vote, no authorization, nothing. That is wrong. Pure and simple. It is wrong. So I want to change the system." Smith, however, could count votes, and he knew that his amendment could not win and that he certainly wasn't going to change the system soon. He withdrew the measure, to Mikulski's and Garn's delight.

The Senate then dealt with nine noncontroversial amendments that Mikulski introduced to appease specific senators. Republican Frank Murkowski, for instance, obtained a provision requiring the Environmental Protection Agency to establish a regional office in his home state of Alaska.

Noting that the VA-HUD bill set aside $16 billion to bail out failed savings and loans, Democrat Tim Wirth of Colorado devoted several hours to the arcane issue of whether federal regulators should release information about the government deals in 1988 that sold bankrupt thrifts to wealthy investors at what critics charged were bargain-basement prices. Jake Garn countered that Wirth's proposed disclosure of private financial records would have a chilling effect on America's banking industry. The senators postured and argued at length—until Garn concluded: "I obviously cannot accept the amendment. We are at an impasse, and it is unfortunate that we could not gain a compromise." The majority leader, sensing the stalemate, decided to change topics once again, and he called forth appropriations for the District of Columbia. Senators quickly approved that legislation with virtually no debate and no roll call.

As Wirth and Garn continued debating privately, Lautenberg demonstrated the extent to which parochial interests pervade appropriations. The New Jersey Democrat spent almost twenty minutes recounting the many items he sponsored within the VA-HUD spending bill that would benefit his state, including $700,000 for water quality activities at Cranberry Lake, $1.6 million for the New Jersey Institute of Technology, and $3.1 million for development of a rotary engine at Wood-Ridge. Although Lautenberg had attended few subcommittee hearings and hadn't even shown up at markup (or later at the conference committee meeting), he claimed credit for a wealth of earmarks.

John Chafee, ranking Republican member of the Committee on Environment and Public Works, engaged Mikulski in a brief colloquy about the bill's directive for the EPA to move its Office of Pollution

Prevention to the administrator's suite. The cardinal, without acknowledging the torrent of complaints from agency officials, agreed to review the provision in the House and Senate conference.

After Wirth finally withdrew his S&L amendment, the entire bill, as amended, was approved on a voice vote by the few senators remaining in the chamber. The cardinal then moved that the "Senate insist on its amendments to H.R. 2519 and agree to a conference requested by the House on the disagreeing votes of the two Houses." The presiding officer appointed members of the VA-HUD subcommittee to be Senate conferees.

Mikulski breathed an audible sigh of relief, but she knew that rough negotiations lay ahead.

6

CONFERENCE

THE HOUSE AND Senate Appropriations Committees usually operate in their own separate realms, but by July, when the panels begin to negotiate the differences among their thirteen subcommittees, more and more appropriators make the three-minute trek across the Capitol between the offices of Representative Jamie Whitten and Senator Robert Byrd. Textbooks on government suggest that representatives and senators assemble in thirteen joint conference committees and simply split their spending differences. The actual bargaining, however, more closely resembles the frenzy of horse trading than the stately order of compromise.

Before Whitten met with his cardinals in mid-May to discuss the 602(b) allocations, his front-office staff had compared spreadsheets with their Senate counterparts. The strict parameters on federal spending ensured that the preliminary numbers for most subcommittees were in the same ballpark. Of the thirteen panels, only the Subcommittees on Agriculture, the Interior, and Energy and Water Development showed significant variation, and the two staffs decided, as appropriators are wont to do, to settle their disagreements later in the process.

The discord percolated in the summer as House and Senate conferees waited for Whitten and Byrd to determine common allocations. Byrd yearned to negotiate quickly in order to finalize his salary increase before Congress adjourned for its traditional August recess. If talk show hosts harassed lawmakers on this contentious issue throughout the five-week break, Byrd worried, his carefully crafted deal would crumble. Whitten, a crafty bargainer, used Byrd's fear of losing the Senate pay raise to demand more money for his agriculture and rural development subcommittee. In fact, the House chairman sent clear signals that no conferences would begin until Byrd returned most of the $394 million in precious outlays he had cut from the agriculture panel.

The central office staffs met twice during the last full week of July to craft a final set of allocations. Little progress came from the first heated session, with the House pushing agriculture stubbornly and the Senate promoting energy and water projects. But after a long session on Wednesday afternoon, July 24, it became clear that the House staff wouldn't back down, and the Senate side blinked.

That blink, formalized at a meeting between Whitten and Byrd the following afternoon, meant that the Senate agreed to provide all but $44 million of the $394 million cut from the Agriculture Department's outlay allocation. As expected, Byrd also restored most of the funds he had stripped from his own Interior Subcommittee's budget authority. To cover these increases, the Senate pared $200 million in budget authority from the labor-health-education panel and $145 million from the energy and water unit. For the VA-HUD subcommittee, Whitten and Byrd essentially split their differences on budget authority but decreased scarce outlays by $15 million compared with the House and $37 million compared with the Senate.

This recutting of the spending pie was an even more closed process than the original 602(b) allocation. Central office staff consulted with neither cardinals nor clerks in either the House or the Senate. Said one senior negotiator: "We had to go back to our subcommittee clerks with new allocations, and yes, some screamed. But, hey, that's simply part of the game." The chairmen's reallocation didn't require an endorsement from the full House, but Whitten obtained approval on July 31 from other appropriators, none of whom dared challenge his authority or these decisions. Byrd needed no one's consent since the Senate committee had previously adopted an overlooked provision that allowed the chairman to employ new allocations anytime he needed to expedite the passage of spending bills. (Whitten and Byrd negotiated another allocation in September to redeploy the small amount of excess money that remained in bills already sent to the White House.)

The new numbers had a minor impact on the VA-HUD panels, but Dick Malow and Kevin Kelly still couldn't proceed until they "scored" the accounting gimmicks that would determine the final size of their available funding. Both clerks predicted their subcommittee members wouldn't meet to endorse a negotiated bill until late September. According to Representative Bill Green, it promised to be "a very difficult conference."

SCORING

Appropriators divide into two camps over accounting gimmicks. One group takes each year at a time, using whatever tricks are necessary to get through. The other worries about the harmful long-term effects of this one-year approach. Sometimes an appropriator or staffer harbors both sentiments. For instance, Stephen Kohashi, minority staff director of the Senate VA-HUD panel, helped Kevin Kelly devise several of the accounting tricks used to fund HOME and the space station, even though he expressed "strong reservations" about postponing budget problems into the future.

Most of Kelly's gimmicks remained unsettled by the first week of September. The subcommittee staff decided to tackle the housing strategem first, sitting down with OMB and HUD officials in the House panel's conference room. (The cardinals and other appropriators were still away on their "district work period," as lawmakers like to describe the summer recess.) All assembled agreed that appropriators could restore and revise the Department of Housing and Urban Development's unobligated $565 million, but the $1.2 billion associated with elderly housing raised several technical questions. Paul Thomson, the House panel's housing guru, argued that it was too early to calculate actual savings since the conversion from loans to grants had just begun. Kelly contended that the change should provide the VA-HUD subcommittee with substantial increases in both budget authority and outlays. OMB accountants rejected early outlay savings since the program's payout spanned fifteen years, but they would permit a $1.2 billion increase in the panel's budget authority if appropriators would assure such savings by mandating the quick conversion of those elderly housing projects already in the pipeline.

The Office of Management and Budget holds the trump cards on scorekeeping at this stage of the annual budget drama since it alone determines if final spending bills exceed their spending caps and spark a sequester. But the OMB doesn't operate in a vacuum. The administration's budget mavens, for instance, had given a wink and a nod in July to the military's paying for NASA's Tracking and Data Relay Satellite System (TDRSS) and for pollution cleanup in Antarctica, but changing world events had introduced doubts by September. During the two-month interval the Soviet Union collapsed and scores of politicians were calling for massive cuts in the U.S. defense budget. Pentagon chief Cheney and his supporters responded by protesting even a small crack in the "fire walls" that protected military money from being drained to popular domestic initiatives.

Headstrong appropriators, moreover, don't countenance rough or arbitrary treatment by OMB "bean counters." Early in the year the House staff argued that substantial expenditures by the Coast Guard, a nondefense division within the Transportation Department, should be classified as military spending. The Coast Guard works in the Arctic, they claimed, only to ensure that navy submarines enjoy access to this strategic region. When the OMB rejected the argument, Whitten's staff called in Barry Anderson, the OMB's chief scorekeeper, and Chuck Kieffer, the agency's liaison to the spending committee, and asserted that the Appropriations Committee could play the scoring game better than the OMB. "What if I went to the head of the Federal Aviation Administration and asked if his air traffic controllers dealt with military aircraft?" hypothesized Dennis Kedzior. The FAA leader, the House aide said, would acknowledge that the civilian agency tracks those planes after they leave their bases.

"What percentage of your total traffic is military-related?" Kedzior proposed to continue. The FAA official might not be sure but would estimate 15 percent. Then appropriators could declare that 15 percent of all FAA appropriations be taken from the defense budget. "We could do it but for the fact that no one wins these pissing contests," Kedzior warned his OMB colleagues, who agreed to reconsider the coast guard transfers.

Scoring for the TDRSS produced complex alliances within Congress and within the administration. Kevin Kelly argued that the air force should pay a $384 million fee to NASA for its use of the space agency's high-orbiting satellites that transmit signals between ground controllers and military spacecraft. The Senate clerk claimed the Economy Act of 1932 made such interagency reimbursements permissible and not subject to the fire wall restrictions of the 1990 budget agreement.

Kedzior and his House colleagues, in contrast, rejected the transfer. "We were frying bigger fish," said the staff assistant, "and we can't allow OMB to pick and choose only a few projects like the space station that they want to help. It would be like Ollie North to the nth degree." However, another clerk suggested Whitten's staff really suffered from the it-wasn't-invented-here syndrome. After the 1990 budget summit the House team had grown increasingly sensitive to the OMB's cutting deals with Senator Robert Byrd and his staffers but not with them. They derogatorily called Byrd's office OMB East.

In an attempt to kill the transfer, someone—and most observers assumed it was a House central office staffer—leaked news of the proposed TDRSS shift to a *Wall Street Journal* reporter. The resulting story declared that "the White House is encouraging a closely held plan to shift hundreds of millions of dollars from classified Air Force accounts to science and satellite programs strained by the costly space station." The article caught the unexpected interest of Representative Dan Rostenkowski, who wrote a snide letter to Richard Darman questioning the transfer in light of the OMB's earlier decision to order a disruptive sequester in response to a $2 million overage in the domestic spending category. The across-the-board spending cut had been particularly embarrassing for the Ways and

Means Committee chairman since it was his request for an earmarked grant to Loyola University in his Chicago district that many perceived to have caused the overage. Rostenkowski's staff showed the letter to Whitten's men beforehand to make sure it was technically correct.

Within the Bush administration the OMB science director, Bob Grady, favored the TDRSS transfer, but his defense counterpart, Bob Howard, objected. Darman, although he didn't want to open the door to massive seizures of the defense budget, leaned toward actions that would assure funding for his beloved space station. In fact, the OMB director's official opinion of the Senate VA-HUD bill, issued in mid-July, failed to mention the air force transfer, reflecting what many considered his tacit understanding that the Defense Department would pick up some costs for the TDRSS.

Across the Potomac River at the Pentagon, Dick Cheney, enjoying enhanced political authority after Operation Desert Storm, declared emphatically that no money should be transfered from the military. After reading the *Wall Street Journal* article, the defense secretary threatened to retaliate against NASA by increasing the space agency's fees for use of the air force's Titan 4 launchers. The debate went all the way to President Bush, who eventually sided with the military. On September 16 Darman responded formally to Rostenkowski, writing that funding for the TDRSS would be taken from domestic rather than defense accounts.

The White House decision, delivered ten days before VA-HUD conferees were to assemble, forced Malow and Kelly to scramble for spending cuts. The clerks focused first on NASA and slashed $330 million from space shuttle operations, later claiming the account had been bloated.

The "Antarctica gimmick" remained a live possibility until the day before VA-HUD conferees convened, when the OMB declared that the navy's logistical expenses would "tentatively" be scored as domestic spending. After having crafted a delicate series of compromises, the clerks and cardinals were in no mood to cut another $75 million from their bill. According to Malow, "We decided to have a Mexican standoff on the Antarctica account." Said Kelly: "We were ready to shut down the program if OMB didn't back down." To force the issue, the maneuvering clerks tried to push the Defense Department into a corner. They crafted report language that eliminated the National Science Foundation's ability to shift money among its own accounts, leaving a DoD transfer as the only means to fund Antarctica research.

Malow and Kelly, moreover, could be cavalier about their Mexican standoff because a special mechanism had been created to handle such a scoring dispute. As part of the 1990 budget deal, appropriators established a $1.5 billion account above the spending caps that subcommittees could tap on a first-come, first-served basis. Even if the OMB ratified its tentative scoring decision against an Antarctica transfer, the clerks assumed a sufficient cushion remained.

NEGOTIATIONS

The fiscal 1992 budget marked the third time Bob Traxler and Barbara Mikulski had negotiated with each other. The two shared a warm relationship, having served together in the House for a decade and having participated in the Steel Caucus and the Northeast-Midwest Congressional Coalition. They were similar political creatures, responsive to their states, and both came from working-class, blue-collar backgrounds. Nonetheless, conference negotiations were business. Concluded a Senate staffer: "Traxler is a wonderful guy, but he can be very intense."

Before Traxler and Mikulski's era, the House clearly dominated VA-HUD conferences. Representative Boland had possessed strong support from representatives and the Speaker, while maverick Senator Proxmire often couldn't deliver votes even from his own subcommittee members. Barbara Mikulski, however, is no William Proxmire. Although relatively junior in seniority, she enjoys the support of Chairman Byrd, knows her bill well, and employs a dogged clerk. She also brought a tremendous advantage to the fiscal 1992 conference—almost $2 billion in "new money"—and she and her legislation had won clear endorsements from the full Senate and its Appropriations Committee, while Traxler had lost several challenges.

Kelly and Malow, although they battle aggressively during conference negotiations, get along well and talk daily. According to the House clerk, "We build on each other's efforts. I learn of things that he can better tackle, and vice versa." Significant tension, however, existed during Kelly's early days. "There's a tradition of honor and honesty that exists between these particular subcommittees," said an associate. "Kevin tested that code several times." Kelly certainly won the honors during fiscal 1992 bargaining for being the more tenacious. Some colleagues said that the Senate clerk haggled with the view that any compromise threatened Mikulski's reelection bid; others, that Malow, a twenty-two-year House veteran, had grown weary of the constant combat.

While lobbyists promoted their favorite programs to appropriators, both House and Senate staffs made use of lobbyists, too. On August 2 Kelly pushed housing activists to pressure House conferees to support HOME since he knew the program would cause the most cantankerous negotiation and he needed all the help he could get. Although Washington-based housing organizations, despite numerous drafts, couldn't agree on a joint letter to Traxler, 250 local groups heeded Kelly's call with separate appeals to their representatives.

Malow and his team, as is the tradition, spent time in August producing "conference notes," an objective description of the Senate's 175 amendments to the original House bill. The list included a few minor variations, such as differing titles for agency programs, as well as all policy and dollar changes.

Toward the end of the first week of September, Malow and Kelly began bargaining on the big issues, especially the Senate's $1.5 billion increase for the HOME Investment Partnerships program. Both men described the following three weeks as pandemonium, with staff working seven days a week, often until midnight. One lobbyist encountered a harried clerk during this period and was told emphatically, "Get out of my face!"

Spending levels for HOME diverged so widely that the clerks brought the cardinals in earlier than normal to settle the final bill's broad parameters. Mikulski and Kelly initially came to Traxler's office for an early-evening meeting on September 10, and later that week the foursome gathered for lunch in the Capitol. The president had requested $1 billion for HOME, the House appropriated only $500 million, and the Senate wanted $2 billion. With moral support from Representative Green, a former regional housing administrator, Traxler argued for expanding current public housing programs rather than financing an expensive new initiative. Mikulski countered that HOME offered needed flexibility to the nation's troubled cities and towns. Aside from the policy arguments, the senator demanded some slack since she and her clerk had identified extra housing money. Traxler finally backed down, agreeing to $1.5 billion.

The space station, despite fierce rhetorical battles in the House, generated little controversy during conference negotiations. Wanting to build the project but not to pressure Mikulski, NASA lobbyists decided against threatening a presidential veto if they didn't get the Senate's $2.03 billion. Even aerospace firms were willing to settle for the House's $1.9 billion in order to avoid angering supporters of other programs who might endanger the station's future funding. Traxler, however, quickly receded to the Senate position on *Freedom,* saying he wanted to demonstrate his loyalty to the "will of the House." But the House cardinal had another and more compelling reason for compromise: Full funding forced additional cutbacks in other NASA programs, allowing Traxler to demonstrate more clearly the financial pain caused by the space station; in effect, he would later be able to say, "I told you so."

Conferees, other than the cardinals, have virtually no role in these critical behind-the-scenes negotiations. House VA-HUD panelists, both Democrats and Republicans, simply sent letters to Traxler highlighting their favorite projects that the Senate had cut. "I leave my fate in the hands of the subcommittee staff to negotiate in my interest," admitted a representative. "I have nothing to do until the meeting of conferees."

The ranking Republican members—Representative Green and Senator Garn—were actively involved during the Boland-Proxmire era, but the more partisan Mikulski limited the minority's role. She and Traxler consulted with the Republicans only after they had finished most of their own deals.

Several appropriators admitted privately that clerks rather than cardinals control conference negotiations. But staffers, being loyal to the bosses, downplayed their power. According to a clerk, "Staffs have authority because they know where the line is. They know what the chairman wants and what his interests are. They know not to compromise these interests on their own."

Malow and Kelly met four additional times during the third week of September to set overall budgets for the twenty-four departments and agencies. To discuss funding for specific accounts within the Environmental Protection Agency, the Senate's Carrie Apostolou walked over to the House panel on Saturday morning, September 21. She and Michelle Burkett had been friends since Burkett worked as a presidential management intern at the Senate subcommittee, but according to the House staffer, "We're firm with each other and go through a good bit of posturing before we define our bottom lines." Apostolou also did some "basic horse trading" with Paul Thomson over programs at the Department of Veterans Affairs. Thomson, who knows the budget inside and out after more than two decades on the job, prevailed on the number of nurses, but Apostolou won her point on quality assurance inspections at VA facilities.

As they cut deals on the 175 amendments, the staff annotated the conference notes with an esoteric script. The most common symbols, "SR" or "HR," signal that the Senate or the House recedes to, or agrees with, the other chamber's position. "HWA," or "House with amendment," denotes a compromise; because the House goes first in the appropriations process, this abbreviation indicates that the conference committee accepts an amended funding level somewhere between the House and Senate versions.

Even more complicated notations are for "amendments in technical disagreement," items that neither the House nor the Senate originally proposed or new programs or legislation that the Senate invented. For instance, since Mikulski added $40 million at the last minute for the Back River Wastewater Treatment Plant in Maryland, a project that had not been authorized or considered by either chamber, the measure was in technical disagreement and had to face a separate vote on the House and Senate floors.

An unspoken rule is that representatives and senators accept each others' earmarks even if, as a staffer explained, "there has to be a bit of paring back to make it all work." The paring back, as might be expected, occurs primarily to those "pork" projects requested by nonconferees. New York Representative Henry Nowak of the Public Works and Transportation Committee, for instance, helplessly learned that $100,000 had been trimmed from the House's original $900,000 for cleanup of contaminated sediments within the Buffalo River. Yet the $1 million allocated for the Saginaw River in Bob Traxler's district remained intact, as did the $1 million for the Small Flows Clearinghouse at West Virginia University in Robert Byrd's home state.

The sway of political connections on conference negotiations also determined the fate of the Laser Interferometer Gravitational Wave Observatory, a National Science Foundation project that House appropriators removed from the fiscal 1991 budget for being too expensive. Malow believed the controversial observatory should be killed for fiscal 1992 as well, but Senate Majority Leader Mitchell called Mikulski three times about the project, one of whose facilities was to be built in his home state of Maine. With Mikulski and Kelly unwilling to compromise, Malow finally agreed to provide $23 million by cutting other NSF research projects. Congressional critics, in response, complained that the conference—in fact, the entire appropriations process—succumbs to such political interference, yet Capitol Hill veterans expressed amazement that the Democratic leader of the U.S. Senate had to place three separate phone calls to obtain a relatively small $23 million.

In an unusual move Traxler and Mikulski placed a joint telephone call to Jack Kemp the afternoon before their conference committee meeting to say they had funded HOME, covered his $1.1 billion shortfall, but cut his request for HOPE by 58 percent. The cardinals' plan to mollify Kemp failed. The housing secretary became so enraged at the reduction to his favorite initiative that he rushed off a letter and press release blasting the appropriators for their "betrayal of low-income families." Declared an agitated Kemp: "I will urge the president to veto this retreat to the failed, scandal-prone housing programs of the past."

CONFERENCE

Bob Traxler assembled his conferees on Wednesday, September 26, at 8:00 A.M., an unusually early hour for federal lawmakers. At this traditional preconference meeting for House appropriators, held in the panel's office on the first floor of the Capitol, the cardinal and the clerk quickly explained highlights of the compromise bill. Many years ago these sessions focused on how House members could band together at the subsequent conference to beat back Senate positions, but Traxler and Malow had already negotiated the controversies. "This was an FYI meeting rather than a strategy session," complained a participant afterward. "We had nothing to do but take notes. The real work had been done."

At 9:10 A.M. Barbara Mikulski entered room 116 of the Dirksen Senate Office Building and uttered the boisterous greeting that had become her trademark: "So where is everybody?" Kevin Kelly, who was arranging bottles of carbonated water, quietly explained that House members had not arrived from their preconference meeting. The very idea of such a session seemed to strike the independent Senate cardinal as odd.

As the final court of spending appeals, House-Senate conferences attract substantial interest from lobbyists and agency officials, yet few ever witness the actual events. One desperate lawyer tried to obtain a seat at the crowded agriculture conference by offering the doorkeeper two tickets to that Saturday's Baltimore and Detroit baseball game; Gerard Chouinard, the House committee's administrative assistant, rejected the bribe, saying politely that he had to work over the weekend. Outside the VA-HUD conference room stood an unusually small group of fifty individuals since few lobbyists knew of the last-minute change in the meeting time that would allow Jake Garn to attend portions of both the Appropriations conference and a Banking Committee hearing.

While Mikulski paced impatiently, Kelly talked with the dozen reporters sitting along the room's south wall. He explained that the conference's moderator and location switched each year between the House and Senate; last year's VA-HUD session had been in the Rayburn House Office Building and Traxler had handled the gavel. Asked about the intensity of recent negotiations, the clerk smiled and replied, "It's all a matter of compromise. When we end this conference, Mikulski and Traxler will leave this room with their hands raised together in a fist."

All nine House representatives arrived together, most looking lost and not knowing where to sit. Traxler headed around the table and wrapped his arms about the shoulders of Mikulski and Garn. After sharing a few words and a quiet joke, the House chairman moved to his side of the room and took off his jacket, his bright red suspenders again gleaming next to an equally red tie.

Mikulski banged her gavel at 9:20 A.M. and welcomed the House conferees. Traxler's side of the table was crowded, with even Jamie Whitten and Joseph McDade making brief appearances. Senate Democrats Bennett Johnston, Frank Lautenberg, Wyche Fowler, and Bob Kerrey (who would announce his candidacy for president four days later) never surfaced, and ranking Democrat Patrick Leahy arrived an hour late and stayed only ten minutes. The panel's Republicans came in force, but even they departed after thirty minutes, leaving Mikulski as the only Senate negotiator for most of the conference. The well-prepared Senate chairman, of course, had obtained proxies from each of the absent Democrats, enabling her to represent the majority if a conflict arose. The nine House conferees stayed for the entire event.

Mikulski read her opening statement, a copy of which was issued to the assembled reporters. The panel's funding problems, she complained, "were compounded by several disappointing and late-breaking developments that were out of our control." One was Jack Kemp's $1.1 billion shortfall. To solve this problem, said Mikulski, the cardinals agreed to "eat an additional $325 million in [rental assistance] renewals in fiscal year 1992, and provide an advance appropriation of over $815 million for fiscal year 1993. That is $325 million that is not available for either new housing initiatives or traditional housing programs." Second, Mikulski and Garn had counted on $384 million from the air force to help cover NASA's

177

satellite tracking expenses. But the cardinal said, "The Department of Defense has [recently] convinced the OMB, at least for the time being, that these funds should not be made available at this time." Finally, the Whitten-Byrd reallocation cut $27 million in budget authority and $37 million in outlays from the Senate panel's original numbers. That meant, explained Mikulski, "Our final 602(b) [the subcommittee's allocation] will be $1.3 billion in budget authority and almost $1 billion in outlays *below* the president's budget request." The cardinal concluded, "So these pressures, coupled with the legitimate requests of our colleagues in both bodies, have made for a tight budget which requires us to make the hard choices for which our constituents elected us." She then invited Traxler and the ranking members to make opening statements.

The House chairman simply expressed brief thanks to his Senate colleagues, saying it always was a pleasure to be associated with Mikulski. Garn again moaned about Byrd's allocation and denounced the OMB's scoring. "Next year," the Senate Republican predicted, "every scoring gimmick that we came up with this year will not be available. It will be very hard next year." The Utah senator, admitting a weariness after fifteen years on the subcommittee, looked across the table at the House clerk and teased, "Dick Malow, however, has been going longer, and he'll outlast us all." Everyone in the room knew that Malow's experience enabled him not only to understand the intricacies of the budget but also to know where the political skeletons lay.

Conference proceedings vary by subcommittee. Malow and Kelly ran one of the most efficient sessions, with virtually all decisions made ahead of time. At the other extreme, labor-HHS conferees bickered for more than three weeks.

Professional staffers quietly dominate conference proceedings, and most hover near the cardinals, nodding their approval or rejection of written amendments from the other side, often without consulting the lawmakers. At the energy and water conference the veteran House clerk Hunter Spillan provided a rare public demonstration of staff power. Near the end of the strained session Senator Bennett Johnston, citing new information, proposed an amendment to his own provision for a small-business set-aside by the Army Corps of Engineers. Spillan, standing in back of the House cardinal, quite firmly said no. "Why do you want a change?" the clerk demanded. "The House agreed with you. It's your language. I don't want the amendment." Although Johnston tried to make light of the staffer's objection, the Senate cardinal backed down.

Despite the tension inherent in these high-stake bargainings, a wry humor pervades most sessions. After Johnston began the energy and water conference by informing two New Jersey representatives that he agreed to their Corps of Engineers projects so "the House would be in a good mood," Senator DeConcini of Arizona quipped, "That's two guys in a good mood. What about the rest of us?" With no need to bully their agendas through, the chairmen tend to be gentlemanly. Representative William Natcher, leader of the House Labor-HHS panel, personifies the cordial cardinal. Sensing the opportunity for compromise, he asked of Senator Tom Harkin, "What do you propose, Mr. Chairman?" And to admonish colleagues, the Kentuckian appealed in a slight mountain twang, "Now, you don't want to do that."

Conferees, some of the most powerful men in the United States, often resort to pathetic pleading before the cardinals, who possess the sole authority to decide if pet projects receive funding or die. Nevada Senator Harry Reid, for instance, wanted an extra $5 million to help his state's universities consider the impact of a federal nuclear waste dump. "I've asked for little in this bill and have gotten very little," begged the Democratic senator. But Representative Tom Bevill, the House cardinal, was not swayed, saying that his mark already topped the president's request. "This is important to me," implored Reid. "The situation is just not fair." The senator's awkward supplications continued for several minutes before the House chairman dismissed the junior senator with an extra $500,000.

Cardinals are clearly the masters of their bills' fate. At the interior conference Representative Sidney Yates rebuffed appeal after appeal from Senator Johnston for more money to be targeted to the Audubon Institute, a research center in New Orleans. Yates pulled an EPA report from his file and complained that the proposed facility would

179

be built on a wetlands. The Louisiana senator protested, but Yates displayed a similar letter from a national environmental group that owned land near the construction site. Johnston tried reading his own letter from a local Fish and Wildlife Service official, but Yates again countered by announcing that the service's national director objected to additional money for the Louisiana project. Johnston, clearly confused and troubled, abandoned his quest, temporarily. The following day he attempted once more, asking that the Audubon Institute's director, who had flown up from New Orleans that morning and was waiting in the hallway, be allowed to enter the conference room and provide financial information about his need for $9.5 million. Yates said he'd rather hear from senior Interior Department officials, who had told him that morning that an expanded project wasn't necessary in fiscal 1992. The House cardinal concluded, "I simply can't agree with your request." Johnston had no appeal.

Negotiations are often complex, but Interior conferees concocted perhaps the strangest compromise. While the House had added a floor amendment to quadruple the fees paid by ranchers who graze their cattle and sheep on federal land, the Senate, at the insistence of Jesse Helms, banned the National Endowment for the Arts from funding projects that depict "sexual or excretory activities or organs." Since western ranchers and senators protested any increase to their costs, and Yates firmly protected the endowment from censorship, conferees haggled for two weeks before they adopted a deal, characterized in the media as "corn for porn," in which appropriators rejected the House's proposed grazing fee increase in exchange for dropping the Senate's antiobscenity language in federal arts funding.

At the VA-HUD conference Bill Green commended the cardinals but raised three items. First, he sagely predicted that proposed funding for the Federal Emergency Management Agency, almost three-quarters of a billion dollars below what was needed to provide disaster relief, would become more troublesome later in the appropriations process. Because the ranking Republican was responsible for presenting the Bush administration's concerns, Green also tried to explain Jack Kemp's requests, but a testy Mikulski cut him off and denounced the housing secretary's prickly letter that threatened a presidential veto. "Through our diligence," she protested, "we have renewed all the Section Eight contracts, and now to come in here as if nothing had happened, nothing counts, is an extremely frustrating situation." Green, unwilling to defend Kemp aggressively, shifted to a question about the space station. What drove the cardinals, Green asked rhetorically, to provide full funding rather than split the difference between the House and Senate marks? Snapped Mikulski: "The president of the United States!"

Before Mikulski could proceed through the conference notes, Garn pleaded that NASA's contribution to the national aerospace plane not be totally eliminated. With no debate Traxler agreed to find $5 million from somewhere in the space agency's research and development account. The clerks nodded and made brief notes.

Mikulski then began reading off the 175 amendments and announcing whether she and Traxler had agreed to an "SR," "HR," "HWA," or an "amendment in technical disagreement." For those without conference notes, including reporters, agency officials, and the half dozen lobbyists, the proceedings quickly became incomprehensible. "Number one, HR," Mikulski declared. "Number two, HWA, providing thirteen billion, five hundred twelve million, nine hundred twenty thousand dollars. . . ." Even those with scorecards, including all conferees and associate staffers, could do little but feverishly record the chairs' agreements on their copies.

While Mikulski read, Kelly periodically flashed a knowing smile to Malow as the two clerks silently remembered their struggles over specific details. Some staff negotiations continued during the conference. After hearing from a House conferee, for instance, Michelle Burkett passed a note across the table to Kelly about an item within the EPA budget. The Senate clerk quickly glanced at the message and silently mouthed a large no.

When the senator came to the segment on HOPE, Joseph McDade, ranking Republican on the full House Appropriations Committee, requested an extra $24 million for HOPE 1, Kemp's key section, which was to help public housing tenants buy their units. Mikulski refused to comment since the Senate had agreed to the House position on this provision. Paul Thomson, the House staffer in charge of housing, grimaced at McDade's suggestion, causing the senior Republican to declare aloud, "It's clear that the staff objects." When McDade asked Traxler to be kind to Kemp, a former appropriator, the House chairman declared, "We really are treating the secretary very well." After enduring several more minutes of pleading, Traxler responded, "Joe, you certainly know how to impose on a friendship. How about if I give you ten million dollars as a compromise, and we'll take it from HOPE two and three." McDade, who was aware that Traxler's "compromise" simply shifted money among the HOPE accounts, knew he couldn't get more, so he thanked the chairman and left the room.

Although short and sharp when her marks were questioned, Mikulski remained jovial throughout the conference. As McDade exited, after having interrupted the meeting's flow by persistently asking for more HOPE money, the Senate cardinal joked, "Glad to see you go, Joe." At 10:35 A.M. Mikulski announced she would have to leave in ten minutes for a floor vote. Suggesting that she had almost completed the conference notes, the cardinal began reading amendments as quickly as if she were practicing to become a tobacco auctioneer.

But discussion of Space Station *Freedom* suspended her surge, with Bill Green arguing at length that conferees should split the difference between the House and Senate marks and provide the saved $65 million to NASA science projects. The House Republican said he wanted not to hurt the station but to obtain the best balance within NASA. The room turned silent and tense as Mikulski paused a moment to prepare her response. While conceding Green's good intentions, the cardinal rejected his suggestion. She noted that the OMB's letter to the conferees identified the space station as the president's top priority, and she argued that the cardinals had not ignored space science. Green persisted, claiming that $65 million would restore several critical science and environmental programs.

Traxler took a deep breath and announced that this item would be

182

Program Appropriations
(in millions of dollars)

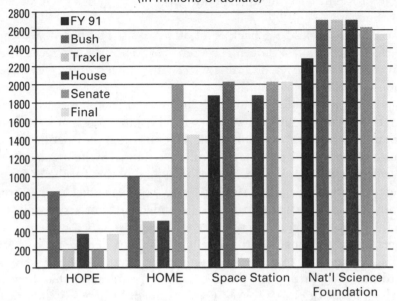

the first on which he disagreed with Green. Admitting that his defense of the station felt awkward, the chairman acknowledged the project's "firm, if not overwhelming, mandate" from the House, and he stated that any delay would only increase the station's total cost. "I'm beginning to sound like a fiscal conservative," said Traxler with a laugh. "I'm getting out of character here. I really regret that we can't keep everything on the plate, but we just can't do it."

After listening to short statements from other representatives, Mikulski declared, "As far as I'm concerned, the issue is closed." Without polling his conferees, Traxler cut off further discussion by stating, "The House will not change its position [of agreeing to the Senate number]." Mikulski then left to vote. During the break Marty Kress, NASA's legislative director; Stephen Kohashi, the Senate panel's minority staff director; and Representative Jim Chapman discussed tactics in case Green persisted when Mikulski returned. Jeff

Lawrence, Green's legislative director, asked a question across the table of Kevin Kelly, who responded loudly, "There's *no* reserve in this budget!"

When Mikulski came back at 11:10 A.M., she huddled in a corner briefly with Traxler, Green, Lawrence, and Kelly. After everyone returned to the conference table, Green announced dryly, "I've been counseled. Let's move on."

Jake Garn appeared again at 11:20 A.M. and complained about the lengthy opening statements that were bogging down his Banking Committee hearing. A smiling Mikulski informed the onetime astronaut, "Traxler and I just saved your spacesuit." Switching subjects, Garn began an appeal on behalf of Alaskan senators for the Environmental Protection Agency to base a new regional office in the forty-ninth state. Admitting that he didn't understand the issue well, the Utah senator jokingly responded to Traxler's detailed questions by threatening to bring Senator Ted Stevens in to defend his own request. Acknowledging the Alaskan's crusty reputation, the House cardinal exclaimed, "Anything but that!" And with that Stevens walked in the door. A shocked Garn pleaded, "I honestly didn't call him." Stevens, not understanding the joke, argued brusquely that an Alaskan office would save the EPA money by reducing airfare costs from the agency's current regional center in Seattle. Traxler thought for a moment and proposed that a new office be established in Alaska if the EPA agreed, a notion that Stevens accepted before leaving.

Frank Murkowski, who arrived several minutes later, objected to Traxler's compromise. Alaska's other senator, clearly wanting credit for bringing a new federal facility to his state, said EPA bureaucrats wouldn't agree to an Alaskan office because they didn't want to move. Traxler, complaining that he was "carrying water" for the administration on this issue, paused again and then suggested new language that would allow the move if the president, rather than the EPA, approved it. Murkowski accepted the new understanding, saying that Alaskans and the EPA could now equally lobby the White House.

Green, making one last request on behalf of Secretary Kemp, suggested transferring money from HUD's low-income housing program to a new "shelter care" initiative. A visibly angry Mikulski protested, "We've done a yeoman's job with HUD, but it seems that enough is never enough at that agency." Traxler, sensing that Green's request was dead, interrupted to say that the Senate chairwoman had made a convincing argument, and he abruptly thanked Mikulski for the conference. She quickly gaveled the session closed at 11:45 A.M.

The cardinals, although smiling, didn't exactly raise their fists together. Instead, as lawmakers and their aides milled about, Traxler called to his Senate counterpart, "I'd hug you, but I can't leap across the table." Mikulski responded, "Come on. You're more of a jock than that."

Outside in the hallway, several reporters confronted Representative Chapman for his opinion of the space station's future prospects. "I expect a real battle next year unless we get significant relief with a great 602(b) allocation," said the cosponsor of the House amendment that saved *Freedom*'s funding. "As evidenced by the cuts we made throughout the budget today, the VA-HUD panel is a difficult place to work. We need help. There's pain everywhere."

Surrounded by journalists, Traxler commented on the ongoing scoring debates, "We're still waiting for a definitive answer from OMB about the navy's work in Antarctica. We could be hanging out there for one hundred five million dollars." The cardinal announced that a meeting with White House officials was expected within two days, and he admitted, "Staff, not I, negotiate such things with OMB." Describing preconference bargaining, Traxler said, "What we were asked to do is fit a size twelve foot into a size nine shoe. Everyone agrees in concept that the budget must be cut, but when it comes down to your own agency, everyone sees it as number one. This subcommittee, however, has a family of agencies, and we must make the tough decisions." The chairman proposed recrafting the 1990 budget agreement so that his subcommittee and others could increase domestic spending. But he acknowledged opposition from Budget Director Darman, a man Traxler said "I don't hold in the highest personal regard."

***

After ushering conferees and reporters from the conference room, the professional staff sat down for the checkout, with Malow and Kelly again reading through the 175 amendments to make sure everyone accepted the same resolution on each and every item. Although associates were not welcomed, Whitten and Byrd had ordered a Republican staffer from each chamber to be present. "We can't leave the room until all the HRs and SRs are settled," said a participant. The seemingly straightforward process produced several minor disagreements, which staffers resolved among themselves. The checkout lasted until almost 2:45 P.M.

Kevin Kelly had agreed to provide a background briefing on the bill's highlights for reporters at 2:30 P.M. He arrived at 3:00 P.M., looking weary and disheveled and admitting to "technical disagreements with the House." The clerk announced that the conference report would be filed the following day, Friday, September 27, and be available to the public over the weekend.

According to Kelly, big and largely unrecognized winners within the compromise bill were the nation's public housing agencies, which obtained a record amount of money to operate and modernize the properties that house 3.5 million poor tenants, as well as enough funds to build an additional seventy-five hundred public housing units. State and local governments also received an unexpectedly high $1.5 billion HOME appropriation to construct rental housing for low- and middle-income families. At the same time the cardinals reserved their most pointed barbs for Jack Kemp and his favorite projects. They cut HOPE's funding 58 percent below the president's request, and they added a record $150 million for "special purpose grants" targeted to their own districts, causing Kemp to complain later that the lawmakers "went too far." Appropriators barred the housing secretary from implementing proposed regulations that would cut operating funds for public housing. They dropped for fiscal 1992 the requirement that local governments match Washington's HOME contribution, despite Kemp's fervent protests. They even restricted the number of staffers the secretary could employ in his Congressional Affairs Office.

NASA saved its prized space station but ended up one of the major

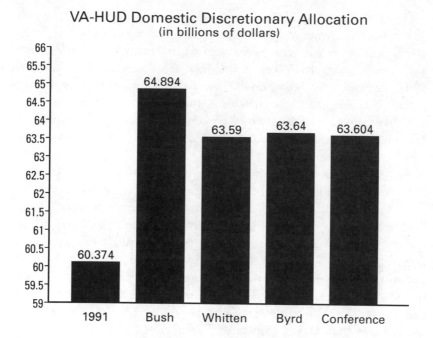

VA-HUD Domestic Discretionary Allocation
(in billions of dollars)

losers. The space agency's overall budget grew just 3 percent, a dramatic decline from the president's request of 13 percent and boosts of nearly 15 percent in fiscal 1990 and 13 percent in fiscal 1991. After accounting for inflation, NASA actually lost money in fiscal 1992. "The Chapman-Lowery amendment proved to be a short-sighted strategy," observed a House appropriator. "NASA should never have put so many of its projects on the chopping block." Conferees cut $330 million from space shuttle operations and eliminated virtually all new NASA projects, including the space infrared telescope, the flight telerobotic servicer, the orbiting solar laboratory, an aerospace braking system for the lunar mission, and an advanced turbo pump for the shuttle. They also provided only $30 million of the $175 million NASA requested for a new rocket engine and just $5 million of the $72 million sought for a hypersonic spacecraft designed to take off and land like an airplane.

Opinion surveys after Operation Desert Storm showed strong public support for military men and women, but veterans fought an uphill funding battle with Senate appropriators, obtaining less than a 1 percent increase. A key critic, Jake Garn, argued that since he didn't depend upon government handouts after serving as a naval officer in the Korean War neither should other veterans. Mikulski, moreover, castigated the quality of veterans' health care, expressing "outrage" over the several deaths linked to mistreatment at the North Chicago Veterans Medical Center.

The state of environmental funding depended upon your perspective. An EPA official argued that "appropriators really hit us this year, increasing the agency's tasks but reducing its troops." Yet a Senate appropriator asserted, "EPA obtained one of its highest budgets in history, and it has records in many accounts." The agency, in fact, secured a $575 million (or 9.4 percent) increase over fiscal 1991, but its core budget for salaries and wages fell $50 million below the president's request. Among EPA accounts, the location of the Pollution Prevention Office, described by a senior EPA staffer as a "silly-assed issue that lacked substance," consumed the most attention during preconference negotiations. Administrator William Reilly decried the Senate's order to move the office under his direct control as congressional micromanaging. Authorizers saw the order as another invasion into their turf. After lengthy altercations with these parties, cardinals called for a complex compromise: A five-person staff would be created in the administrator's office to guide and direct all pollution prevention efforts, a Pollution Prevention Policy Council would be chaired by the deputy administrator, and twenty-one staffers within the pollution prevention unit would move to the Toxics Office, which would be renamed the Office of Pollution Prevention and Toxics.

The National Science Foundation fared well, but not as well as scientists had hoped. The president proposed a substantial $406 million increase compared with fiscal 1991. The House cut that request by only $1.2 million, but the Senate slashed $76.5 million. Conferees, desperately looking for money to support space station and HOME, ended up below both the House and Senate marks and $144.5 million from the president's behest. Still, the science agency obtained a re-spectable $261.5 million, or 11.3 percent, boost from the previous year.

READOUT

As Kevin Kelly went to meet the press, Dick Malow, Paul Thomson, and Michelle Burkett headed back to their offices and began writing. As was the custom, House staff assumed the bulk of postconference responsibilities, crafting the sixty-one-page "joint explanatory statement of the committee of conference," while Kelly and Carrie Apostolou wrote the four-page conference report that listed the disposition of the 175 Senate amendments.

The joint explanatory statement, although filled with specific instructions to the agencies, is relatively clear to a lay reader. Conference action on amendment number 3, for instance, reads, "Restores language proposed by the House and stricken by the Senate earmarking $8,750,000,000 for [veterans] personnel and compensation and benefits costs, amended to earmark $8,740,000,000." In contrast, consider the virtually incomprehensible legalese on the same provision in the conference report: "That the House recede from its disagreement to the amendment of the Senate numbered 3, and agree to the same with an amendment, as follows: Restore the matter stricken by said amendment amended as follows: In lieu of the sum named in said amendment insert $8,740,000,000; and the Senate agree to the same." Beyond crafting such technical jargon, professional staffers try to eliminate conflicting signals between the House and Senate reports. "We take care to provide no wiggle room for the agencies," explained Malow.

Another task is deciding which items can be protected within the comprehensive conference report, subject to a single up or down vote in each chamber, and which are "disagreement amendments" that require separate votes. An item's germaneness and scope—whether it violates the conference's general authority or the special authority of the Appropriations Committee—are deciding factors, but it sometimes becomes a judgment call by staff. Mikulski's addition of $40 million for the Back River Wastewater Treatment Plant in Maryland was clearly not germane since neither the House nor the Senate had approved an authorization or an appropriation. If the staff had slipped such an amendment into the conference report, an individual lawmaker could have protested and blocked the entire spending package. To avoid such a disaster, clerks sometimes obtain informal rulings from the parliamentarians.

Malow, Thomson, and Burkett worked virtually nonstop from 2:45 P.M. on Thursday to Friday at 8:00 P.M. Kelly and Apostolou, after finishing the short conference report, waited in the wings to read draft sections of the joint statement. Pressed for time, Malow and his crew took the unusual step of asking the Senate staffers to craft some of the policy language; for most subcommittees, Senate employees see only the final version.

Congressional rules require that the conference report be filed for at least three legislative days before the House and Senate can vote on the compromise measure. The VA-HUD staff wanted to file the documents by midnight Friday, thus making it one of the mandatory three days, and to have the chambers consider the final spending bill on the following Wednesday. Explained a clerk: "We do things fast so there's no time for others to plan an attack."

At 8:00 P.M. on Friday, September 27, an extra ten staffers from the House Appropriations Committee arrived at the VA-HUD conference room for the readout, a grueling several-hour process to check for mistakes and to ensure that everyone agrees with the policy directives in the conference report and joint statement. "We demand silence in the room," explained Dennis Kedzior of the House panel. "It's Gestapolike." One reader recites the conference report line by line, while the fourteen other staffers check their copies for typos and errors. Another reader tackles the joint statement. (Despite the diligent effort, Traxler later admitted a "printing error" had misdirected a $575,000 earmark to Ashburn, Massachusetts; it was supposed to go to Auburn.)

"There always are disagreements," said Kedzior. "Some subcommittees have had minor fistfights late at night over different interpretations." Tempers flared only a few times among exhausted VA-HUD staffers. Still, the readout dragged on for almost four hours, sending House and Senate employees on a mad dash to file the conference report at their respective chambers by the midnight deadline.

HOUSE FLOOR

At 11:00 A.M. on Wednesday, October 2, Bob Traxler took to the House floor to explain provisions within his revised VA-HUD spending bill, which he claimed touched everyone in the country "in some fashion and to some degree." Acknowledging that not everyone would be happy with every aspect of the legislation, the cardinal declared, "It is the very best we could do under trying financial circumstances."

Traxler admitted that H.R. 2519 contained some $2.5 billion in one-time scorekeeping gimmicks, and he cautioned, "We will not be able to sustain the program levels for next year that we are establishing this year under current budget practices." Laying the groundwork for future fights over the space station's funding, the cardinal went out of his way to list NASA's science programs curtailed because of *Freedom*. "We cut space shuttle operations by three hundred thirty million dollars," Traxler lamented. "We are not proud of that at all. We have delayed the advanced X-ray astrophysics facility for more than a year. That was one of my favorite projects."

Bill Green announced that OMB Director Richard Darman could not yet say if the president would sign or veto the VA-HUD spending bill. Announcing the presence of "loose ends," Green warned that none of the legislation's numerous scoring gimmicks had been fully resolved. Yet Joseph McDade, the full committee's ranking Republican, casually described this $2.5 billion uncertainty as "a minor and technical matter and, in my judgment, can be taken care of as we move forward." The VA-HUD legislation, Green also disclosed, failed to provide some $700 million that the Federal Emergency Management Agency needed for disaster relief since the cardinals wanted

191

"emergency" funds outside the budget caps to cover those expenses. Although a hurricane or other natural disaster might appear to be an emergency, Green explained the power of budget semantics: "The administration takes the position that the $700 million gap exists because in the past the Congress funded FEMA at lower levels than the administration had requested." These concerns aired, the New York Republican demonstrated the bipartisan nature of appropriators. "This is an excellent agreement," he declared. "It represents the good hard work of the members of this subcommittee, and I urge that it be adopted."

George Brown, who helped defend the space station in June, had expressed skepticism about the project recently, and some lawmakers assumed he would use this floor debate to make peace with Traxler. The Science, Space, and Technology Committee chairman, in fact, began by promising to support the conference report, but he quickly blasted the "unauthorized, unrequested earmarks for personal interest items" that squeezed higher-priority initiatives. While conceding that pork barreling is "a time-honored tradition of this body," the authorizer criticized appropriators for forcing NASA to pay $100 million for bizarre projects that often had nothing to do with space. "It includes seven and a half million dollars in continued funding for the Wheeling, West Virginia, Jesuit College," Brown said. "I do not believe anyone in Congress or in NASA knows what this will be for." He also condemned the space agency payments to a center for environmental research in Traxler's backyard as well as the Christopher Columbus Center in Mikulski's hometown of Baltimore. The angry congressman concluded his "jihad against appropriators" by reading a list of questionable earmarks and by calling the VA-HUD conference report "a sad exercise in the abuse of that power" of Congress to appropriate funds.

Traxler ignored Brown's broadside and issued his own charge. "The problem," the cardinal said, "is that each one of the authorizing chairmen thinks that his area of concern is the only one in the entire U.S. budget, and that is not true."

The Republican whip, Newt Gingrich, delivered another assault, scolding the VA-HUD panel for micromanaging the Department of Housing and Urban Development. He described as "terribly petty" the subcommittee's decision to cut the number of Jack Kemp's legislative assistants from twenty-eight to fifteen. The ever-ready Traxler responded that as a proportion of total staff, HUD's fifteen was twice what other agencies had.

Several representatives overlooked the policy debates and used the occasion to highlight provisions within the bill that benefited their districts. Nancy Pelosi, a new appropriator, submitted a statement that she later crafted into a press release, bragging about how her efforts ensured $25 million for earthquake rehabilitation, $4.1 million for an AIDS program, $4 million for a homeless shelter, and $2 million for an estuary—all within her San Francisco district. Even Jamie Whitten boasted that the VA-HUD bill contained money—in fact, $265 million more than the president's $200 million request—for a NASA rocket project headquartered in Yellow Creek, Mississippi.

Traxler called for a roll call vote on the conference report after the customary hour of debate. At this last public scene in the annual budget drama, representatives are loath to oppose any appropriations bill that funds key agencies and popular programs. The VA-HUD motion carried overwhelmingly, 390–30.

The cardinal then proceeded to address individually the sixty-seven amendments in disagreement. Most were dealt with perfunctorily, with Traxler offering a motion and the Speaker pro tempore quickly recognizing a favorable voice vote from the few representatives in the chamber.

Sonny Montgomery, however, objected to Senate amendment 21 requiring the Department of Veterans Affairs to accept laboratory standards set government-wide by the Department of Health and Human Services. The chairman of the House Veterans Affairs Committee, protecting his authority and bending to the power of the veterans' lobby, declared, "We have no intention of allowing the secretary of another department to determine whether the standards to be applied in VA laboratories have been met." Giving voice to the House's frequent frustration with Senate appropriators, Gerald Solomon added, "Let us not necessarily cave in to some of the pompous members of that other body that just want to get their way all the time."

Traxler provided a weak defense of the provision, suggesting that he had hurried to an agreement with the Senate in order not to be last in line for the special pot of money that accommodates scoring differences between the Congressional Budget Office and the Office of Management and Budget. Said the cardinal: "I feel very much like a person who is sort of caught in the center, who wants to support my House colleagues and at the same time wants to get the conference report done so we can utilize the special set-aside."

In the course of making a final plea, Montgomery admitted, "I never really have quite understood the scoring that they are talking about today." It didn't matter. The House voted, 390–24, to reject the Senate's amendment, forcing Mikulski to give in or propose another conference to debate the issue.

Such struggles between appropriators and authorizers are growing more intense. "The Appropriations Committee always walks a thin line regarding its policy directives," admitted Dick Malow. "We're now closer to the brink." Some turf-protecting authorizers want to be appointed to appropriations conferences. Others demand new House rules that would require a two-thirds vote to approve Senate amendments. Several believe the Speaker should use his power to slow down the process, rally his troops, and block nongermane riders. Setting their sights on House appropriators, too, chairmen of several legislative committees have asked their staffs to prepare lengthy reports on how to circumvent, restrain, or overpower the cardinals. Most of the recommendations—multiyear program authorizations, core funding requirements, and bell-shaped expenditure plans—are esoteric and offer no illusion of a quick fix.

Appropriators, meanwhile, quietly wage their own campaign against bickering authorizers, remarking frequently on the declining relevance of their legislative colleagues. "Authorizers have lost their objectivity and become nothing more than lobbyists for their programs," said one. "If you want a yes, go to an authorizing committee," noted another. "There's not enough money in the Treasury to satisfy authorizers"; "Authorizers contemplate their navels while appropriators act"; "Since authorizers can't get it together to make decisions, someone has to run the government," the comments continued.

Earmarks are perhaps the major source of strain between authorizers and appropriators since the escalating costs of pork confine agency programs dear to the legislative committees. Because pork provides enormous political benefits to the local politician, out-of-the-loop authorizers also resent that the beneficiaries tend to be appropriators. Authorizers and reporters revel in ridiculing the multi-million-dollar scheme to capture electrical power from the aurora borealis in Alaska, the $2 million earmark to stimulate the sale of Native Hawaiian handicrafts, and the $1 million study on why more people don't bicycle or walk. Surprisingly, several Appropriations Committee staffers also complain about the pork barreling trend. "One of the biggest changes in the appropriations process over the past ten years is the ravenous increase in pork," lamented a clerk. "Earmarks in this year's legislation are nauseating," moaned another. "We try to develop a good bill, but the chairman's piggish ways are eating into ongoing programs."

Cardinals dismiss pork busters as frustrated men who wish they controlled the appropriations process. They relish catching these critics appealing for special favors, and they conclude cheerfully, "Everyone seeks pork." Most appropriators argue forthrightly that earmarks are justified. "The legislative branch is simply substituting its judgment for the administration's, and that is its constitutional right," pronounced a subcommittee chairman. "Directed spending is not like Imelda Marcos giving contracts to her brother," added a clerk. "These projects are legitimate."

Even some authorizers admit that congressional pork has its benefits. George Brown, for instance, assailed science earmarks—which totaled a record $810 million in fiscal 1992, up from less than $50 million a decade before—but he confessed that without such congressional directives, review panels of leading scientists would send all federal science grants to a monopoly of elite universities. According to Daniel Greenberg, editor of *Science & Government Report,* "Quite a few of today's highly regarded research centers were long ago conceived in the pork barrel. And quite a few wastrel projects in the federal research inventory . . . are plastered with approving peer review reports."

***

Traxler and Mikulski doubled the money devoted to special housing projects from $73 million in fiscal 1991 to $150 million in fiscal 1992, including $1.5 million for a regional medical center in Jamie Whitten's backyard, $3.9 million for low-income apartments in Traxler's Bay City, and $300,000 to promote rural economic development in Jim Chapman's northeastern Texas district. When the House came to Senate amendment 35 affecting those earmarks, Dan Burton began his oft-repeated diatribe against pork by displaying to the C-SPAN television audience a large poster depicting a hog eating the Capitol dome. The Indiana Republican then castigated appropriators for "taking this country down the road to financial and fiscal ruin."

Traxler ridiculed Burton as "the supporter of the B-2," an expensive military aircraft the cardinal considered wasteful. Gene Taylor, a Democrat from Mississippi, added his scorn, accusing Burton of earmarking $150 million for the Sikhs of India while objecting to housing construction projects for Americans. Burton became flustered, repeating several times, "There was no money sent to Punjab, India. Where is the gentleman getting that?"

Traxler revealed his New Deal sympathies by declaring, "I am a member of this body who believes that now is the time to do a public works bill for America." Claiming that Burton and his pork-busting colleagues oppose "public purpose projects" that put Americans to work, the cardinal announced, "I believe that is what our nation is about and what we ought to do. I believe this with all of my heart and fervor that I can muster." Now worked up, Traxler attacked Burton for failing to criticize the billions wasted in the defense budget. Proclaimed the cardinal: "When those of us who put domestic concerns and the people of America ahead of foreign concerns and being the policeman of the world, when we rise to do something on health and education, on physical infrastructure, they say that is waste. I say to them, 'Shame, shame on you for attempting to mislead the American public as to what your true intentions and purposes are. How can you possibly relegate this nation to second rate in health, education, public facilities and buildings?' "

Even Burton was blown away by the cardinal's diatribe. "Boy, can you demagogue an issue," he concluded. Lawmakers approved

Traxler's motion, earmarks intact, on a voice vote. Burton's defeat proved to be the norm. In fact, all of Traxler's and Mikulski's earmarks within the VA-HUD spending bill—including $20 million for the space agency's undersea research center in Baltimore—survived House and Senate scrutiny.

Without other objections, the chairman breezed through the remaining amendments by 2:15 P.M. After eight months of work, Bob Traxler had completed his most difficult legislative assignment. No doubt he had been battered and bruised along the way, but approval of the conference report marked a significant achievement. Reporters, however, wanted to know only whether Traxler had written bad checks at the House Bank, the most recent scandal tarnishing the public image of Congress and a topic the cardinal sought to avoid. No journalist called to ask about the $81 billion VA-HUD bill that funded programs touching everyone in the country. The chairman's press secretary complained, "In the media's mind the legislation is nickel-and-dime stuff—no pun intended—compared to check bouncing."

SENATE FLOOR

A short time later, on the other side of the Capitol, Barbara Mikulski introduced the same conference report to her Senate colleagues. "We faced compelling needs from virtually every agency and advocacy group with an interest in this legislation," the cardinal announced. "From our aging veterans who fought to save our freedom to the pioneers of the new frontiers in space, we had significant causes among which to choose."

Jake Garn praised the bill, calling it a "remarkable feat," but he expressed deep concern about America's future "budgetary burdens." While endorsing the legislation's accounting gimmicks, he admitted, "I think it is important that we put ourselves, and the public, on notice that this measure probably represents the highwater mark of funding for these programs." The ranking Republican, moreover, warned about the still-unsettled transfer of money from the U.S. Navy to the National Science Foundation for work in Antarctica. "Unless this issue is resolved favorably," Garn said, "we may well have to secure funding on an emergency basis to avoid a catastrophic shutdown of this critical program."

Virtually no debate ensued. Frank Lautenberg once again bragged about the many projects he had obtained for New Jersey, and Howell Heflin conducted a scripted colloquy with Mikulski about a NASA project he wanted for a corporation in his home state, Alabama. Mikulski urged NASA officials to address Heflin's questions when they submitted their "operating plan," due thirty days after enactment of the bill.

The conference report was agreed to on a voice vote with only a few senators on the floor. Mikulski then packaged en bloc all but one of the amendments in disagreement and again heard no objection from the nearly empty Senate chamber.

All that remained was the amendment, 21, that had been rejected by the House. Dismissing the claim that VA labs consistently performed quality work, Mikulski charged, "This is the same medical care operation that presided over the horror stories that we saw at Cleveland Hospital, where it resulted in terrible injury, deaths in a Chicago hospital, and in a Boston hospital, where female patients were not given the VA-mandated Pap smears and mammograms." The cardinal criticized the VA bureaucracy for manipulating the legislative process, but she couldn't overcome the House's objection in what she described as "a very prickly parliamentary situation." In the words of another senator, the chairwoman "caved" and dropped the amendment. In Mikulski's own words, "I do not want to hold up the VA-HUD bill because of the internal politics of the House of Representatives and the U.S. Senate. . . . I am proud of the bill. I am willing to do the compromise because I will tell you: I want to make sure that we meet the high tech needs of the United States of America. This bill has done it. I am proud to chair it."

With that, Congress sent the $81 billion bill, making appropriations for the departments of Veterans Affairs and Housing and Urban Development and for sundry independent agencies, commissions, corporations, and offices, to the White House for the president's signature. The budget drama, however, was far from over.

7

THE BUCKS NEVER STOP

SINCE PRESIDENT GEORGE Bush identified the space station as his highest priority within the VA-HUD bill, few expected him to veto the final measure that fully funded *Freedom*. Nevertheless, Jack Kemp, some conservative organizations, and a coalition of pork-busting lawmakers mounted a campaign to produce such a veto. The housing secretary, just before the VA-HUD conference committee meeting, declared in a press release, "This appropriations bill amounts to a back of the hand to the most significant policy initiatives included in the Cranston-Gonzalez National Affordable Housing Act, which President Bush signed less than a year ago with the support of an historic bipartisan coalition." Kemp also complained directly to Bush, White House Chief of Staff Sununu, and OMB Director Darman.

The Heritage Foundation widely distributed a two-page alert in mid-October entitled "The Housing Bill: Waiting for a Bush Veto." The right-wing group, which clearly favored Kemp over the more moderate Bush, wrote that the president's failure to issue a veto threat "signals Capitol Hill that he perhaps is more interested in spending billions of dollars on a space station than on backing his own HUD secretary, Jack Kemp, who is fighting to retain the central provisions of landmark housing reforms enacted last year."

On Capitol Hill, Harris Fawell, Republican representative from Illinois, and sixty-four other congressional representatives urged the

199

president to exercise a line-item veto and excise the 133 "special purpose" housing grants targeted primarily to the districts of appropriators. Bush had long sought a line-item veto, believing he did not have the authority but should. The members of Congress, however, asserted that the Constitution already provided the president with such powers, and they suggested the VA-HUD legislation was "a perfect opportunity for a test case." Several appropriators expressed surprise that Fawell's letter was endorsed by so many members. One suggested he saw "Kemp's fingerprints all over it." Another worried that the letter signaled a rank-and-file revolt against pork. But most dismissed Fawell's attack because of the questionable legality of a line-item veto.

It normally takes ten days to "enroll" a bill, so appropriators grew nervous as several weeks passed without the president's signing the VA-HUD spending legislation. At first they assumed delays resulted from unforeseen technical problems, including the postponed delivery of special parchment, made from a two-hundred-year-old recipe, on which bills are officially printed. But Kemp and his colleagues began spreading rumors about Bush's objecting to the housing earmarks. According to a cardinal, "We started to fear that a veto would focus more attention on our pork barreling."

Since the president had not signed several spending bills when the new fiscal year began on October 1, Congress adopted stopgap measures to keep federal agencies operating. A few lawmakers tried to affix to these must-approve legislative vehicles an array of unrelated and often controversial amendments, including an extension of unemployment benefits, a banking reform bill, and a Democratic proposal to alter the distribution of federal matching money to presidential candidates. Yet Whitten and Byrd refused to consider any riders, demanding that the continuing resolutions (CR) remain "clean." The stopgap bills, therefore, stated simply that federal agencies without approved appropriations could continue working at the lowest of three funding levels: fiscal 1991 appropriations, the House's fiscal 1992 proposal, or the Senate's version. Congress adopted the first CR in late September, keeping the government running through October 29. On October 24, with only four of the thirteen regular spending bills signed, it quickly cleared a second stopgap bill, hoping that lawmakers and the administration would soon complete work on the remaining appropriations.

Shortly after Congress approved the second CR, White House "sources" squelched the rumors about a veto of the VA-HUD spending bill. An OMB official said that veto appeals from cabinet secretaries "are never taken lightly" but that rejecting the entire legislation to protest the destruction of Kemp's housing reforms was not worth upsetting the bill's delicate balance or threatening the president's pet space station.

The issue within the administration then became what the president should say on signing the bill. Several NASA officials urged Bush to complain about the space agency's small 3 percent increase. But Darman, who drafted the presidential statement, believed the administration had to honor its deal with Mikulski: If the senator supported the space station, the president would support the legislation. The budget director wrote simply, "Although [the bill] does not fully fund the administration's request for civil space activities, the act provides the funds necessary to maintain a balanced and forward-looking space program."

Some individuals within the EPA wanted the president to oppose congressional earmarks. Here Darman believed the administration was boxed in since it had initially requested unauthorized grants for sewage treatment facilities in New York, Los Angeles, San Diego, and Seattle. The president's statement, as a result, failed even to mention the money appropriators added for Detroit's Rouge River and Baltimore's Back Water.

Kemp argued for strong rhetoric, something like "the president condemns" or "denounces" various housing provisions within the bill. The best he got from Darman was an expression of concern. "I am disappointed that the Congress continues to support housing programs that are very costly and that do not offer choice to poor families because new buildings, rather than poor families, receive subsidies," the final statement declared.

With funding battles theoretically over for the year, Bush's diplomatic statement ended with praise for appropriators balancing diverse and competing priorities. It expressed the president's willingness to continue working with Congress "to seek solutions to the problems I have noted and to attend to the priorities I have identified." The collegial Bush often invited congressional leaders to the White House to witness the signing of major pieces of legislation, but no such invitations were extended for the VA-HUD or other spending bills. According to an OMB staffer, the Republican administration had no interest in giving too much praise or favorable publicity to Democratic cardinals.

Bush quietly approved the VA-HUD bill, as well as appropriations from four other subcommittees, on Monday, October 28. H.R. 2519, the 139th bill to pass the 102d Congress, finally became Public Law No. 102-139.

ICING ON THE CAKE

To cover emergencies or expand preferred projects before a new fiscal year begins, Congress can approve supplemental spending bills that offer another opportunity for cardinals to wield their capital clout. Supplementals, as well as regular appropriations, theoretically must stay within spending caps for defense, international, and domestic categories. But the 1990 budget accord included large loopholes to increase funding for the Persian Gulf War, the savings and loan bailout, and any designated "emergency." Significantly it also allowed the OMB, rather than appropriators, to define which emergencies were exempt from the spending caps.

The OMB occasionally wielded its emergency designation sword to suit the administration's political ends. Favoring the State Department's international diplomatic work over the Commerce Department's domestic development efforts, White House budgeteers declared that expenses for evacuating State Department personnel from Middle East embassies during Operation Desert Storm would be counted as emergency spending, but they refused to provide the same treatment for Commerce Department personnel evacuated from the same embassies. The State Department, as a result, obtained extra money, while Commerce officials had to reduce their existing budget accounts to cover evacuation costs.

The year's first supplemental provided $42.6 billion to help pay for Operation Desert Shield/Desert Storm. When Congress marked up spending bills the previous spring, obviously no one expected Iraq to invade Kuwait or the United States to enter a Middle East war. After the combat began, therefore, White House and congressional budget negotiators agreed that associated military expenses would not be counted against the regular spending caps.

To address domestic demands, appropriators considered a concurrent dire emergency supplemental. Knowing that this legislation, in some form, would pass and be signed into law, many lawmakers sought to define emergency spending broadly and to insert special-interest provisions. Dairy state legislators, for instance, tried to alter federal milk marketing orders and boost falling milk prices, while Housing Secretary Kemp sought to shift nearly $500 million to the new HOPE initiative. Appropriators rejected both pleas. The end result was a $5.4 billion bill that included an extra $100 million to bail out the District of Columbia, $1.5 billion for more food stamps, and $150 million to help states administer unemployment insurance programs overwhelmed by the recession. The president signed both the dire emergency and Desert Storm measures on April 10, 1991.

The third—and largely noncontroversial—supplemental responded to the plight of Kurds in northern Iraq. Linking the measure to the Middle East war, the OMB allowed the entire $572 million aid package to be exempt from the budget caps. But lawmakers, growing testy that additional money was being spent overseas rather than in the United States, demanded that the president quickly compile another list of unfunded dire emergencies that would require a fourth supplemental. "Rather than look around the world for places to spend our money," declared Whitten, "it is absolutely essential that we start at home and take care of our own people."

On June 28 Bush requested another $693 million for FEMA to respond to thirty-five domestic natural disasters, including tornadoes in Mississippi, ice storms in New York, flooding in Washington, and typhoons in Guam. The president, however, designated only $151 million as emergency spending, charging that Congress—specifically Bob Traxler and Barbara Mikulski—had underfunded FEMA, had caused the agency's current shortfall, and should be required to make offsetting cuts within other accounts. (The cardinals responded by criticizing the agency's competence and accusing Bush of filling it with Republican political hacks who knew nothing about emergency response procedures.) The White House also sought an additional $2.9 billion to replace or repair combat equipment damaged during Operation Desert Storm, as well as $55.3 million to restore a Kansas air force base destroyed by a tornado. To offset some of the $3.7 billion supplemental, the president proposed rescissions or spending cuts at NASA and the departments of Transportation and Housing and Urban Development.

The "college of cardinals" met on July 10 and decided to challenge the administration's assumptions. Rather than identify offsets, Traxler labeled the entire $693 million FEMA request as emergency funding exempt from the spending caps. "We have a definition problem, clearly, with the administration," Traxler was quoted as saying. Predicting a confrontation with the White House, he continued, "It's like warfare. You can be damn sure I'm going to be ready for them." Six other cardinals joined the action, and the supplemental quickly expanded to $5.6 billion, more than 50 percent above the administration's proposal. The biggest addition was Whitten's $1.75 billion for farmers and ranchers who lost their crops or herds as the result of droughts, floods, or freezes.

On July 17, the evening before the full Appropriations Committee was to mark up the supplemental spending bill, OMB Director Darman threatened a presidential veto over the "unwarranted" $1.75 billion for domestic agricultural disasters. Whitten abruptly canceled his markup, arranged another strategy session with the cardinals, and called the White House to schedule a meeting with President Bush. William Lehman was quoted as saying after the cardinals' meeting, "It's eyeball to eyeball—who's going to blink." The transportation cardinal predicted the president would back down because he needed the extra money for military equipment, but administration officials faced little pressure to negotiate since they could satisfy their immediate needs by transferring funds from other defense accounts.

Exposing a philosophical and generational rift among appropriators, the cardinals debated at length the wisdom of confronting Bush with a large supplemental that he'd veto. Wanting the committee to make a political point, David Obey, chairman of the Foreign Operations Subcommittee and leader of the panel's younger generation, argued for a showdown with the White House to demonstrate Democratic commitment to social programs and Bush's insensitivity to Americans in need. But Whitten, the pragmatic inside player, preferred a compromise bill that would distribute at least some money to farmers and other worthy recipients. The chairman worried that Bush, then at the height of his popularity, would continue his string of twenty-one vetoes that Congress had failed to override. Despite his age and growing frailty, Whitten won this and most arguments about committee strategy.

The chairman began his White House negotiations on July 24 with an afternoon phone call from President Bush, who offered only kind words and a promise to send the OMB's Richard Darman and Agriculture Secretary Edward Madigan to Whitten's office the following day for continued discussions. That hourlong meeting proved inconclusive. Asked by a *Congress Daily* reporter as he left Whitten's office if he and the chairman had reconciled their differences on the supplemental spending bill, Darman said, "No. I expressed our point of view. We were just really explaining our positions to each other—no more than that." As explanations continued and frustrations increased, Whitten derided the president publicly for sending more than $1 billion in emergency appropriations to foreigners but less than $39 million to Americans. The chairman's enlarged supplemental gained support steadily on Capitol Hill, even from farm state Republicans anxious for the agricultural disaster relief. Still, Darman refused to budge.

Three months passed, and what was to have been a supplemental to the fiscal 1991 budget became additions to 1992 spending bills, several of which had not yet been enacted. Whitten finally gathered his committee in mid-October to mark up an even larger and more controversial bill. Democrats, for instance, wanted more federal matching money distributed to their presidential candidates in early 1992 in order to "level the playing field"; appropriators approved the contentious amendment on a party line vote, but Republicans predicted a presidential veto of the entire supplemental if this partisan measure remained. The now-bulky bill went beyond appropriations to order arms sales halted within 120 days to Saudi Arabia and Kuwait if those countries didn't deliver their promised contributions toward the cost of Operation Desert Storm. It even demanded that those nations pay the many parking tickets imposed on their diplomats in New York City and Washington, D.C. Traxler added several relatively minor provisions of his own. Tweaking Jack Kemp one more time, he cut $250,000 from HUD's salary account in order to create the National Commission on Severely Distressed Housing. Responding to pleadings from Native American advocates, the cardinal also allowed up to 1.5 percent of the Environmental Protection Agency's wastewater treatment loan fund to be used for direct grants to Indian tribes.

When the supplemental reached the House floor on October 29, other legislators added even more "emergency" provisions, including an extra $1.4 billion to Head Start and other programs for low-income children, sending the bill's total cost to $7.5 billion, or some $4 billion more than Bush had requested four months before. Even the FEMA segment grew to $943 million, reflecting Whitten's last-minute additions to help cover the costs of recent fires in California, Washington, and Virginia.

The House approved the dire emergency supplemental by a healthy margin, but not without a heated debate. Whitten began the proceedings by again raising his favorite issues: how the Committee on Appropriations since 1945 had reduced presidential funding requests by more than $180 billion and how the Office of Management and Budget unreasonably ordered a sequestration of thirteen ten-thousandths of 1 percent. Arguing that the nation's economy was in worse shape than at any time since the 1940s, the chairman stated that emergency funding was needed "to get our country moving, to increase production, to again export more than we import."

But Joseph McDade, the ranking Republican appropriator, labeled the disaster relief supplemental "a bill that has been waiting for a disaster to happen." He and others attacked the cardinals for intentionally failing to set aside funds for disaster relief within their regular appropriations bills in order to spend that money on other programs; he described the Democrats' plea for emergency funds as a cynical ploy to spend more federal money than the budget caps allowed. The VA-HUD panel, for instance, provided no money in its fiscal 1991 bill for FEMA's disaster relief account and only $184 million in its fiscal 1992 bill. Whitten's subcommittee also slighted similar relief programs at the Department of Agriculture, while Interior, using an obvious back-door route to increased funding, cut its regular appropriation to clean up abandoned mine sites by nearly $9 million, only to turn around and request $10 million in emergency funds for the same purpose. "So of course, there is a shortfall," explained McDade, "and, my friends, it is created not by an act of God but by an act of Congress."

Ignoring McDade and challenging the White House, most representatives voted on October 29 to have the supplemental's entire $7.5 billion be exempt from the spending caps. Yet Darman continued to argue that emergency funds should cover only the war's mopup and a small portion of FEMA's disaster relief. Everything else, he maintained, should be paid for by cutting existing programs.

Two weeks after the House vote Robert Byrd ran his version through the Senate Appropriations Committee with virtually identical spending levels: some $3.5 billion for military equipment, $1.75 billion for farm disaster assistance, $1.4 billion for low-income children, and $943 million for FEMA. Yet the Senate chairman, wanting to avoid a Republican filibuster, removed the disputed provision regarding funds for presidential candidates.

The dire emergency supplemental, after five full months of consideration, came to the Senate floor on Friday, November 22, 1991, just days before Congress planned to adjourn for the year. Frantic legislators tried to attach scores of unrelated amendments. Byrd beat back most, but another contentious item survived: allowing military women to obtain abortions at Defense Department health clinics.

Feeling substantial pressure from farm state Republicans, military contractors, and disaster-ravaged communities, Darman spent the weekend crafting a compromise letter. He informed House and Senate cardinals on Monday morning that the administration would consider emergency spending for farm disaster assistance "in the range of $500 million to $900 million." Regarding funding for FEMA, Darman wrote, "In a spirit of comity we would be willing to raise our emergency amount [from $151 million] to a somewhat higher level," later said to be "in the neighborhood of $690 million." The OMB director, however, rejected other emergency spending, including funds for Head Start.

Conferees made little progress during their first negotiating session other than to strip the supplemental of its abortion provision and $1.4 billion for children's programs. Rather than trim further, the cardinals, with the OMB's blessing, added $400 million of "emergency" funds to help the Soviet Union dismantle its nuclear weapons and another $100 million for the U.S. military to transport humanitarian aid to that beleaguered country.

On Tuesday afternoon, November 26, Whitten announced that he and Darman had settled on $995 million for emergency farm assistance, down from the chairman's initial $1.75 billion request but far above the OMB's opening offer of zero. The final supplemental, approved by both chambers the following morning just before adjournment, totaled roughly $6 billion.

The agreement on FEMA placed particular pressure on Traxler and Mikulski. Although the compromise measure increased the agency's emergency funding from Bush's first request of $151 million to $800 million, it called for annual appropriations of at least $320 million to FEMA's disaster relief account. Negotiators, in short, directed the VA-HUD cardinals to stop underfunding the agency. According to Kevin Kelly, the settlement was "a disaster."

POWER TO THE SCOREKEEPERS

A concurrent ordeal for the VA-HUD panels was the OMB's final scoring of accounting gimmicks in the regular 1992 spending bill. Even after the president had signed their legislation on October 28, Traxler, Malow, Mikulski, and Kelly had to endure a monthlong roller coaster ride of uncertainty. Mikulski complained that she spent enormous time dealing with "glitches." Frustrated by not controlling the legislation's fate, Traxler asserted, "The scorekeepers set the rules."

Despite heated arguments from appropriators, the OMB remained steadfast that the air force would make no payment to NASA for the Tracking and Data Relay Satellite System. The White House budget office also continued to say that accounting tricks within HUD offered extra budget authority but no additional outlays.

Yet scoring for the National Science Foundation's research operations in Antarctica remained unsettled. Before conference, Darman had ruled that the navy would pay $30 million of the $105 million account to cover its responsibility for environmental cleanup at the South Pole project. The remaining $75 million, however, was "tentatively" scored as domestic rather than defense. Of that $75 million in budget authority, the OMB estimated $40 million would be spent or outlaid in fiscal 1992.

The VA-HUD clerks provided no Antarctica money in their spending bill. From Kelly's perspective, Bob Grady had indicated the Defense Department would cover the entire $105 million. Dick Malow felt the OMB officials "gave us every signal in the world they would score it as defense." The UNF, hoping for additional spending authority, certainly promoted that interpretation. Even the Congressional Budget Office endorsed the navy's transfer as a legitimate military expenditure. More important, Senator Daniel Inouye's Defense Appropriations Subcommittee obliged Mikulski and had the navy assume the full $105 million for Antarctica research.

Within the administration, however, Grady's argument lost ground steadily. Part of the setback involved internal OMB politics; according to one agency official, "Grady was being considered for the open slot as deputy director, so his challengers had their knives ready to slash his proposals." Another White House staffer suggested that Defense Secretary Dick Cheney blocked the transfer by throwing "temper tantrums against any reduction in his budget." Moreover, Darman grew increasingly troubled that the navy would be stuck with Antarctica expenses forever and that approval of this "foot-in-the-door proposal" would encourage others to break down the fire walls between defense and domestic spending. Just before the defense conference committee meeting on November 15, Darman insisted that no additional Antarctica money could be taken from the defense budget.

The OMB director's newfound resolve forced Mikulski and Traxler to find $75 million in budget authority and some $40 million in outlays. Since the VA-HUD bill had already passed Congress and been signed by the president, the cardinals had two options: amend their own bill at the defense conference committee meeting, or, preferable, push the spending into the $1.5 billion cushion that the budget agreement established for scoring items on which the OMB and CBO disagreed. Budget negotiators in the autumn of 1990 created this cushion as a way to appease appropriators worried that the OMB would abuse its new scorekeeping powers. In effect, the complex provision enabled appropriations to spend a bit more money than the well-publicized caps allowed.

Access to the $1.5 billion domestic cushion essentially occurs on a first-come, first-served basis. Traxler and Mikulski rushed through the VA-HUD conference to assure their place near the front of the line, and they felt confident that a substantial reserve remained to cover the Antarctica gimmick if the OMB didn't ultimately approve its defense scoring. Late-moving subcommittees face more constraints since the last dollar appropriated over the caps and cushion will incite an across-the-board cut of domestic spending. Although such sequestration would be spread across most subcommittees, no cardinal wants to trigger the disruptive event. Much to their regret, Traxler and Mikulski had become the Johnny-come-latelies as Antarctica funding now depended upon the slow-moving defense bill, which was delayed because of grand debates about the role of the U.S. military after the collapse of the Soviet Union. Access to the special allowance, in fact, evolved into a sluggish race between the defense and Labor-HHS subcommittees. (Ongoing controversies with both bills required Congress on November 13 to clear a third and final continuing resolution.)

The labor-HHS conference finished first, despite chaotic sessions that featured weary representatives and senators bickering at length over small earmarks. Since Representative Natcher refused to cut education and Senator Harkin held firm on health care, conferees adopted scores of accounting gimmicks to make it through the year. Despite fervent pleas from Traxler and Mikulski, the labor-HHS appropriators exhausted the remaining cushion and left no money for VA-HUD's Antarctica scoring dispute. According to Mikulski, "It left a bad taste."

The VA-HUD chairs again faced problematic options. If they kept the $75 million Antarctica provision within the defense bill, the OMB would score it as domestic spending, the caps would be busted, and a sequester would be ordered. On the other hand, Traxler and Mikulski had little interest in the defense panel's cutting $75 million of budget authority and $40 million of outlays from their own delicate package of compromises that had just been enacted. With their backs to the wall, the cardinals decided to fight. Unless they gained access to the $1.5 billion cushion, Traxler and Mikulski threatened to cut from the very NASA programs that the Bush administration held most dear.

The tactic worked, to the surprise of both cardinals and clerks. The night before the president was to sign the labor-HHS bill and formally exhaust the cushion, OMB officials called Malow and Kelly to announce they had located an extra $40 million in available outlays. The news meant that the VA-HUD panel was home free—at least on the outlay front.

Where did the $40 million come from? OMB staffers claimed their scoring of the final labor-HHS bill freed up funds. But according a clerk, the discovery "resulted from pure politics." He said, "Remember that you can rejigger the numbers to produce virtually anything. Now if you wanted a large number, it would attract attention and could be difficult. But forty million dollars is not even at the noise level."

Since the OMB "discovery" affected only outlays, Malow and Kelly quickly had to locate $75 million in budget authority within their own bill. Finding $75 million may sound difficult to the uninitiated, but veteran budgeteers understand that an amazing amount of money floats around the agencies. HUD's assisted housing account, for instance, then contained some $3.3 billion in unobligated funds largely because the department was notoriously bad at estimating expenses.

The questions for Traxler and Mikulski became where to take the money from and whom to blame for the decision. Both cardinals decided that the National Science Foundation should absorb $5 million; an NSF official characterized this judgment as "a slap on the hand for having created the Antarctica scoring problem in the first place." Noting the large unobligated carryovers at HUD and their own antipathy toward Jack Kemp, Traxler and Mikulski wanted the remaining $70 million to be taken from the Department of Housing and Urban Development—as long as they could create what one staffer called plausible deniability.

The cardinals quietly presented two options to the Office of Management and Budget: seize the $70 million from either the NSF or HUD. Despite some fear that the OMB would split the charge between the two agencies, Traxler and Mikulski gambled that Darman, knowing President Bush's strong support for scientific research, would choose to nip HUD. Their judgment proved correct. The tactic allowed the defense bill to pass without sequestration, and it made Jack Kemp believe that the White House rather than the Appropriations Committee was the heavy. An Appropriations staff member described these final machinations as a revealing glimpse into budget politics. "You can make things happen," he said proudly, "when there's synergy between the OMB, the Senate, and the House."

By late November Malow and Kelly were more frustrated than fascinated by the prolonged process, yet they absorbed several lessons from the irritating machinations. Asked whether appropriators set a dangerous precedent by allowing the OMB to make a funding decision between the NSF and HUD, Kelly responded firmly, "Such a choice will never happen again." Malow resolved not to work through a subcommittee he didn't dominate. Both clerks agreed they'd avoid all scoring gimmicks without ironclad agreements from the Office of Management and Budget.

REPROGRAMMING

Those clerks who passed their bills early and avoided scorekeeping gimmicks took extended vacations, played golf, or traveled across the country, often on boondoggle tours of federal facilities. Malow and Kelly, however, had little rest before their twenty-four departments and agencies delivered requests to reprogram appropriations. These operating plans, due thirty days after the president signed the VA-HUD spending bill, offered the administration a final appeal on fiscal 1992 spending and appropriators another level of oversight. "We take operating plans very seriously," said Kevin Kelly. According to Dick Malow, "Reprogramming takes a fair amount of my time, but it's a vital, if little understood, step in the budget process."

Reprogramming typically doesn't address major policy changes. It's a nonstatutory process that recognizes the fluidity of budget assumptions that must adjust to emerging opportunities, disasters, new legal requirements, or shifting economic conditions. It enables federal agencies to spend money on items they didn't initially request or appropriators didn't specify.

The rule of thumb is that administration managers have the authority to shift up to $250,000 between programs within an appropriations account. Above that level (which varies a bit by agency), changes must be formalized in operating plans or reprogramming requests approved by senior appropriators. The initial operating plan, developed by the budget officer and reviewed by OMB officials, lists the agency's accounts and requested changes, known as puts and takes; a short accompanying text justifies the proposed modifications. Subsequent reprogramming applications usually surface two or three times during the year as the real world catches up with the budget. Petitions from the Department of Veterans Affairs, for instance, tend to update changing hospital construction plans.

Reprogramming review procedures vary by the Appropriations subcommittee, although clerks uniformly make most of the judgments. The defense panel involves all subcommittee members, while only the cardinals play an active role for VA-HUD. Traxler and Mikulski do consult with their ranking Republican members, but they approach junior appropriators only if a reprogramming request affects a project in their districts. One panel member admitted not knowing the process even occurred.

Traxler and Mikulski jointly sign letters back to each agency approving the reprogramming requests or listing their contingencies. Those letters also clarify unclear segments of the original legislation or report. Said the House cardinal: "We want to make sure the agencies don't tinker with Congress's directives."

According to Representative Bill Green, "The reprogramming process is quite unconstitutional, but it's a system that works." On the one hand, Green said, such control by a select few members of Congress can be seen as an illegal legislative veto on the power granted to cabinet secretaries and agency directors. Yet if a secretary insists on his or her right to move money at will among accounts, appropriators will retaliate the following year by rejecting his or her favorite projects or limiting his or her flexibility.

The Department of Housing and Urban Development offers an instructive example. Although previous secretaries carefully sought permission to reprogram money, Kemp battled the cardinals constantly and issued numerous legal briefs challenging their authority. "The secretary may be technically correct," admitted a senior HUD official, "but he fails to realize that appropriators have taken to establishing lots of little accounts with specific funding levels. The end result of Kemp's struggle for independence is that the agency enjoys far less autonomy."

Most agency budget officers, despite the legal uncertainties associated with reprogramming, want to maintain comity with powerful cardinals for philosophical as well as practical reasons. According to one veteran, "Appropriators have the constitutional responsibility to ensure that the federal budget is implemented as enacted."

Review of operating plans drags on for several weeks. In late January 1992, just days before President Bush was to submit his new budget, Dick Malow sat in his office dictating responses to repro-gramming requests, as well as questions for Traxler to ask at the upcoming hearing on fiscal 1993 spending by the American Battle Monuments Commission. "The appropriations process," observed the clerk, "is continuous."

ENDURING TURF WARS

The struggle for control of the federal purse also never ceases. In fact, the cardinals' evolving relationships within Congress and with the administration help define the ebb and flow of political power in Washington.

Consider the conflict between appropriators and authorizers. On one front, Representative George Brown led a surprisingly successful charge at the end of 1992 against $95 million of energy and water earmarks, only to discover that appropriators later inserted the very same earmarks in the defense spending bill. "What arrogance!" de-cried a frustrated authorizer. "The audacity of appropriators will come back to haunt them." In fact, representatives changed House rules in early 1993 to allow authorizing chairman preferential treat-ment to challenge a cardinal's conference report. Pressure also is building to have authorizers sit on appropriations conference com-mittees, particularly to debate legislative amendments from the Sen-ate.

Yet pork busters may have lost visible targets after the Democrats gained control of both the White House and Congress. "Much of my motive to earmark was my lack of confidence that past Republican administrations would direct funds to quality projects," stated one Democratic cardinal. "More consultations between the branches of government will mean fewer congressional directives." Increased leverage, however, may be an equally important factor, according to another cardinal, who fondly remembered having Democratic cabi-net secretaries accept his informal spending recommendations. With a Democrat in the White House, this cardinal asserted, Democratic

215

appropriators don't need to rely solely on earmarks to direct federal spending. Predicted a clerk: "Pork will not disappear, but it will be removed from political radar screens as a major issue."

Tensions remain with the White House, even though a Democratic president delights Democratic cardinals. Appropriators are still haunted by the threat of a line-item veto, which would transfer enormous authority to the executive branch. Senator Robert Byrd attacked the proposal vehemently in a six-hour speech that described Congress's power of the purse as "the taproot of the tree of Anglo-American liberty." Despite Byrd's oratory, forty-four senators supported a line-item veto in 1992, and that number may increase in response to a grass-roots demand for political reform. A less severe change, what some call "expedited rescission," would require Congress to vote up or down on the specific items that the president wants to eliminate; proponents assume public exposure would eliminate the worst pork abuses. As a candidate, Bill Clinton supported a line-item veto, but some appropriators think the new president won't antagonize powerful lawmakers whom he needs to court.

Term limits, adopted in fourteen statewide initiatives during the 1992 elections, are an emerging threat to the seniority system that has long prescribed how power is allocated on Capitol Hill, particularly within the Appropriations Committee. If term limits are adopted throughout the country (and found to be constitutional), cardinals would still hold substantial authority, but control would shift further to entrenched clerks and budget officers who know the intricacies of federal budgeting.

Cardinals, of course, enjoy new opportunities as well as challenges. Budgetary fire walls fell in 1993, with prospects for appropriators transferring defense savings to popular domestic programs. The cardinals also may benefit from an emerging consensus that restraining entitlements—which are managed by authorizing committees—would nick the federal deficit more than domestic spending caps or line-item cuts. Even former OMB Director Richard Darman offered a deficit reduction deal that pleased appropriators: caps on entitlements in exchange for more domestic spending. A bipartisan commission headed by Senators Sam Nunn and Pete Domenici also endorsed a ceiling on mandatory spending but increases for children, education, and research and technology development—all accounts controlled by the cardinals.

The House Appropriations Committee faces these tests with twenty fresh faces, or one-third of the panel. Some lawmakers suggest the new blood will shake up the panel's traditions. One veteran, however, predicted, "Once new appropriators learn they need the cardinals to get things done, the committee will return to business as usual."

The fresh faces on Appropriations reflect the anti-incumbent mood pervasive during the 1992 election campaign. To some, appropriators are the epitome of what's wrong with Washington: entrenched, tradition-bound politicians who greedily direct spending to their own districts. No doubt appropriators grab too much pork and resort to too many accounting gimmicks. Yet the cardinals of Capitol Hill have several attributes that serve our nation well. Unlike most politicians in the nation's capital, they make tough spending decisions. They get things done, setting government priorities year in and year out. They provide regular and detailed oversight of federal programs. And since their bipartisan ways limit nonproductive squabbles, they are one of the few groups in Washington that concentrate on governing.

EPILOGUE

ON JANUARY 6, 1992, Representative Jamie Whitten broke the record for longest service in the House of Representatives: fifty years, two months, and two days. About a month later and just a few days after President Bush's fiscal 1993 budget arrived on Capitol Hill, Whitten suffered a stroke and entered the Walter Reed Army Medical Center in Washington. Then eighty-one years old, the appropriations chairman stayed in the hospital for a month and returned part-time to his committee office in late March, looking pale and gaunt. Under pressure from other appropriators, the weary Whitten maintained his title but transferred day-to-day oversight of the committee to the ranking Democrat, William Natcher of Kentucky. Whitten, despite his frailty, won his reelection handily, but the Democratic Caucus for the 103d Congress, which began in January 1993, took away his chairmanship of both the full committee and his agriculture subcommittee. Although the eighty-three-year-old Natcher now formally controls the central office, the ascension of forty-eight-year-old Richard Durbin to cardinal of the agriculture panel portends a generational shift on House Appropriations.

William Natcher, a hard-working and scrupulous lawmaker known for never having missed a vote on the House floor, may change some of the committee's operating procedures. Having steadfastly refused to add pork to his labor-HHS spending bills, the new chairman, for instance, may discourage other cardinals from ear-marking. But like Whitten, Natcher defends the Appropriations Committee staunchly from any and all critics. Responding to calls for authorizers to obtain more control over federal spending, Natcher protested: "It wouldn't work. It would be a complete disaster, and I say that to you frankly."

Senator Robert Byrd suffered a rare pork-barreling setback when federal investigators concluded that CIA officials had selected a West Virginia location solely to endear themselves to the Senate's chief appropriator. Following protests from angry authorizers and critical reporters, CIA Director Robert Gates rejected in late March 1992 the chairman's plan to move three thousand jobs to Jefferson County.

Representative Bob Traxler's congressional district remained es-sentially intact after redistricting, and he seemed headed toward an easy reelection victory. On the last day of April 1992, however, the VA-HUD cardinal took to the House floor and announced he wouldn't run again. "I need some time for myself," Traxler explained obliquely. "It has been a long, wonderful life of public service. But I feel if I served one more year, I'd be there for ten." An unspoken reason for the surprise departure was the chairman's 201 overdrafts at the House Bank, which placed him among the worst offenders. Not long after his announcement Traxler was attacked by robbers as he left a Capitol Hill restaurant. The resulting head injury required thirty-two stitches and kept the cardinal away from congressional action for several weeks, causing the fiscal 1993 VA-HUD markup to be delayed. In November 1992, a healthy Traxler won election to the Board of Trustees of Michigan State University.

Louis Stokes, a veteran Democrat from Cleveland, took over the House VA-HUD panel in early 1993, becoming the first African American to chair a major Appropriations subcommittee. Elected to Congress in 1968, Stokes had distinguished himself by tackling deli-cate assignments, including investigations of the Kennedy and King assassinations, as well as the House Ethics Committee's review of the Abscam scandal. The new cardinal has been a strong advocate for public housing subsidies and educational programs in poor commu-nities.

Dick Malow, Paul Thomson, and Michelle Burkett remain professional staff members on the House VA-HUD panel, ready to break in the new chairman.

Senator Barbara Mikulski won her reelection by a substantial margin. Kevin Kelly, still the youngest clerk, continues to hound agency officials.

Both ranking Republicans on the VA-HUD subcommittees left Congress. Senator Jake Garn retired, and Representative Bill Green lost his reelection bid after his New York City district was reconfigured following the 1990 census.

A record nineteen House appropriators did not return to Washington in 1993. They included two other cardinals: transportation's William Lehman and Edward Roybal of the treasury panel. The VA-HUD panel lost five of its nine members, including Traxler and Green. Bill Lowery, cosponsor of the fiscal 1992 House amendment that restored the space station's funding, announced he would not seek reelection to Congress the day before it was revealed he had 300 overdrafts at the House Bank. Chester Atkins, with 127 overdrafts, lost his Democratic primary. Lawrence Coughlin, the subcommittee's second most senior Republican, retired out of frustration with the House's increasingly partisan squabbles.

Joseph McDade, top Republican on the House Appropriations Committee, was formally indicted in May 1992 on racketeering, bribery, and corruption charges associated with his alleged receipt of about $100,000 in campaign gifts, speaking fees, and gratuities from three defense contractors. The criminal investigation had lasted nearly four years, and the indictment stated that McDade used his influence on Appropriations to help the firms win and retain lucrative government contracts. Despite the controversy, McDade won reelection to his sixteenth term.

Quentin Burdick, chairman of the Senate agriculture and rural development subcommittee, died in September 1992. He was replaced by Dale Bumpers, who led the unsuccessful Senate fight against the space station.

Representative George Brown has continued to support *Freedom*, despite his personal doubts about the project's priority. During consideration of the fiscal 1993 budget, the science chairman admitted, "If I have to make a choice between space science and the space station, then I'll come down for space science every time." But Brown and most members of the House of Representatives rejected such a choice, as well as a Traxler-Green motion to abandon the space station project.

Richard Truly received a surprise on February 12, 1992, when President Bush announced that the NASA administrator would be replaced. "I'm floored. I can't explain it," Truly was quoted as saying. "It was not my idea." Numerous press accounts suggested that Vice President Dan Quayle and his National Space Council orchestrated the shift to David Golden, an executive with TRW. Well respected in the aerospace industry, Goldin was virtually unknown in political circles, although he proved his mettle by saving the space station's funding in the fiscal 1993 budget.

Leon Panetta, chairman of the House Budget Committee, and a key supporter of Traxler's efforts to kill the space station, became President Clinton's OMB director, replacing station advocate Richard Darman. After learning in March 1993 that the space station program had gone another $1 billion after budget, Panetta forced NASA to devise another new design that would cut *Freedom*'s cost approximately in half while maintaining its scientific research mission. Some NASA officials and congressional supporters wondered aloud whether the project could be saved.

The 602(b) Coalition nearly disbanded in June 1991 after the bitter House floor fight over *Freedom*. Yet most of the assembled lobbyists concluded that the group provides enough benefits to continue meeting, even if less frequently. "You never know what you'll learn," resolved an environmentalist. "I can't afford not to be there." An aerospace executive was more glib: "Appropriators may come and go, but lobbyists endure."

President Bill Clinton proposed an economic program in February 1993 designed to reduce the deficit, provide a short-term economic stimulus, and encourage long-term investment. Congress adopted a budget resolution in March that calls for a record $496 billion in deficit reduction over five years. Without additional measures, however, the deficit is expected to stand at $192 billion in fiscal 1997, the last year of Clinton's term, and to soar in subsequent years. In April 1993, Congress raised Washington's debt ceiling by $225 billion to $4.370 trillion—providing the federal government with just enough borrowing authority to last until the end of fiscal 1993.

ACKNOWLEDGMENTS

MANY PEOPLE DESERVE my sincere thanks. Scores of appropriators, congressional staff, agency officials, political scientists, and lobbyists generously offered their time and perspectives on the federal budget drama. The board of directors of the Northeast-Midwest Institute and the cochairs of the Northeast-Midwest Congressional Coalition kindly allowed me the independence and leave of absence needed to write this book. Among those providing sage comments on early drafts were Don Ryan, a former Appropriations staff member who directs the Alliance to End Childhood Lead Poisoning; Joe White, of the Brookings Institution; and Judy Schneider, of the Congressional Research Service within the Library of Congress.

Leona Schecter, my literary agent, helped mold the original proposal. Jason Conte and Justin Lawrence, my interns from the University of Michigan, located valuable information amid countless government reports. Glenn Starnes, the Northeast-Midwest Institute's computer guru, created the charts and tables. Walt Bode, my editor at Grove Press, vastly improved the book's organization and style. Diane MacEachern, my wife, provided support, critical reviews, and encouragement.

ABOUT THE AUTHOR

SINCE 1987 Richard Munson has been the director of the Northeast-Midwest Congressional Coalition, a regional center that conducts policy research and drafts legislation on energy, environmental, trade, and economic development issues. In 1985 he published *The Power Makers*, an inside look at America's power industry and its struggle to control tomorrow's electricity. *The Power Makers* was selected by the *Washington Monthly* as one of the year's best political books. In 1989 Munson published *Cousteau: The Captain and His World*, an unauthorized biography of the underseas explorer. He has been executive director of the Solar Lobby and the Center for Renewable Resources, co-coordinator of Sun Day, an international event to advance alternative energy development, and director of the Environmental Action Foundation. He also has taught history at the University of Michigan. He lives outside Washington, D.C., with his wife and their two children.